Commentaries on Obscenity

Edited by

Donald B. Sharp

The Scarecrow Press, Inc.
Metuchen, N.J. 1970

ISBN 0-8108-0316-X

Editor's Preface

Laws pertaining to so-called "obscene" material have been relaxed in recent years, largely because of decisions by the United States Supreme Court; repeatedly, the Court has declared in favor of liberal standards and has denied local authorities the power to suppress "obscene" material by infringing upon Constitutional rights. However, progress has not always been consistent, nor entirely coherent. Thus, the scholar of obscenity law, whether casual or serious, finds no easy path through the welter of cases, opinions, and citations which now constitute obscenity law. Each new case proceeds from virtually all previous cases; like a family tree inverted, each case has antecedents which have more antecedents, each with its own peculiarity.

This anthology has been gathered to aid the scholar concerned with obscenity law and issues pertinent to freedom of the press. The introductory essay by the editor reviews the recent developments in obscenity law, as these developments have proceeded from opinions rendered by the Supreme Court. The introductory essay is followed by articles by legal scholars who comment on the issues raised in these recent Supreme Court opinions. Thus, the reader is provided with material from a series of opinions, and with extensive commentaries, which point out problems resolved adequately, poorly, or, in some cases, not at all. Hopefully, the quotations from opinions, plus the commentaries, will aid the convenience of persons interested in obscenity law. Most of all, the anthology may remind every reader that the law, however mysterious and occasionally perverse remains the product of serious efforts by sincere men; that is, while one may not always agree with a legal opinion, he can be encouraged by the fact that questions of obscenity law do receive searching study.

The comments are given in chronological order, so that the past is surveyed, the present analyzed, and the future tentatively suggested. Each item is prefaced by a short note which indicates its contribution. Throughout, the editor has attempted to retain that which was significant to the development of the law; sometimes, he has retained that which was merely cogent. Hopefully, a proper balance has been achieved. The form of the original has been generally maintained. Italics are as in the original. Any adjustment effected by the editor is indicated by ellipsis, or by the use of the square brackets. For example, the symbol for "section," as commonly used in a legal code, not being available to a typist, has been indicated by [Sec.]. Footnotes have been retained only in part; thus, the sequence of footnotes in the anthology will not correspond to the original texts. Interested readers are urged to consult the originals, since the footnotes, particularly in legal journals, contain a wealth of citations and droll commentary.

In conclusion, and in final justification of the editor's efforts, the editor submits Justice William J. Brennan's observation in Roth v. United States, 354 U.S. 476 (1957) at 488, that: "The fundamental freedoms of speech and press have contributed greatly to the development and well-being of our free society. . . . Ceaseless vigilance is the watchword to prevent their erosion. . . ." Hopefully, this anthology will promote that "ceaseless vigilance."

In closing this prefatory note, the editor offers appropriate credit to several people who have been of great help to him in the preparation of the anthology. Thanks are due to Professor Leon Carnovsky, of the University of Chicago Graduate Library School, for suggestions which prompted the project itself; to Howard W. Winger, editor of the Library Quarterly, for reminders about subtle points that might have been overlooked; to Henry Knepler, of the Department of Humanities of Illinois Institute of Technology, who gave encouragement; to Miss Diane Nousanen, of the University of Chicago Law School Library, for much assistance in locating materials; and to Miss Janet Kamer, of Chicago, for extensive assistance in preparing the manuscript. The editor feels his own efforts pale in comparison to these named.

Donald B. Sharp
Librarian
Carlow College
Pittsburgh,
Pennsylvania
November, 1969.

Table of Contents

PART I:

OBSCENITY LAW AND THE INTRANSIGENT THREAT OF GINZBURG

By Donald B. Sharp

And therefore the ill and unfit choice of words wonderfully obstructs the understanding. Nor do the definitions or explanations wherewith in some things learned men are wont to guard and defend themselves, by any means set the matter right. But words plainly force and overrule the understanding, and throw all into confusion, and lead men away into numberless empty controversies and idle fancies.

Francis Bacon,
Introduction to the Novum Organum.

Introduction

The law of the land, like the Sabbath, was made for man, and like the Sabbath, is often put to mysterious uses. However clear statutes may seem, a court may render a decision that appears contrary to statute; likewise, case decisions sometimes contradict all precedents. The average man, or even the lawyer, cannot always find absolute guides to conduct simply by searching statutes and cases at law. Such uncertainty is the price society pays for a dynamic, flexible legal system: for a mutable society must have a legal system which responds to change yet retains its eternal principles. Likewise, while law, essentially, expresses the "majority rule" concept, it also expresses the "protection of minorities" concept. Thus, legal codes have inherent conflicts, and these conflicts produce the sometimes confusing decisions rendered by courts.

In practice, law attempts to satisfy its conflicts by giving attention to the facts which create problems. The law applies a statute (i.e., a stated part of the social code to which society may forcibly require adherence) to the facts of a case at bar. However, since cases and judges differ, since those men who wrote the statute may be long dead, and since society must recognize that law is largely subjective, the law does not rest on absolute adherence to statutes. It also looks into previous cases which involved similar circumstances. These previous cases, or <u>precedents</u>, which connect the demands of the present with the wisdom of the past, provide a judge with authority for a decision, so that law is not merely his whim. A judge can no more take the law into his own hands than can anyone else.

Thus, if a judge does render an unpopular decision, his decision will be accepted because, on the one hand, the contenders have no choice, and because, on the other hand, they recognize that precedent gives the judge authority for his decision. However, if a judge renders a decision contrary to precedent, claiming that the circumstances require such a decision, his decision upsets everyone, for not only has a revered precedent been denied but a new one has been created. In future cases, the judge must decide which precedent holds; as precedents increase, the task of lawyer and judge becomes more difficult, and the position of the average man less certain. Sometimes, the new precedent is so dubious that no one depends on it, and the old precedent survives. However, when a decision of the highest court of appeal in a given society produces confusion, the difficulties are particularly serious, since the ruling affects the whole society.

Such uncertainty has arisen in recent years from United States Supreme Court decisions involving so-called "obscenity." After several years of liberal decisions, the Court handed down the _U. S. v. Ginzburg_ decision in 1966, upholding the conviction of Ralph Ginzburg on the charge of mailing "obscene" material. In its decision, the Court virtually wrote a new statute, and threw obscenity law into the confusion out of which the Court had been leading it.

The possibility that the _Ginzburg_ decision constitutes a "clear and present danger" to the freedom to read motivates this essay. The primary concern is to measure the effect of the _Ginzburg_ decision, by contrasting it with previous decisions and by invoking the opinions that able lawyers expressed about it. At the present time, the practical effect of the decision is vague, since statistics which would indicate exactly how many prosecutions have depended on _Ginzburg_ are inconclusive. Putative authorities contradict; hence, the potential of _Ginzburg_ for making trouble can be suggested only be observing what competent men of law have said about it.

Since authorities themselves are divided and uncertain, this essay can hardly offer a definitive statement about the present legal status of "obscenity"; indeed, a flexible legal system prevents such a statement. However, simply to make a coherent statement about chaos, and to account for such chaos in terms of law, precedent, and possibility, will possibly make the situation more comprehensible.

1. Before *Roth*

Egyptian monarchs plastered over or chipped off the stone-carved records of their predecessors in one of the earliest efforts of the state to control the reading material to which citizens were exposed. The state has maintained its interest in what citizens read, but in the last 300-odd years, particularly in the West, the aim of censorship has shifted from political writings to material that deals with the human body and its processes in a way that is called "obscene." In Christian-oriented societies, citizens typically have greater access to political writings of any persuasion than they do to materials which present anything other than a Mosaic or Pauline view of sex. In many developing nations, such as India and the African states, censorship has been written into the constitution, and the power of the state is invoked as often against obscene material as against political.[1] This attitude is particularly curious in these countries, since their art and temple sculpture show a candid acceptance of sexual matters.

Why the state should restrict sex from the reading of the citizens is not clear. The underlying assumption is that to read obscene material incites the reader to lustful thoughts; the enthymeme involved is that lustful thoughts can result in anti-social behavior.[2] Thus, if a book incites the reader to think about sex in any way except the conventional, the book is "obscene." That such law is filled with subjectivity does not hinder prosecutors. In the United States and its third-cousins, the Caucasian-dominated countries of the British Commonwealth, the drift toward censorship of obscene[3] material may have been an outgrowth of the Puritan ascendency. Supreme Court Justice William O. Douglas, in his concurring opinion in the *Fanny Hill* case,[4] in which the Supreme Court ruled that the Commonwealth of Massachusetts could not prohibit the sale of the book, observed:

> The extent to which the publication of "obscenity" was a crime at common law is unclear. It is generally agreed that the first reported case in-

> volving obscene conduct is the King v. Sir Charles Sedley. Publication of obscene literature, at first thought to be the exclusive concern of the ecclesiastical courts, was not held to constitute an indictable offense until 1727 [in footnote: Dominus Rex v. Curl. 2 Strange 789 (K. B. 1727)][5]

In any event, prosecutions involving obscene material began, and continued, in England. In 1857, Lord Campbell's Act specifically made the distribution of obscene literature a crime;[6] the problem since then has been the definition of the term "obscene." In the Hicklin case, Lord Cockburn declared:

> I think the test of obscenity is this, whether the tendency of the matter...is to deprave and corrupt those whose minds are open to such immoral influences, and into whose hands a book of this sort [pamphlets involved] may fall.[7]

In the United States, the history of obscenity statutes and the legal status of obscenity are no more clear than in England. Justice William J. Brennan, writing the opinion of the Court in the Roth case,[8] contended that obscene writing was prohibited by a 1712 Massachusetts statute which rendered criminal the publication of "any filthy, obscene, or profane song, pamphlet, libel, or mock sermon...."[9] However, a question exists whether "obscene," in the statute, is a gratuitous synonym, or denotes a class of material distinct from "libel" or that which is "filthy." Brennan further pointed out that the constitutions of many of the original thirteen colonies proscribed various behaviors under the terms "vice" or "immorality." Brennan thus perceived a consistent development of obscenity law from the beginning to the present, and found ample precedent for suppression of obscenity.

Justice Douglas found less, however, arguing that:

> ...there is an absence of any federal cases or laws relative to obscenity in the period immediately after the adoption of the First Amendment. Congress passed no legislation relating to obscenity until the middle of the nineteenth century.[10]

Douglas refers to the Tariff Act of 1842 (5 Statutes 566), which prohibited the importation of "obscene prints." Justice Douglas' point was that the First Amendment was absolute and that the Supreme Court should not be party to suppression of printed material.

In any event, after 1842, Congress passed many laws restricting obscenity, so that by 1958 about 20 laws and amendments thereto were available to control the distribution of obscene material through the mail or in interstate commerce; these laws included material pertinent to such medical topics as abortion and birth control.[11]

Throughout this period of time, numerous books were suppressed, such as the novels of Theodore Dreiser and the various marriage manuals published up to about 1930. Generally, these cases turned on whether the word "obscene" had been defined accurately, or whether it had been applied appropriately. Thus, Judge John M. Woolsey decided in favor of Margaret Stopes' Married Love[12] because he felt it would be helpful to married people, and decided in favor of James Joyce's Ulysses because "...whilst in many places the effect of Ulysses is emetic, nowhere does it tend to be aphrodisiac."[13]

The law of obscenity developed its own guidelines and peculiarities. In some cases, such as Fanny Hill and Ulysses, the action was against a book, with the state attempting only to prevent the distribution of the book within the state, and with the state taking pains not to penalize either bookseller or publisher. Conversely, some cases aimed against a person, and conviction resulted in a fine or imprisonment for the bookseller, while the book apparently could be sold by someone else, at least until he was haled into court. Judicial proceedings would declare a book "obscene," but neither the private ownership of the book nor its right to exist were in issue; the issue was the sale or distribution of the book by a person, and the person was held at fault. Roth and Ginzburg exemplify this second type of case.

The precedents of obscenity law seem to have been the Hicklin case, which established the "isolated passages" and the "most susceptible person" doctrines, i.e., that obscene material was to be judged according to the effect that isolated passages might have on the most susceptible person who might likely get his hands on it. The Hicklin rule was gradually modified to the "prurient interest rule,"[14] and the "most susceptible person" test was thrown out bodily in Butler v. Michigan,[15] by Justice Felix Frankfurter's observation that:

> The State insists that, by thus quarantining the general reading public against books not too rugged for grown men and women in order to shield juvenile innocence, it is exercising its power to promote the general welfare. Surely, this is to burn the house to roast the pig.... The incidence of this enactment is to reduce the adult population of Michigan to reading only what is fit for children.[16]

The "prurient interest rule" survives, however, and remains the basis of many obscenity trials. The use of the "prurient interest" test did not actually clarify the law a great deal, since the difficulty of defining "obscene" shifted to the problem of defining "prurient interest." The American Law Institute (ALI) has offered a fairly rigid definition of "prurient interest," but the Supreme Court, invoking the ALI definition in Roth, carefully invoked only as much of the definition as would support a conviction, rather than the whole, which directly contradicts the Roth finding.[17]

Until the Roth case in 1957, as obscenity cases came before the Supreme Court the issue of the First Amendment being abridged was not raised; apparently, the appealing attorneys accepted the law and its tacit premises, and appealed on the basis of whether the obscenity statute actually applied, i.e., whether the material was actually obscene, or on procedural grounds. For example, in Butler v. Michigan, appellants contended that conviction would violate the "due process" clause of the Fourteenth Amendment. Generally, if obscenity cases reached the Supreme Court, they were decided in some way other than by relying on the First Amendment. Thus, when Samuel Roth appealed his conviction under 18 U. S. C. A., Section 1461, the federal statute prohibiting the mailing of obscene materials, on the basis that his First Amendment rights had been abridged, the Court was called upon for a new approach to the question. Because, in Justice Brennan's words, "The dispositive question is whether obscenity is utterance within the area of protected speech and press. This is the first time the question has been squarely presented to this Court....,"[18] the Roth case was likely to produce a landmark decision, to set a precedent that would invite defenses in obscenity cases to be based on the First Amendment. Therefore, the Roth case, and the precedent it became, deserve particular attention.

Notes

1. See Peaselee, Constitutions of Nations (1956), re Burma, Ireland, India, Nigeria, Zambia, et al.

2. Henkin, "Morals and the Constitution: The Sin of Obscenity," 63 Columbia Law Review 393 (1963).

3. "Obscene" is not used here as a pejorative term; indeed, the word can hardly be called "denotative" at all; here, the term simply refers to that body of printed material to which the word "obscene" has been applied, which ranges from Deuteronomy to Fanny Hill.

4. A Book Named "John Cleland's Memoirs of a Woman of Pleasure," et al, v. Commonwealth of Massachusetts, 383 U.S. 413 (1966).

5. Ibid., 429.

6. Kalven, "The Metaphysics of the Law of Obscenity," 1960 Supreme Court Review, 2 (1960).

7. [Queen v. Hicklin, L. R. 3 Q. B. 360 (1868)]; cited by Rembar, The End of Obscenity, 20 (1968).

8. Roth v. United States, 354 U. S. 476 (1957).

9. Idem, 483.

10. 383 U. S. 430 (1966).

11. See Roth v. United States at 485, note 17; and Cairns, Paul, and Wishner, "Sex Censorship: The Assumptions of Anti-Obscenity Laws and the Empirical Evidence," 46 Minnesota Law Review, 1010, note 2 (1962). These various laws have rarely been invoked against scientists, research-

ers, and doctors, for a consistent assumption of the courts has been that such people have a "proper" use for obscenity, while the average person does not. Ginzburg v. U. S., 383 U. S. 463 (1966), makes the practice virtually a legal doctrine.

Another important element of these laws is that they make censors out of customs and postal officials, leaving execution of the law up to civil servants, with disturbing results. See Cairns, et al., supra, and Leon Friedman, "The Ginzburg Decision and the Law," 36 American Scholar, (1966-67), 80.

12. U. S. v. One Obscene Book Entitled "Married Love," 48 F. 2d. 821 (1933).

13. U. S. v. Ulysses, 5 F. Supp. 184 (1933).

14. Monaghan, "Obscenity, 1966: The Marriage of Obscenity Per Se and Obscenity Per Quod," 76 Yale Law Journal, 129, at note 14 (1966); also, 354 U. S. 489 (1957).

15. Butler v. Michigan, 352 U. S. 380 (1956).

16. Ibid., 383.

17. 354 U. S. 488 (1957); cited by Brennan from ALI Model Penal Code para. 207.10 (2): "A thing is obscene if ... its predominant appeal is to prurient interest, i.e., a shameful or morbid interest in nudity, sex, or excretion, and if it goes substantially beyond customary limits of candor...." Justices Douglas and Hugo L. Black, dissenting, at 354 U. S. 513 (1966), provide the remainder of the ALI definition: "We reject the prevailing tests of tendency to arouse lustful thoughts or desires [as a test of prurient interest]...."

2. Roth

Samuel Roth conducted a business in New York, selling books, photographs, and magazines which, presumably, appealed to "prurient interest." He was tried and convicted of violating the federal statute (18 U. S. C. A. 1461) which prohibits mailing of obscene materials. His conviction was sustained by the Second Circuit [New York] Court of Appeals, from which he appealed to the Supreme Court. His case was argued on April 22, 1957, and decided on June 24, 1957.

Roth's case was heard and decided on the same day as that of David S. Alberts, of Los Angeles. Alberts was convicted under a California statute which declared illegal the "keeping for sale"[1] of any "obscene or indecent picture or print," and had appealed to the Supreme Court from the Superior Court of the State of California. Roth and Alberts were in the same kind of business, but Alberts' attorneys relied on the Fourteenth Amendment, contending, as in Butler v. Michigan, that the "due process" clause of the Fourteenth Amendment prevented the states from abridging any right guaranteed by the Constitution: in Alberts' appeal, the freedom to publish.[2] His counsel argued that the Fourteenth Amendment prohibited the states from abridging any Constitutional privilege, and that California had abridged Alberts' First Amendment privileges. Ultimately, the appeal depended on whether the First Amendment was included in the Fourteenth.

The Roth and Alberts cases, while often cited as one, are actually two cases; the Court affirmed Roth's conviction with a six to three vote, and affirmed Alberts' with a seven to two vote. However, in Roth, Chief Justice Earl Warren concurred for reasons other than those of the majority, and wrote a separate opinion; Justice John M. Harlan, while admitting a dislike for obscenity, dissented in Roth but stood with the majority in Alberts. Justices Douglas and Black, both absolutists about the First Amendment, dissented in both cases. Thus, Roth produced four opinions, and Alberts two, since Justices Douglas and Black joined in one opinion. Even though Roth became a major precedent, the division of opinion left the status of obscenity uncertain. The task of future cases was thus rendered more difficult, despite the fact that Roth liberalized earlier precedents.

A third obscenity case heard along with Roth and Alberts was Kingsley Books, Inc., v. New York,[3] which involved slightly different questions. The City of New York had ordered that books be seized until a determination could be made whether they were obscene. According to the New York Penal Code (Section 22-a), the matter would be brought to trial in two days, and a decision rendered in two more, making four days between the time that books were seized and their legality established. The defendants contended that such a procedure was a "prior restraint" on freedom of the press, and appealed to the Supreme Court. Appellants did not raise the question whether their merchandise was legally obscene, but argued solely that "prior restraint" violated "due process," and that a judgment in violation of due process could not stand. The Court, unimpressed, affirmed their conviction on the basis that four days was not so long that it could be called "prior restraint," and also because the lower-court had clearly refused to enjoin any future books the defendants might sell.

Kingsley produces some interesting questions, such as, for example, whether a day's run of a newspaper could be enjoined from distribution for four days, until a determination was made whether it was obscene. However, its interest to the Roth case is that in Roth and Kingsley, Chief Justice Warren raised the issue of conduct, an issue which arose nine years later as "pandering" to uphold Ralph Ginzburg's conviction. Warren, dissenting, wrote: "There is totally lacking [in this case] any standard for judging the book in context. In my judgment, the same object may have wholly different impact depending on the setting in which it is placed.... It is the conduct of the individual that should be judged." The question of "conduct" and "setting" in Ginzburg threw obscenity law back into the confusion out of which the Court had been leading it.

As Justice Brennan stated, the "dispositive question" in Roth was whether obscenity was protected by the First

Amendment. The Court settled that question fairly quickly:

> ...expressions found in numerous decisions indicate that this Court has always assumed that obscenity is not protected by the freedom of speech and press.[4]

Brennan cited 18 cases which had come before the Court to validate this conclusion, then proceeded into a historical analysis of colonial statutes, citing via footnotes about 50 constitutional provisions, statutes, and cases which, he believed, supported his conclusion. To lay the matter more clearly to rest, Brennan denied another contention of Roth's attorneys:

> It is insisted that the constitutional guaranties are violated because convictions may be had without proof either that obscene material will perceptibly create a clear and present danger of antisocial conduct, or will probably induce its recipients to such conduct.[5]

The clear and present danger doctrine comes from Schenck v. United States, 249 U. S. 47 (1919). Schenck involved pacificist tracts which urged disruption of the armed services in World War I. Justice Oliver Wendell Holmes held that "The question...is whether the words used [in the tracts]...create a clear and present danger that they will bring about the substantive evils that Congress has a right to prevent."

Following Brennan's statement, the reviewer of Roth expects some strong statement on the question of incitement to behavior; instead, he finds one of Roth's weaker points (although the point has not been particularly important to the results of Roth, simply because it has not been raised in defense of obscenity, no doubt because of Roth). Brennan wrote:

> But in light of our holding that obscenity is not protected speech, the complete answer to this argument is in the holding of this Court in Beauharnais v. People of the State of Illinois.... Libelous utterances not being within the area of constitutionally protected speech, it is unnecessary

> ...to consider the issues behind the phrase "clear and present danger." Certainly no one would contend that obscene speech, for example, may be punished only upon a showing of such circumstances. Libel, as we have seen, is in the same class.[6]

Brennan's example from Beauharnais proves nothing except, perhaps, that the Court considers speech and writing the same. Brennan simply transferred the circular logic of Beauharnais to Roth. Many people might well contend that obscene speech need not be punished at all unless someone is specifically offended by it, as in a tort case. "Offense" would amount to "circumstances" which lead to "evils" that "Congress has a right to prevent." However, according to Beauharnais, obscene speech may be punished without evidence of circumstances which involve evils. Thus, obscene speech, *per se*, is not protected.

Brennan transferred this last conclusion to Roth. However, he ignored the question of "why" obscene speech is not protected; his casual analogy between libel and obscene speech in Beauharnais, in which the question was not answered, does not answer the question in Roth. Brennan's method of dealing with the "clear and present danger" question saved the Court from having to seek a scientifically verifiable rationale for suppressing obscene literature, and blocked the introduction of empirical evidence into obscenity cases. However, by evading the question, Brennan strengthened the assumptions that obscene literature *does* cause antisocial behavior, and kept law at some distance from the work of those scholars who find no connection between obscenity and antisocial behavior.

Roth, nevertheless, was not a loss to the cause of freedom of speech and press. Had Brennan stopped with his historical survey and his denial of the "clear and present danger" test, obscenity law would have been little changed from its previous state. However, Brennan felt required to go further, since the First Amendment was involved, and since he knew many worthwhile books involving sex had been subject to prosecution. Therefore, he wished to clarify the status of such materials. Furthermore, since the Roth brief had raised First Amendment questions, Brennan *had* to distinguish between protected speech and nonprotected speech; though he could not explain why obscenity was not protected, he could explain why other materials were. He thus engaged the "exposition of ideas" concept, and proceeded from it to a new (in 1957) definition of obscenity. He prepared for his definition in his beginning remarks:

> The protection given speech and press was fashioned to assure unfettered interchange of ideas for the bringing about of political and social changes desired by the people.[7]

Here, Brennan identified two aspects of speech and writing: 1) that they deal with ideas, and thus, 2) have value to society. These germs became a theory later on, but first Brennan had to justify them:

> All ideas having even the slightest redeeming social importance... have the full protection of the guaranties, unless they encroach upon the limited area of more important interests. But implicit in the history of the First Amendment is the rejection of obscenity as utterly without social importance.[8]

Now, one question here is whether the free exchange of ideas was the <u>only</u> purpose of the First Amendment, and a second question is who shall determine when an utterance encroaches upon some "more important interest"; furthermore, who shall say what interests are most important? Brennan left such questions to the casuists,[9] and proceeded:

> This is the same judgment expressed by this Court in Chaplinsky v. New Hampshire, 315 U. S. 568 [1942]... [that]:
>
> ... There are certain well-defined and narrowly limited classes of speech, the prevention of which have never been thought to raise any Constitutional problem. These include the lewd and obscene... It <u>has been well observed that such utterances are no essential part of any exposition of ideas, and are of such slight social value as a step to truth that any benefit that may be derived from them is clearly outweighed by the social interest in order and morality</u>.... [Emphasis added by Brennan.][10]

Brennan followed his precedent almost to the letter, accepting without question that the classes of speech identified are "clearly defined"; he used his precedent to declare them so. To this point, he was a good lawyer, and still honest; however, he did not remain so. He omitted, as indicated by ellipsis, a key part of the Chaplinsky opinion; the reader must insert into the ellipsis the words:

> ...the profane, the libelous, and the insulting or fighting words -- those which by their very utterance inflict injury or tend to incite an immediate breach of the peace.[11] [Emphasis added.]

Thus, Chaplinsky actually concerns the possibility of speech leading to action, and is, therefore, consistent with Schenck, but neither is consistent with Roth, since no proof exists that obscenity ever caused a breach of the peace, immediate or otherwise. Brennan misused his precedent to deny obscenity the protection of the First Amendment. However, Brennan was pursuing a promising train of thought; he was working toward the concept that nothing could be obscene if it had the characteristics defined in Chaplinsky such characteristics as being a part of "exposition" or of having "social value." He was, thus, genuinely attempting to balance what were, in his view, the needs of society with concepts of freedom; thus, he may be partially forgiven for his ellipsis.

After these observations and the reference to Beauharnais, supra, Brennan came to his defense of material dealing with sex:

> However, sex and obscenity are not synonymous. Obscene material is material which deals with sex in a manner appealing to prurient interest. The portrayal of sex, e.g., in art, literature and scientific works, is not itself sufficient reason to deny material the constitutional protection of freedom of speech and press. Sex, a great and mysterious motive force in human life, has indisputably been a subject of absorbing interest to mankind through the ages; it is one of the vital problems of human interest and public concern.[12]

Having declared that material was not automatically

obscene because it dealt with sex in a candid manner, Brennan pointed out that Hicklin depended on the most susceptible person and on isolated passages, but that the lower courts which tried Roth and Alberts had not been so guilty. He cited the original prosecutor in Alberts, to the effect that the material at issue was obscene only if it offended "...the common conscience of the community by present day standards."[13] Thus, at this point in the opinion, Brennan had established that material was obscene if it: 1) did not involve exposition of ideas; 2) had no social value; and 3) offended community standards. These three conditions have become enshrined as the "Roth Test," and have been the basis for obscenity trials since.

However, Brennan did less well with some other objections which arose. To the claim that the law was imprecise because "obscene" was difficult to define, he invoked Petrillo v. United States, 332 U. S. 1 (1947), to the effect that:

> [T]he law does not require impossible standards; all that is required is that the language 'conveys sufficiently definite warning as to the proscribed conduct when measured by common understanding and practices....' That there may be marginal cases in which it is difficult to determine the side of the line on which a particular situation falls is no sufficient reason to hold the language too ambiguous to define a criminal offense....[14]

Brennan's short shrift to the difficulties of definition seems grossly unjust in obscenity cases; certainly, in a close case, a man can guess whether he is committing a robbery, but he cannot necessarily predict whether the material he sells, by which commerce he earns his living and pays his taxes, is obscene or not. The mere presence of his case in the Supreme Court, and the fact that the Court does decide unanimously, proves that the law does, indeed, "require impossible standards." If the Supreme Court cannot decide what is obscene, then the layman can hardly be expected to.

The quotation from Petrillo did add, by implication, another element to the obscenity formula, i. e., the legal concept of scienter; that is, that a person must know he is committing a crime; else, he may not be guilty. Now, scienter does not apply to all criminal acts, but in Smith v. California, 361 U. S. 147 (1959), the Court concluded that a bookseller could not read all the books in his stock, and could not, therefore, know with certainty if one particular book was obscene, and therefore, could not be convicted simply because a few books in his shop were obscene. Brennan wrote the opinion of the Court in Smith, and perceived an inhibition on the exchange of ideas (a reflection of Roth) if book sales were held up until the seller could read them. Thus, the discussion of legal standards in Roth helped to liberalize obscenity law in future cases.

The discussion of standards in Roth, apparently, aimed at the public, and not at the Supreme Court, for the Court took no notice of the travail that occurs when a layman fails to guess the Court's attitudes. Kalven points out that Samuel Roth was faced with a possible $5,000 fine and a five-year sentence because he did not know what was obscene, and that the Court failed to appreciate these difficulties.[15] However, the presumed clarity of standards came back to confound all in the Ginzburg case: virtually everyone aware of the case assumed the Supreme Court would overrule Ginzburg's conviction; their thinking was based on the assumption that a reasonable man, judging by community standards, could determine what was obscene. Now, in Ginzburg, the Court admittedly did not deal with the question of whether Ginzburg's merchandise was obscene, but instead invoked the issue of pandering; the consternation in legal circles, and elsewhere, arose partly from the fact that Ginzburg had never been indicted for "pandering." Indeed, Ginzburg's advertising, the very proof of his certainty about the law, was used to convict him of pandering. Certainty did him no good, but actually added to his troubles.

Weaknesses in Roth were noticed at once; while Chief Justice Warren concurred, he was unhappy about the basis of the decision. Justice Harlan would have preferred to join the decision, but could not because of its implications; Justices Douglas and Black rejected it completely. Thus, while Roth did become a landmark decision, dissenting opinions weakened its value as a precedent.

Chief Justice Warren, concurring, suggested the Court should limit itself "to the facts before us and to the validity of the statutes in question as applied."[16] As an introductory remark, Warren's observation seems a <u>non sequitur</u>. However, he proceeded to explain himself:

> The history of the application of laws designed to suppress the obscene demonstrates convincingly that the power of government can be invoked under them against great art of literature, scientific treatises, or works exciting social controversy.[17]

Warren did not want to encourage censorship by upholding convictions against obscenity, since some people, and courts, might interpret "obscene" too broadly; however, he did, definitely, desire to punish Roth and Alberts, and sought some basis upon which to do so:

> But there is more to these cases. It is not the book that is on trial; it is a person. The conduct of the defendant is the central issue, not the obscenity of a book or a picture. The nature of the materials is, of course, relevant as an attribute of the defendant's conduct, but the materials are thus placed in context from which they draw color and character. A wholly different result might be reached in a different setting.[18]

At first reading, Warren seems to be merely offering a discursive comment on a legal case; however, his reader realizes with shock that a Supreme Court justice is speaking, that the speaker is serious, and that the justice has completely shifted the ground of the case. If Roth and Alberts were guilty of selling "obscene" material, then, presumably, the nature of the material is the central issue; however, Warren says "Not so," and raises the matter of "conduct." Now, presumably, the only relevant conduct was the selling, and the selling is prohibited conduct only if the article sold is prohibited, as is the case with liquor sales to minors. However, Warren perceives some curious situation in which the "nature" of the materials is "relevant" to "conduct," but that "conduct" gives the materials "character," an instance of logic that is circular at best. Warren may mean that the law can restrict "conduct involving obscene materials." If so, then the specific circumstances of the sale (i. e., how brash were the sales techniques of the respective men?) should be discussed;

however, Warren does not discuss that, but returns to the statutes:

> The personal element in these cases is seen most strongly in the requirement of scienter. Under the California law, the prohibited activity must be done 'willfully and lewdly.' The federal statute limits the crime to acts done 'knowingly.' In his charge to the jury, the district judge stated that the matter must be 'calculated' to corrupt or debauch. The defendants in both these cases were engaged in the business of purveying textual or graphic material openly advertised to appeal to the erotic interest of their customers. They were plainly engaged in the commercial exploitation of the morbid and shameful craving for materials with prurient interest. I believe that the State and Federal Governments can constitutionally punish such conduct. That is all that these cases present to us, and that is all we need to decide.[19]

Warren's whole treatment here is cavalier; one looks in vain for some system of legal statute or precedent which would integrate the discussion and lead syllogistically to the conclusion; contrarily, the discussion jumps from one point to another without transition or logic, and without validation of its claims. Warren's introduction of scienter is irrelevant, since the question was presumably settled in the lower court; neither Roth nor Alberts had claimed that they did not know what they sold was obscene; they contended that they should be allowed to sell it because of Constitutional guarantees. In any event, the means by which the materials were obviously "calculated" to "corrupt or debauch" deserves some legal establishing, according to rules of evidence. Next, the equation between "corrupt" and "erotic interest" ought to be validated before the term "erotic interest" is stretched, absurdly, to suddenly mean "morbid and shameful craving for materials with prurient interest." Justice Brennan, only eight pages earlier, had declared that sex and obscenity were not synonymous; whence, then, this logic of Warren's?

Warren's opinion received surprisingly little attention at the time he wrote it; legal commentators examined Brennan minutely but virtually ignored Warren. In view of the dissenting opinions, perhaps the fact that Warren concurred created a feeling that his opinion added little to the majority opinion.[20] This oversight was serious: first of all, Warren appears to uphold convictions on charges for which the defendants were not tried; he convicts them of an act which involves more than mere selling; and he convicts them for satisfying a purchaser's "erotic" or "prurient" interest, thus shifting the legal emphasis from the nature of a thing to a matter of personal behavior. To separate conduct from an object is usually simple; the murderer is guilty, not his weapon. However, Warren brings conduct and object together, and obscures the distinction.

The important feature of Warren's opinion is that it became legal midwife to Ginzburg. Apparently, legal scholars and Ginzburg's own advisors must have never come across this passage by Warren in Roth; had they done so, Ginzburg might have put aside his flamboyance and proceeded with the dignified circumspection with which Grove Press marketed the Kama Sutra and The Story of O. In Ginzburg, the obvious irritation, bordering on anger, which Warren had shown in Roth, burst forth with apocalyptic vengeance, and when it did, the people most surprised were the very ones who should have been most familiar with Roth: the Constitutional lawyers and the publishers. Possibly, the shock after Ginzburg was shock at the Court's effrontery in turning against precedent. In any event, Warren's opinion in Roth predicted Ginzburg; nor did Warren attempt to conceal his beliefs, the better to waylay unsuspecting purveyors of prurient material. In Jacobellis v. State of Ohio, 378 U. S. 184 (1964), Warren joined Justice Tom C. Clark in a separate, dissenting opinion in a case which reversed the conviction of Nico Jacobellis for possession of an obscene film. Warren and Clark spoke of the difficulty of defining "obscene," and said that while defining was underway:

> Meanwhile, those who profit from the commercial exploitation of obscenity would continue to ply their trade unmolested.
>
> In my opinion, the use to which various materials are put -- not just the words and pictures themselves -- must be considered in determining whether or not the materials are obscene. A technical

> or legal treatise on pornography may well be inoffensive under most circumstances but, at the same time, 'obscene' in the extreme when sold or displayed to children.[21]

Here, again, is the same attitude and the same lack of connecting logic: the introduction of a personal concept of the law which is not validated by either statute of precedent, a situation bad for law and men. Besides its numerous legal repercussions for books, censors, trial judges, and lawyers, the Warren opinions seem to outlaw "erotic" interest, at least if it becomes "prurient."

If the conduct of a person is a deciding factor, beyond the nature of the materials, and if to gratify "erotic" interest is illegal and may be punished, then the state should also punish the person who has this "erotic" interest. In the case of prostitutes, male and female, for example, the law may punish both solicitor to prostitution and solicitee; why not, then, punish the buyer as well as the seller, since they are both acting to gratify "erotic" interest? Such, then, are some of the issues Warren ignored. However, the formulae provided by Brennan for defining obscenity were unharmed by Warren's opinion, and went on to become the defining precedent of future obscenity cases.

Notes

1. West's California Penal Code Annotated, 1955, section 311; cited by Brennan, 354 U. S. 480 (1957).

2. However, in Butler v. Michigan, the issue was not freedom of the press, but whether freedom had been abridged by the State's insistence on a standard appropriate only to children.

3. 354 U. S. 436 (1957).

4. 354 U. S. 445-446 (1957)

5. Idem, 486.

6. Beauharnais v. Illinois is at 343 U. S. 240 (1952); cited by Brennan, 354 U. S. at 486-487.

7. 354 U. S. 484.

8. _Idem._

9. Since Brennan was the judge, perhaps he need not explain himself, since the matter was for his disposition; which reminds one of the apochryphal anecdote of the man who confronted a judge and a priest with the question: "Which is worse: for the priest to say 'You be damned,' or the judge to say 'You be hanged.'?" "Well," the judge told him, "If a judge says 'You be hanged,' you may usually depend on being hanged."

10. _Idem_, 485.

11. Pointed out by Monaghan, _supra_, 132; Monaghan does not attack Brennan's omission so _much_ as the validity of classifying kinds of speech as in _Chaplinsky_; however, he concludes that _Chaplinsky_ provides"...weak scaffolding for any theory that obscenity is beyond the First Amendment simply because it is worthless."

12. 354 U. S. 487; Kalven, _supra_, 10, jocularly calls the first clause in the last sentence"...the least controversial utterance in the Court's history."

13. _Idem_, 490.

14. _Idem_, 491.

15. Kalven, _supra_, 17.

16. 354 U. S. 494.

17. _Idem_, 495.

18. _Idem_; _cf._ _Kingsley Books v._ _New York_, p. 10, _supra_.

19. _Idem_, 495-496.

20. See the various periodicals cited up to this point in this study for examples of neglect of Warren's opinions.

21. _Jacobellis v._ _Ohio_, 378 U. S. 201 (1964); cf. _Kingsley Books v._ _New York_, 354 U. S. 436 (1957), _supra_.

3. Dissent in *Roth*

In a study aimed at *Ginzburg*, the attention given here to *Roth* may appear excessive; however, the significance of *Ginzburg* is that it deviated grossly from the strong precedent laid down in Roth; hence, the strength of the Roth precedent must be clearly defined. Furthermore, *Ginzburg* has by no means become a respectable precedent; indeed, the Supreme Court seems almost ashamed of it, and *Roth* continues to be the precedent cited. Thus, analysis of *Roth* is, perhaps, more important than analysis of *Ginzburg*.

For similar reasons, the dissenting opinions in Roth are important; they could be ignored, since they did not affect the outcome of the case, and, since they were minority opinions, lawyers do not invoke them to establish new precedents. As in any majority-rule system, the wisdom of the minority, however cogent, tends to be neglected. Nevertheless, the dissenting opinions in *Roth* are worth attention, because they are cogent, and because they anticipate many of the weaknesses of *Roth*.

Justice Harlan opened his dissent with:

> My basic difficulties with the Court's opinion are threefold. First, the opinion paints with such a broad brush that I fear it may result in a loosening of the tight reins which state and federal courts should hold upon the enforcement of obscenity statutes.[1]

Harlan's second point pertained to the relationship of state and federal authority; the relationship is subtle, and has not been significant in obscenity cases. But his third point was more telling:

> Third, relevant distinctions between the two obscenity cases here involved, and the Court's own definition of 'obscenity' are ignored.[2]

Harlan returned to this point later, but in getting there, pointed out that the Court had accepted the lower court's assertion that the materials in question were, indeed, "obscene," and had only addressed itself to the question of whether they were constitutionally protected. Harlan felt the Court had abrogated its own responsibility to determine whether the materials were obscene, and he realized the dangers of leaving the determination up to lower courts:

> I do not think that reviewing courts can escape this responsibility by saying that the trier of facts, be it a jury or a judge, has labeled the questioned matter as 'obscene,' for, if 'obscenity' is to be suppressed, the question [is]...not really an issue of fact but a question of constitutional judgment of the most sensitive and delicate kind. Many juries might find that Joyce's 'Ulysses' or Bocaccio's 'Decameron' was obscene...[and] no such verdict could convince me...that these books are 'utterly without redeeming social importance.'[3]

Harlan recognized the danger of accepting a lower court's finding that a given piece of work is "obscene." His next point was that the formulae assembled by Brennan were inconsistent with the American Law Institute formula on which Brennan partly depended. He noted that the ALI expressly rejected the "deprave and corrupt" and the "sexual thoughts" tests; both tests, of course, had been relied on by the lower courts, and had been endorsed by Brennan.

Harlan proceeded into his discussion of state and federal authority, his main point being that the federal government should not participate in any action unless the federal government, under the Constitution, "has a direct substantive interest, that is, the power to act, in the particular area involved."[4] He went on to say that the states should have the power to experiment with obscenity law, for, since some would be liberal and some strict, experiments leading to sound principles could occur in the various states. Furthermore, he believed that national freedom of speech would still be served, since a book banned in one state might be available in another. He believed the Roth decision might preempt the rights of the states, and lead to federal censorship. While he agreed that the possibility of sex-oriented literature might damage society, through long-run effects on morals, he felt the matter was a state concern:

> The Federal Government has no business, whether under the postal power of commerce power, to bar the sale of books because they might lead to any kind of 'thoughts.'[5]

In closing his dissent, Harlan suggested the federal government bar the sale of "hard-core" pornography but he did not pause to distinguish that from "obscenity."

Harlan's opinion has one serious danger: that if the states determine what is "obscene," publishers will have to litigate in every state in defense of their books. Grove Press faced this problem in regard to Tropic of Cancer, which was subject to legal action in numerous states and localities.[6] However, Harlan did declare that the federal government should not be concerned with regulating "thoughts," a refreshing change from Warren's concern with "thoughts." Thus, while Harlan is no absolutist, and does not mind seeing some material suppressed, he does recognize that people should have freedom to think, and freedom to choose what stimulates their thinking.

Justice Black and Douglas, absolutists about the First Amendment, declared:

> When we sustain these convictions, we make the legality of a publication turn on the purity of thought which a book or tract instills in the mind of the reader.[7]

> ...punishment is inflicted for thoughts provoked, not for overt acts nor antisocial conduct. This test cannot be squared with our decisions under the First Amendment.[8]

> The tests by which these convictions were obtained require only the arousing of sexual thoughts. Yet the arousing of sexual thoughts and desires happens every day in normal life in dozens of ways.[9]

> The test of obscenity the Court endorses today

> gives the censor free range over a vast domain. To allow the state to... punish mere speech or publication that the judge or the jury thinks has an undesirable impact on thoughts but that is not shown to be a part of unlawful action is to drastically curtail the First Amendment.[10]

The two justices noted the dearth of proof that obscene material caused antisocial action, quoting a study by Lockhart and McClure[11] at length. They went on to deplore local suppression of material on the basis of the thoughts it provoked, pointing out that in any "... battle between the literati and the Philistines, the Philistines are certain to win."[12] They recommended that the Court avoid taking sides in a dispute between free-expression advocates and advocates of suppression, to avoid putting its weight behind one side or the other:

> Government should be concerned with antisocial conduct... the First Amendment... must allow protests even against the moral code that the standard of the day sets for the community. In other words, literature should not be suppressed because it offends the moral code of the censor.[13]

Black and Douglas pointed out that to encourage censorship on the basis of "thoughts" that reading might "instill" in the reader would necessarily exalt the status of the censor, to the detriment of literary freedom. They denied that obscenity was excluded, historically or otherwise, from First Amendment protection, and submitted:

> Freedom of expression can be suppressed if, and to the extent that, it is so closely brigaded with illegal action as to be an inseparable part of it.[14]

Several cases were cited to support the foregoing statement; their opinion was concluded with what was, perhaps, the most sensible statement in the record:

> I would give the broad sweep of the First Amendment full support, I have the same confidence in the ability of our people to reject noxious literature as I have in their capacity to sort out the true from the false in theology, economics, politics, or any other field.[15]

Douglas and Black need no explicators. Their opinion is so direct and straightforward that it is difficult to quarrel with. The opposing view requires, as in Brennan's and Warren's opinions, tortuous logic and careful selectivity of supporting evidence. Granted, Brennan and Warren set themselves a more difficult task, but the very difficulty of validating their position indicates some of its weakness. This is not to claim that the obvious is always the true; however, truth does not repose in casuistic logic, omitted quotations, and law by fiat and preference of justices.

Notes

1. 354 U. S. 496 (1957).

2. *Idem*, 497.

3. *Idem*, 497-498.

4. *Idem*, 504.

5. *Idem*, 506.

6. See Rembar, *supra*, 168-215; also, Hutchison, *Tropic of Cancer* on Trial (1968).

7. 354 U. S. 508.

8. *Idem*, 509.

9. *Idem*.

10. *Idem*.

11. Lockhart and McClure, 38 *Minnesota Law Review*, 295 (1954); for a more recent discussion by Lockhart and McClure, see 45 *Minnesota Law* Review 5 (1960).

12. 354 U. S. 512.

13. *Idem*, 512-513.

14. *Idem*, 514.

15. *Idem*.

4. Post-Roth

The Roth decision and its definition of obscenity as material not granted protection of the First Amendment, and as material that 1) has no "redeeming social importance," 2) appeals to "prurient interest," and 3) offends the community standards, immediately became a vigorous precedent. The Supreme Court used it at least 19 times up to 1968, and it was invoked over 300 times in federal districts and state courts up to 1968.[1] In some instances, Roth was invoked to sustain a conviction; however, most of the citations of Roth which appear in subsequent Supreme Court decisions are used to reverse lower-court convictions for distribution of obscene literature. Charles Rembar discusses at length the significance of the Roth decision to his defense of Lady Chatterley's Lover for Grove Press.[2] Thus, Roth caused rejoicing among friends of freedom of the press, including the purveyors of "material appealing to the prurient interest."

The Court added some footnotes to Roth, too. In Roth, Justice Harlan had raised the question of jurisdiction, of whether the federal government was encroaching on a state responsibility. He noted, in his dissenting opinion:

> ...the Court fails to discriminate between the different factors, which, in my opinion, are involved in the constitutional adjudication of state and federal obscenity cases.[3]

However, Harlan's position gained no weight with the rest of the Court; in two cases, the Court glossed Roth enough to imply that any conviction of obscenity cases which appeared to abridge Constitutional rights was appropriate for the attention of the Court. In Smith v. California,[4] in reversing a conviction for selling an obscene book, the Court demanded that state processes not conflict with the Constitution; they noted:

> ...the question here is as to the validity of this ordinance's elimination of the scienter require-

> ment -- an elimination which may tend to work a substantial restriction on the freedom of speech and of the press.[5]

> ...our holding in Roth does not recognize any state power to restrict the dissemination of books which are not obscene.[6]

Their point was that to require a bookseller to know the contents of every book he sold would limit his ability to sell books, and would thus restrain thought; however, their opinion strengthened the concept of federal jurisdiction in the obscenity cases. Not long after, in Marcus v. Search Warrant,[7] the Court cited Smith to deny a conviction based on an improper search, and added:

> ...under the Fourteenth Amendment, a State is not free to adopt whatever procedures it pleases for dealing with obscenity as here involved without regard to the possible consequences for constitutionally protected speech.[8]

The direction the Court was taking clearly threatened the ease with which lower courts might prosecute distributors of obscene material.

The trend was developed even more specifically in Bantam Books, Inc. v. Sullivan,[9] and in a Quantity of Books v. Kansas.[10] In Sullivan, the Court decided that the State of Rhode Island was restraining freedom of the press through the activities of the Rhode Island Commission to Encourage Morality in Youth. The Commission followed a practice of surveying booksellers' shops, noting the titles they sold, and then sending them notices asking them to remove offending books so that the Commission would not be troubled with seeking prosecution under obscenity laws. The Court said of this procedure:

> The Commission's practice provides no safeguards whatever against the suppression of the nonobscene and constitutionally protected matter; and it is a form of regulation...which may be applied only after a determination of obscenity has been made in criminal trial....[11]

Of the Quantity of Books case, the Court declared:

> . . . since the warrant here authorized the sheriff to seize all copies of the specified titles, and since P-K [the distributor] was not afforded a hearing on the question of the obscenity even of the seven novels before the warrant was issued, the procedure was likewise constitutionally deficient.[12]

What the Court was asserting here was that neither local indignation nor the censor's zeal could substitute for due process of law. The Court was demanding strict adherence to legal process in exactly the same spirit in which they demanded the criminals be advised of their rights. However, the net effect was to strengthen the position of the Court and to cause anguish among partisans of suppression.

The Court did not stop with books and printed matter. It reversed a New York ruling that prohibited showing of the movie Lady Chatterly's Lover. The New York court had depended upon a New York statute which declared illegal any movie ". . . which portrays acts of immorality. . . as desirable, acceptable, or proper patterns of behavior."[13] The Court held that such a ruling suppressed ideas, and reversed. In Jacobellis v. Ohio, the Court also reversed conviction for possession of an obscene film, on the basis that the film was not obscene according to Roth. The Court broadcast its precedent with good effect.

Nor was the Court satisfied to reverse state convictions; it treated federal authorities with equal disapproval. The Postmaster General found his own prosecutions under 18 U. S. C. A., Sec. 1461 reversed. In a per curiam[14] decision in Sunshine Book Co. v. Summerfield,[15] the Court reversed a federal court conviction without comment. The justices likewise reversed the conviction in One, Incorporated v. Olesen, Postmaster of Los Angeles,[16] with equal casualness. Another significant reversal was the conviction in Manual Enterprises v. Day,[17] upon which the Court discussed the issues at some length.

At issue in Manual Enterprises was whether the Postmaster General could substitute administrative procedure for legal process. In question were a series of magazines obviously aimed at a homosexual audience, and which carried advertisements which indicated where putatively obscene pictures could be obtained. Postmaster J. Edward Day assumed that 18 U. S. C. A., Sec. 1461 empowered him to close the mails to material which appeared obscene to him, but the Court concluded that:

> ...18 U. S. C. Sec 1461 does not authorize the Postmaster General to employ an administrative process of his own to close the mails to matter which, in his view, falls within the ban of that section.[18]

Manual Enterprises has some interesting aspects, besides the element of administrative suppression.[19] For one, it crystallized the Roth formula into an integral unit. The Court noted:

> The Court of Appeals was mistaken in considering that Roth made 'prurient interest' appeal the sole [emphasis added] test of obscenity.[20]

The opinion goes on to state that "community standards" and the "average person" must be considered also, and that unless the material offends these criteria it cannot be obscene. Thus, Manual Enterprises made the Roth test a unit of inseparable parts, a doctrine which was firmly repeated in Ginzburg.

Manual Enterprises anticipated Ginzburg in two other ways; first, the Court raised the issue of advertising (since the advertisements in the magazines were charged with indicating where obscene materials could be obtained), and pointed out that the publisher could not know whether the materials advertised in his magazines were obscene, could not reasonably investigate them all, and could not be held responsible if his advertisers purveyed obscene material. Advertising contained in magazines, and for magazines themselves, had not been a major consideration before. The question sprouted in Manual Enterprises, or how material was used and by whom, and flowered in Ginzburg.

Next, in concluding the opinion, the Court added a personal footnote, a footnote almost chilling in its implications, but one that apparently went unnoticed at the time. The Court opined:

> ...nothing in this opinion of course remotely implies approval of the type of magazines published by these petitioners, still less the sordid motives [emphasis added] which prompted their publication.[21]

The judicial recognition of "sordid motives," and the admission that the Court was aware of them, presages Ginzburg and the "pandering" charge raised there; however, this subtle note was ignored, which is one reason why Ginzburg surprised so many people.

During the period of time under discussion, several more obscenity cases were adjudicated by the Court, and Roth was cited as the controlling precedent. In Times Film Corp. v. Chicago,[22] Mounce v. U. S.[23] and Tralins v. Gerstein,[24] the Court gave per curiam reversals to several convictions, each time citing Roth. Even Henry Miller's Tropic of Cancer, which had fought its way through a dozen state courts, finally had its day before the Supreme Court in Grove Press v. Gerstein.[25] For all the sound and fury it generated elsewhere, Miller's novel rated only a per curiam reversal of its Florida conviction. After the searching debate in Roth, Alberts, Manual Enterprises, all of which involved material with no literary appeal, Miller's novel got no more than a sideways glance from the Court; the Court missed its opportunity to offer some immortal critical judgments.[26]

Notes

1. As indicated in Shepard's United States Citations: Case Edition, Supplements, 1943 - 1964, and 1964 - 1968 (Shepard's Citations, Inc.: Colorado Springs).

2. Rembar, op. cit., 45-58.

3. Roth v. United States, 354 U. S. 496 (1957).

4. 361 U. S. 147 (1959).

5. Ibid., 150.

6. Idem, 155.

7. 367 U. S. 717 (1961).

8. Ibid., 731.

9. 372 U. S. 58 (1963).

10. 378 U. S. 205 (1964).

11. 372 U. S. 59 (1963).

12. 378 U. S. 210 (1964).

13. Kingsley International Pictures Corp. v. New York, 360 U. S. 685 (1959).

14. Per curiam, or "by the court," implies an element on unanimity, or ease in reaching a decision; per curiam opinions usually give only the barest pertinent facts, and seem almost perfunctory.

15. 355 U. S. 372 (1958).

16. 355 U. S. 371 (1958).

17. 370 U. S. 478 (1962).

18. Ibid., summary at 479.

19. Postmaster Day's use of administrative procedure illustrates how material may be suppressed without ever coming to bar, and, thus, suggests one method of illegal suppression open to censors. The issue will be considered more fully in a subsequent chapter.

20. 370 U. S. 486 (1962).

21. Idem, 495.

22. 355 U. S. 35 (1957).

23. 355 U. S. 180 (1957).

24. 378 U. S. 576 (1964).

25. 378 U. S. 577 (1964).

26. In the _Grove Press_ case, specific reliance was placed on _Jacobellis v. Ohio_, 378 U. S. 184; however, _Jacobellis_ depended largely on _Roth._

5. Ginzburg and His Enemies

Had he not run afoul of the courts, Ralph Ginzburg would probably have become a significant member of American publishing circles. He began his career with Esquire, and helped raise it from its salacious past to its present sophistication. He later joined Look magazine, and was partly responsible for the change of its format about 1960, at which time Look changed from being a quasi-pulp family magazine to one with pretensions of intellect. He left Look in 1961 to form his own publishing firm.[1] Besides being called "brilliant" and "creative," Ginzburg was a flamboyant, possibly egregious person whose very self-confidence worked against him, even before he went into court.[2]

In any event, Ginzburg formed a corporation and set about publishing material devoted to sexual candor.[3] He published a hardcover periodical entitled Eros which was devoted to the erotic in art and literature; a weekly newsletter entitled Liaison which promised salacious news and commentary; and The Housewife's Handbook of Selective Promiscuity, a book by Mrs. Helen Rey, of Phoenix, Arizona. Mrs. Rey's Handbook concerned her own sexual adventures and misadventures, which apparently began at the age of three and continued without interruption to middle age. Mrs. Rey had originally published her book privately, and sent personal letters to psychologists, doctors, and marriage counselors, offering it for sale. About 12,000 copies were sold before Ginzburg gathered the Handbook into his publishing list.[4]

Ginzburg veritably flooded the country with mailed advertisements for his material. He tried, with poor wit and no success, to mail these advertisements from Blue Ball and Intercourse, Pennsylvania, but could not secure bulk mailing permits because of the quantity of material involved; he did secure a permit at Middlesex, New Jersey. Thereupon, thousands of advertising brochures were sent to academics and other people who might have had an intellectual interest in the material. However, large numbers went everywhere else. Ginzburg apparently bought his mailing lists from firms which prepare them, but did not investigate the names on the lists; as a result, a large number of his advertisements went to school-age children.[5]

Eventually, Ginzburg was charged with mailing obscene materials and was brought to trial in Pennsylvania. Ginzburg contended in Fact that the venue was chosen carefully, to inconvenience him, since he lived in New York, and also to assure that a conservative prudish judge would be sitting. The venue was chosen according to a 1958 amendment to Section 1461 of the U. S. Code which allows a publisher to be prosecuted at both the place of mailing and the place of delivery.[6] Ginzburg was found guilty, and appealed. The appelate court, the U. S. Court of Appeals, Third Circuit, upheld the conviction,[7] and Ginzburg appealed to the Supreme Court. At first, the Court denied *certiorari*, refusing to hear the case at all, but then reversed itself and agreed to hear the case. The case was heard with *Mishkin v. New York* (383 U. S. 502) and *Memoirs of a Lady of Pleasure [Fanny Hill] v. Massachusetts* (383 U. S. 413). Mishkin sold "bondage" books, aimed at homosexual and sado-masochistic audiences; his conviction was upheld. *Fanny Hill*, once threatened by suppression in Massachusetts, emerged with her conviction reversed, free to circulate among the brahmins.

The publishing world generally assumed that Ginzburg would be acquitted. The feeling was that the original conviction was an error, that *Roth* demanded Ginzburg's conviction be reversed. Charles Rembar, defending *Fanny Hill* in the same Supreme Court session, felt Ginzburg's chances for reversal were better than his own.[8] Perversely, on March 21, the first day of Spring, 1966, the Court upheld Ginzburg's conviction. To uphold his conviction was surprise enough, but the circuitous path by which the Court did so was more surprising. Four justices dissented. Justice Potter Stewart, who rarely defended obscenity, who dissented on several obscenity reversals, and who stated in a Court opinion, "I can't define hard-core pornography, but I know it when I see it,"[9] was provoked to take sharp exception with the majority. Justice Harlan, no friend of obscene material and an advocate of state authority, delivered an opinion accusing the Court of failing to follow its own guidelines. Justices Black and Douglas, consistent with earlier positions, dissented; Black sadly, Douglas almost bitterly. Clearly, the decision divided the house, even if not along its normal lines. Of particular surprise to some people, however, was the fact that Justice Byron R. White, appointed by the late President John F. Kennedy in 1962, and Justice Abe Fortas, appointed by President Lyndon B. Johnson, in 1965, both voted with the majority. Justice Fortas had been particularly admired as a non-parochial man, and certainly his position in the Ginzburg case is not consistent with any position he has taken vis-a-vis obscenity since.[10]

Nor did the Court find accord in Mishkin and Fanny Hill. In Mishkin, Justices Black, Stewart, and Douglas dissented; Douglas, however, wrote a single opinion for Ginzburg and Mishkin, while Black and Stewart wrote separate opinions for each case. In Fanny Hill, Justices Brennan, Warren, and Fortas reversed for reasons expressed in a tripartite opinion, Justices Black and Stewart concurred for the reasons given in their dissent in Ginzburg, and Douglas wrote a separate, concurring opinion. Justice Tom Clark, relatively silent in such matters, wrote a separate dissenting opinion, as did Justices Harlan and White. The three obscenity cases produced thirteen different opinions, fourteen if Douglas' are counted in both Ginzburg and Mishkin. Thus was the law asserted by the nation's definitive court.

Beyond the Court, in the public arena, the decision gained the approval of Time magazine, Cardinal Francis Spellman, Norman Vincent Peale, the Citizens for Decent Literature (CDL),[11] and numerous religious leaders and publications. The law journals recorded negative reactions to the decision. Of 24 law journals examined for this study,[12] 19 denounced the decision as erroneous and confusing; four hedged, seeking logic in the confusion, rather than offering to dispute the Court's finding; only one of the 24 gave unqualified approval to the Court's decision: the Villanova Law Review.[13] As a final note, the respected London Economist called the decision "astonishing."[14] Surely, the Court wrought ill that day.

Since the decision did create somewhat of a legal tempest, it requires full attention; thus, despite the offense to patience and logic, the opinion, delivered by Justice

Brennan, deserves extended quoting (documentation omitted; numbers in brackets are page numbers of the opinion):

[465]

> We affirm [Ginzburg's conviction]. Since petitioners do not argue that the trial judge misconceived ... the standards... enunciated in Roth... the only [sic] serious question is whether those standards were correctly applied.
>
> In the cases in which this Court has decided obscenity questions since Roth, it has regarded the materials as sufficient in themselves for the determination of the questions. In the present case, however, the prosecution charged the offense in the context of the circumstances of production, sale, and publicity and assumed that, standing alone, the publications themselves might not be obscene. We agree that the question of obscenity may include consideration of the setting in which the publications were presented as an aid to determining the question

[466]

> of obscenity.... we view the publications against a background of commercial exploitation of erotica solely for the sake of their prurient appeal....
>
> [footnote 6, 466] It is suggested that petitioners were unaware that the record being established could be used in support of such an approach [i. e., pandering charge], and that petitioners should be afforded a new trial. However, the trial transcript clearly reveals that at several points the Government announced its theory that made the mode of distribution relevant to the determination of obscenity....

[467]

> ... Besides testimony as to the merit of the material, there was abundant evidence to show that each of the accused publications was originated

or sold as stock in trade of the sordid business of pandering -- 'the business of purveying textual or graphic matter openly advertised to appeal to the erotic interest of their customers....'[15]

[468]

The 'leer of the sensualist' also permeates the advertising for the three publications [which]... stressed the sexual candor of the respective publications, and openly boasted that the publishers would take full advantage of what they regarded an unrestricted license allowed by law in the expression of sex and sexual matters....[16]

[469]

...The solicitation [for the Handbook] was indiscriminate, not limited to those, such as physicians or psychiatrists, who might independently discern the book's

[470]

therapeutic worth. Inserted in each advertisement was a slip labelled 'GUARANTEE' and reading 'Documentary Books, Inc. unconditionally guarantees full refund...if the book fails to reach you because of U. S. Post Office censorship interference.' Similar slips appeared in the advertising for EROS and Liaison; they highlighted the gloss petitioners put on the publications, eliminating any doubt that the purchaser was being asked to buy.

This evidence, in our view, was relevant in determining the ultimate question of obscenity and in the context of this record serves to resolve all ambiguity and doubt [sic]. The deliberate representation of petitioner's publications as erotically arousing, for example, stimulated the reader to accept them as prurient...the brazenness of such an appeal heightens the offensiveness of the publications to those who are offended by such material....Where the purveyor's sole emphasis is on the sexually provocative aspects of his publications, that fact may be decisive in the determination of obscenity. Certainly in a prosecution, which, as here, does not necessarily imply suppression

[471]

of the materials involved, the fact that they originate or are used as a subject of pandering is relevant to the application of the Roth test....

[472]

...Petitioners...deliberately emphasized the sexually provocative aspects of the work, in order to catch the salaciously disposed. They proclaimed its obscenity; and we cannot conclude that the court below erred in taking their own evaluation at its face value and declaring the book as a whole obscene despite the other evidence [that it was not].

The decision in United States v. Rebuhn, 109 F. 2d 512 [1940], is persuasive [sic] authority for our conclusion.....[17]

[474]

...in close cases evidence of pandering may be probative with respect to the nature of the material in question and thus satisfy the Roth test ....the fact that each of these publications was created or exploited entirely on the basis of its appeal to prurient interests strengthens the conclusions that the transactions

[475]

here were sales of illicit merchandise, not sales of constitutionally protected matter. A conviction for mailing obscene publications...explained in part by this element, does not necessarily suppress the materials in question, nor chill their proper distribution for a proper use....All that will have been determined is that questionable

> publications are obscene in a context which brands them as obscene as that term is defined in Roth . . . .
>
> It is important to stress that this analysis simply elaborates [sic] the test by which the obscenity vel non of the material must be judged.

Thus the majority opinion, an opinion based on: 1) gross extrapolation from the lower court's interest in circumstances; 2) interpolation of the concept of "pandering" into the Roth test, where it does not exist (that is, the Court stepped back to Roth, added "pandering" to Warren's concurring opinion, and then cited the freshly revised precedent); and 3) a selective quotation from the ALI Model Penal Code, that omits significant material, material which would have virtually required another decision. Last, for a precedent, the Court is reduced to citing Rebuhn v. U. S., a 26-year-old case.[18]

To detail these points: the lower court had accepted evidence to support a conclusion that "pandering" was present and that circumstances of distribution were important; however, the issue was not a part of the formal charge; hence, Ginzburg's attorneys, on appeal, and also the dissenting justices, contended that Ginzburg had been convicted of a crime of which he had not been accused. The only point at which the Court faces this objection is in footnote 6, page 466. Now, if a man is to be convicted, certainly the objections of four Supreme Court Justices to his conviction deserve more than a footnote; they deserve searching analysis. Instead, the Court took the "pandering" bit in its teeth, and ran.

Furthermore, the term "pandering" does not occur at all in the Roth opinions. Justice Warren, concurring for reasons not relied on by the Court, and for reasons he continued to advance, but which had not, so far, been accepted by the Court, said in Roth:

> The defendants in both these cases [Roth and Alberts] were engaged in the business of purveying textual or graphic matter openly advertised to appeal to the erotic interest of their customers.[19]

Warren did not use the word "pandering," but Brennan introduced it into the *Ginzburg* opinion in such a way that it becomes an appositive to the phrase "purveying... matter... to appeal to the erotic interest of their customers." The manipulation is crude, and one wonders how the Court could offer such a gross piece of work as a product of serious logic. Likewise, just as Warren, in *Roth*, equated "erotic interest" and "prurient interest" in contradiction to the ALI Model Penal Code, so Brennan repeated the error in *Ginzburg*.

The Court had invoked, in *Roth* and in documentation in *Ginzburg*, the ALI *Model Penal Code* often enough to indicate that they were influenced by it; in both cases, the *Code* is quoted, and in *Roth* the "prurient interest" phrase is borrowed from it; however, in *Ginzburg*, as in *Roth*, the Court took only as much of the *Code* as would support their finding. The *Code* actually defines "pandering" as "... the deliberate stimulation and exploitation of emotional tensions arising from the conflict between social convention and the individual's sex drive."[20] Such being the ALI definition, the Court should examine for evidence of "tension" arising from these factors, since *Roth* plainly declared that "Sex and obscenity are not synonymous,"[21] and since Ginzburg's materials could hardly create any more tension than other materials to which the Court had granted First Amendment protection. Indeed, one commentator has suggested that expert testimony from psychiatrists might be introduced into a trial to determine whether such a tension has been created.[22] Even so, the tension might be considered a mental aberration of the subject who feels the "tension," rather than a crime requiring imprisonment of the distributor of the tension-creating material.

As another disturbing element of the opinion, the evidence presented has been perverted to sustain the conviction. Brennan says "petitioners... proclaimed its obscenity...," in reference to the *Handbook*; now Brennan's term "obscenity" is his own generalization of other terms petitioners did use; granted, they "stressed" the "sexual candor" of their material, but they did not at any point declare that "These materials are obscene." Thus, Brennan accuses them of more than they did. Next, he points out that petitioners were promised a refund if the *Handbook* were held up by postal censorship; in various footnotes he cites phrases from the advertising in which Ginzburg stated that the material was available only because of recent liberal decisions by the Supreme Court.[23]

Brennan claims these advertising promises prove the material was obscene, when what they do prove is that Ginzburg firmly believed they were not, that he believed so strongly that the materials were legal under recent decisions that he boldly said as much. Granted, if material is required to pass court review, people will wonder what makes it suspicious, and will perhaps desire to read it; however, that material is expected to pass court tests to be acceptable for mailing is hardly a declaration of its obscenity; it is quite a contrary sort of statement, and Ginzburg invested about $500,000 of his and his backers' money in their faith in their interpretation of the state of the law. Yet, the best Brennan could say for all their effort was that it proved the "obscenity" of the works in question, or, at least, "pandering." Granted, a penchant for rigid logic has not characterized Brennan's opinions; even so, some limit to absurdity ought to exist, but those limits should not be established by Supreme Court decisions.

Another factor arises in the _Ginzburg_ decision: that the justices did not like Ginzburg and/or his business, and were determined to punish him one way or another. Friedman reports of the Court session:

> Those who witnessed his [Justice Brennan's] reading of the opinion were struck by his anger and emotion. There was no question that he was offended by what Ginzburg had done.[24]

Toward this same point, Epstein observed:

> In its choice of such prejudicial epithets as 'pandering' and 'the leer of the sensualist' to describe Ginzburg's activities, the Court seems to be saying that Ginzburg's crime was no more than a function of his personality: that he was a vulgarian... and had no right to trade in a market whose delicate and dangerous products must be limited to gentlemen and scholars. Such an _ad hominem_ judgment can hardly have been what the Court intended, no matter how the obscurity and occasional

> passion of Justice Brennan's language may seem to support such an interpretation.[25]

For several obvious reasons, then, the majority opinion that upheld a conviction that would imprison Ginzburg for five years seems poorly motivated and inconsistent with precedent. However, the best objections came directly from the dissenting justices and, curiously, the dissenting justices were in closer agreement than usual.

To the point that Ginzburg was convicted of a crime for which he had not been charged, nor had the opportunity to defend himself against, Justice Black declared:

> One stark fact emerges with clarity... That fact is that Ginzburg, petitioner here, is now finally and authoritatively condemned to serve five years in prison for distributing printed matter about sex which neither Ginzburg nor anyone else could possibly have known to be criminal.[26]

Justice Harlan objected:

> What I fear the Court has done today is in effect to write a new statute, but without the sharply focused definitions and standards necessary in such a sensitive area. Casting such a dubious gloss over a straightforward 101-year-old statute (see 13 Stat. 507) is for me an astonishing piece of judicial improvisation.[27]

To which Justice Stewart added:

> But Ginzburg was not charged with 'commercial exploitation'; he was not charged with 'pandering'; he was not charged with 'titillation.' Therefore, to affirm his conviction now on any of those grounds...is to deny him due process of law.... Neither the statute under which Ginzburg was convicted nor any other federal statute...makes 'commercial exploitation' or 'pandering' or 'titillation' a criminal offense.
>
> Today the Court assumes the power to deny Ralph Ginzburg the protection of the First Amendment

> because it disapproves of his 'sordid business.' That is a power the Court does not possess.[28]

Thus, while the majority seemed satisfied to convict Ginzburg for his "sordid" business of "pandering," many questions were left unresolved. Justice Black objected to the Roth standards in general, and their application in Ginzburg in particular, observing that:

> In the final analysis the submission of such an issue as this to a judge or juror amounts to nothing more than a request for the judge or juror to assert his own personal beliefs.... Upon this subjective determination the law becomes certain for the first and last time.[29]

Justice Harlan warned of this same subjectivity in obscenity cases:

> [According to this decision] The First Amendment ... no longer fully protects material on its face nonobscene, for such material must now also be examined in the light of the defendant's conduct .... This seems to me a mere euphemism for allowing punishment of a person... because a judge or jury may not find him or his business agreeable.[30]

Justice Stewart pointed out that the Constitutional mandate given the Court required "restricted" views of suppressible material, and suggested that only "hard-core" pornography be suppressed. Justice Douglas devoted his dissent to a general analysis of the question of whether any material could be suppressed; since his dissent applied also to Mishkin, in which a seller of "bondage" books had been convicted of selling obscene materials, he included in his opinion an eloquent plea for the rights of the aberrant members of society to read what they wished:

> Why is it unlawful to cater to the needs of this group? They are, to be sure, somewhat offbeat, nonconformist, and odd. But we are not in the realm of criminal conduct, only ideas and tastes. Some like Chopin, others like 'rock and roll.' But why is freedom of the press and expression

> denied to them [the aberrant ones]? Are they to be barred from communicating in symbols important to them? When the Court today speaks of 'social value,' does it mean 'value' to the majority? Why is not a minority 'value' cognizable? ...Why is communication by the 'written word' forbidden [to them]? If we were wise enough, we might know that communication may have greater therapeutic value than any sermon that those of the 'normal' community can ever offer. But if the communication is of value to the masochistic community or to others of the deviant community, how can it be said to be 'utterly without redeeming social importance'? 'Redeeming' to whom? 'Important' to whom?[31]

By raising the question of a privileged class of readers who can restrict the reading of others, Douglas raises a consideration which weakens the _Rebuhn_ precedent.[32] By indicating in _Rebuhn_ and in _Ginzburg_ that materials have a "proper" or "legitimate" use, the Court endorses the privileges of one group over another. Scholars, doctors, and psychologists may read obscene material, but the layman may not; likewise, doctors and scholars presumably have no prurient interest or are incapable of "titillation," and thus may examine illegal material while _hoi polloi_ may not. The Court does not regard at all the problem of how scholars will acquire such material if it is illegal to sell it. Rather, it asserts that: 1) "Some material, as Roth's or Mishkin's, is illegal in any circumstances," and 2) "Some material, as Rebuhn's or Ginzburg's, is illegal only if it is sold in such a way that it appeals to 'prurient interests' or 'titillates'." Such concepts suggest that if the scholar uses his obscene material to entertain himself, the seller, at the moment, becomes guilty of a crime, whereas as soon as the scholar returns to objective study of the material, the seller is no longer guilty. Such a situation is analogous to the one in which a professor studies _Hamlet_ on one occasion, reads it for pleasure on another, and permits it to appeal to his "prurient interest" on another.

Now, throughout all Supreme Court cases, until Justice Douglas raised the question in _Ginzburg_, the question of whether the scholar, or layman, enjoyed having his "prurient" interest stimulated was never considered. Instead, the Supreme Court clearly outlawed "prurient" interest, except that of scholars, an exception that clearly violates the "equal protection of the laws" clause of the Fourteenth Amendment, a clause which ought to apply to literate and illiterate, just as it must apply to Negro and Caucasian. The Rebuhn conviction also depended on such an assumption. However, the Court does not believe so, and distinguishes between those whose "prurient" interest may be appealed to, and those who must suffer.[33]

Ginzburg opens another Pandora's Box of legal difficulties in its admission that Ginzburg's conviction did "not necessarily imply suppression of the materials involved," nor " chill their proper distribution for a proper use." Up to Roth, the question in obscenity cases was whether the materials were obscene; if they were, either they could be suppressed, or the distributor could be jailed, or both. In his concurring opinion in Roth, Warren raised the question of persons: a shift from an in rem (the thing) to an in personem (the person) orientation. In cases after Roth, Warren reiterated this preference but the Court did not endorse it: it was simply too great a shift of law; no precedents, except perhaps Rebuhn, and U. S. v. 31 Photographs,[34] which Warren did not cite in Roth, could be interpreted to support such a finding. However, in Ginzburg, the Court specifically accepted an in personem interpretation of the case.

By establishing an in personem precedent, the Court unduly confuses obscenity law; advertising and use of material determines its obscenity. Thus, the hardest of Justice Stewart's "hard-core" pornography might be legal, if decorously advertised, while approved books, such as Tropic of Cancer, might be illegal if advertised in a manner to appeal to "prurient" interest. Grove Press thought of this possibility, and kept their advertising for Lady Chatterley's Lover and Tropic of Cancer discreet and dignified. However, they were seeking to imply that they really did not believe people would buy these books because they were possibly obscene. The method was a ploy in the game that pretends scholars have no "prurient" interest and that illiterates will buy Tropic of Cancer because it has been praised by Karl Shapiro. The worst legal possibility, though, is that the in personem precedent in Ginzburg could set off a spate of local and state prosecutions on the basis of advertising. Indeed, since Ginzburg, one federal circuit judge sought to suppress a book entitled _Lust Job_ because its cover presumably titillated.[35]

One commentator, addressing himself to these problems, applies _Ginzburg_ to several hypothetical cases, which may be paraphrased thus:

> Case 1. _Eros_ or the _Handbook_ is sold without use or knowledge of the publisher's advertising.
>
> Case 2. Prosecution for selling the _Handbook_ without objectionable promotion.
>
> Case 3. Selling the _Handbook_ with advertising substantially similar to Ginzburg's.
>
> Case 4. A statutory action to have the Handbook declared obscene _in rem_.
>
> Case 5. Prosecution of the head of Ginzburg's firm for selling _Eros_, _Liaison_, and the _Handbook_ at any future date.[36]

The commentator's full exegesis would occupy an undue portion of this paper; suffice it to say that while the above hypothetical cases seem clear, i.e., that only Case 3 invites successful prosecution, still a competent legal commentator perceives possibilities for prosecution in the other cases. The particular commentator was analyzing the _Ginzburg_ opinion line-by-line, noting the legal implications of its various phrases. He finds it a "confusing, self-contradictory opinion," of which he observes: "As an attempt to rationalize an anomalous result, the device [Brennan's logic] and its accompanying reasoning are a failure; whether they will endure is another question."[37]

Notes

1. For a short biographical sketch, see "Playboy Interview: Ralph Ginzburg," 13 _Playboy_ (July, 1966), 47ff.; curiously, _Look_ magazine, in the early 1960's, became devoted to hagiographic treatment of the late President John F. Kennedy, at the same time that the President's brother, the late Robert F. Kennedy, was devoting himself to the

prosecution of obscene material, including Ginzburg's.

2. See the issue of Fact magazine published in 1965 in which Ginzburg recounts hostility toward him; he also contends that anti-Semitism and insinuations that he was homosexual (insinuations apparently based on his manner of dress) were partly responsible for his conviction. This writer recalls the irritation of faculty members at the University of Alaska, in early 1962, at receiving Ginzburg's advertising material; their offense arose from the fact that Ginzburg's material emphasized the keyhole-peeping aspect of his work, and the faculty members felt patronized; many would have liked to have subscribed, but did not because they did not want to accept membership in the group that Ginzburg identified as interested in his material.

3. Ginzburg had privately published a bibliographical cum critical work entitled An Unhurried View of Erotica (New York: Helmsman Press, 1958); he contended that preparation of this work convinced him of the need to strip sex of its guilty cover; see the "Interview" in Playboy.

4. 383 U. S. 472 (1966); idem, at 468 indicates that 5,000 more copies were distributed by Ginzburg.

5. Day, [J. Edward, Postmaster General], "Mailing Lists and Pornography," 52 American Bar Association Journal 1103 (December, 1966); Day's jaundiced attitude toward obscenity warps his objectivity in this article. For example, he reports that his office received 35,000 letters complaining about Ginzburg's advertising, but says nothing about how many of these were exactly identical and came from whole classes in parochial schools, from school children who could have had no awareness of the issues involved; compare Ginzburg's comments in Playboy, supra, note 1. Curiously, these 35,000 letters were never mentioned as appropriate evidence to Ginzburg's conviction.

6. H. R. 6239 (1958); Day, op. cit., takes great pride in this law as a form of justice; most others see it as means of suppression through financial drain; see Hutchison and Friedman, supra. However, the venue question was not raised by Ginzburg in his own defense; see 383 U. S. 464 (1966), at note 1.

7. 338 F. 2d. 12 (1965)

8. Rembar, op. cit., 425; Rembar's observation, that "The materials [sold by Ginzburg]...put less of a strain on the law than did Fanny Hill," is not offered in defense of Ginzburg, but as part of a straw man that Rembar invokes every ten pages or so, the better to reflect on his own brilliance as a lawyer. In view of decisions after Roth, neither Ginzburg nor Rembar had much to worry about. In re the public feeling about Ginzburg's case, see Friedman, supra, 72, and Jason Epstein, "The Obscenity Business," Atlantic Monthly (Aug. 1966), p. 56-60.

9. Jacobellis v. Ohio. 378 U. S. 197 (1964).

10. Note, for example, that the U. S. Senate refused to confirm Justice Fortas for the position of Chief Justice in 1968; a significant issue in the denial was Fortas' alleged sympathy for obscene material. Someone should have pointed out Ginzburg to the senators. As another curiosity, Fortas filed an amicus curiae brief in Roth, in the name of the law firm to which he belonged, in which he espoused Black's absolute position; granted, a lawyer need not believe in every brief he files, but the fact raises the difficulty of predicting how a judge will apply the law.

11. Cited by Armstrong, op. cit., 148.

12. About 35 individual law journals responded to Ginzburg in either commentary or article, but not all these could be encompassed within the investigation from which this paper proceeds. In contrast, only nine journals specifically responded to Roth, and about six more in a general way; all saw Roth as clarifying the difficulties of obscenity law.

13. Greiner, 11 Villanova Law Review 874 (1966).

14. April 2, 1966, 39.

15. A footnote gives Roth at 495-496 as the source of the quotation; it is from Warren's Roth opinion, and gives to Warren an undeserved legislative authority.

16. The source of the phrase "leer of the sensualist" is not provided; Rembar used it in his brief for Fanny

Hill, too, also as a quotation, without documentation; it comes from Judge Woolsey's opinion re Ulysses.

17. The significant doctrine of Rebuhn: "Most of the books could lawfully have passed through the mails, if directed to those who would be likely to use them for the purposes for which they were written.... They might also have been lawfully sold to laymen who wished seriously to study the sexual practices of savage or barbarous peoples, or sexual abberations; in other words, most of them were not obscene per se.... the defendants had indiscriminately flooded the mails with advertisements, plainly designed merely to catch the prurient.... the circulars were no more than appeals to the salaciously disposed...."

18. A more recent precedent was available in U. S. v. 31 Photographs, 156 F. Supp. 350 (1957), which involved photographs imported for the use at the Indiana University Sex Research Institute; cited by Schiller, 16 American University Law Review 127, (1966), at note 57.

19. 354 U. S. 495-496.

20. Cited by Friedman, op. cit., 89.

21. 354 U. S. 487.

22. Ross, "Expert Testimony in Obscenity Cases," 18 Hastings Law Journal (1966), 173-174; see also Justice Harlan, dissenting at 383 U. S. 496: "...as I read the Court's opinion, the burden would be on the Government to show that the motives of the defendant were to pander...." In any event, the ALI Code aims elsewhere: the Code is concerned with the purveyor who promises something and does not deliver, rather than the man who delivers. If Ginzburg's matter did appeal to prurient interest, he was not exploiting the tension, but satisfying it; he was not promising something arising from tension, and failing to deliver, as the ALI Code envisioned; thus, the Code was not appropriate to the case at all, unless Ginzburg's material was obscene, and if the material was obscene the conviction cannot be upheld on grounds of "pandering." However, see Schwartz, "Morals Offenses and the Model Penal Code," 63 Columbia Law Review (1963), 669; and Petersen, "Notes: Constitutional Law," 41 Tulane Law Review (1966) 129.

23. 383 U. S. 468, note 9.

24. Friedman, *op. cit.*, 74.

25. *op. cit.*, 59.

26. 383 U. S. 476.

27. *Ibid.*, 494-495.

28. *Ibid.*, 501.

29. *Ibid.*, 479

30. *Ibid.*, 494.

31. *Ibid.*, 489.

32. See also "The Supreme Court, 1965 Term," 80 *Harvard Law Review* (1966), 193, at note 37, which denies similarities between *Ginzburg* and *Rebuhn*.

33. Epstein, *op. cit.*, 59, discusses this same question briefly.

34. 156 F. Supp. 350 (1957). One may also ask: Why did the Court refuse to use the phrase "*in personem*," even though it used the concept? Because *in personem* is a recognized legal doctrine with its own interpretations, and *Ginzburg* was counter to the accepted attitude toward *in personem* cases?

35. Cited by McPheeters, "Recent Cases," 32 *Missouri Law Review* (1967), 130.

36. Dyson, "Looking-Glass Law: An Analysis of the Ginzburg Case," 28 *University of Pittsburgh Law Review* (1966), 1.

37. *Idem*, 15-16.

6. Motivations for Ginzburg

The critic's umbrage at the Supreme Court's finding in Ginzburg must be tempered with the caveat that the decision did not occur in a vacuum. The very anomaly of the decision indicates some kind of origin, for so peculiar a decision could hardly have been accidental.

The first possibility, most easily disposed of, is that the Court was responding to public pressure. J. Edward Day's objections to obscene material have been noted; that a high government official feels so strongly about such material indicates some pressure on the Court. Furthermore, Ginzburg said in his interview with Playboy magazine:

> ... soon after I began publishing Eros, Bobby [sic] Kennedy, then Attorney General, and J. Edward Day, then Postmaster General, decided they had better crack down on literature dealing forthrightly with sex.[1]

Leon Friedman, writing in the American Scholar, dared suggest:

> Somewhere not very far back in the justices' minds is an awareness of the danger in frustrating too often the conservative elements of the country in every area that concerns them. Why not throw them a bone once in a while? Who cares about Ralph Ginzburg?[2]

The ad hominem element has been mentioned earlier in this study.[3]

Beyond these possibilities, one can suggest that Warren finally persuaded the Court to accept his view, but such a suggestion begs the question of why the Court accepted Warren's view.

A better explanation exists in the concept of "variable obscenity," that obscenity varies according to circumstances. This concept is the virtual brainchild of Professors William B. Lockhart and Robert C. McClure, of the University of Minnesota Law School. Professors Lockhart and McClure have established their reputations as legal experts in obscenity law by virtue of various articles on the matter, two in particular: "Literature, The Law of Obscenity and the Constitution" (38 Minnesota Law Review, 1954), and "Censorship of Obscenity: The Developing Constitutional Standards" (45 Minnesota Law Review, 1960). The substance of these articles was summarized by Professor Lockhart in an address at the University of Utah in 1961, and reprinted in 7 Utah Law Review (1961) under the title "Obscenity Censorship: The Core Constitutional Issue -- What is Obscene?" In this address, speaking for both himself and Professor McClure, and repeating almost *verbatim* some of their 1960 article, Porfessor Lockhart suggested:

> Constitutional freedom of expression requires that [D. H.] Lawrence's novel [*Lady Chatterley's Lover*] be free from censorship when sold to a primary audience...of mature, adult buyers. ... But when it is marketed in such a manner as to appeal to...sexually immature kids to nourish their craving for erotic fantasy, then...there is reason for censorship. This variable obscenity approach requires that in each instance the finding of obscenity be based upon the nature of the primary audience to which the sales appeal is made and the nature of the material's appeal to that audience.[4]

More of Professor Lockhart's address could be quoted, but the above quotation suffices to show that legal circles entertained an attitude that considered circumstances important to obscenity cases. The question of why "sexually immature kids" should be prevented from "nourishing" their fantasies is not examined. In *Roth*, the Court cited the 1954 article, and in *Fanny Hill*, a companion case to *Ginzburg*, both the 1954 and 1960 articles were cited. Thus, the Court was apprised of the work of Professors Lockhart and McClure, and may have cobbled up a philosophy from them. Had the Court done its homework as well as the professors (who, granted, did not have a deadline as the Court did), the attempt might have worked. Instead, it excluded from its "variable approach" the careful definitions and delineations that Lockhart and McClure considered necessary to such an approach. C. Peter Magrath discusses this exclusion, and its problems, in his study of the Court's 1966 decisions.[5]

The point of the foregoing is not that the Court did depend upon Lockhart and McClure, but only that if it did, that dependence would partially explain an otherwise unexplainable decision; however, the point must also be made, that if it did depend upon Lockhart and McClure, it did so in the same spirit and extent to which it depended on the ALI Model Penal Code: by taking what was suitable to the decision, and omitting the troublesome remainder.

Notes

1. op. cit., 120.

2. op. cit., 79.

3. Chapter V, page 47, note 27.

4. op. cit., 299; the full address contradicts the Ginzburg decision, but since the purpose here is not to compare Professor Lockhart and the Court, the contradiction will not be presented. Also, see 45 Minnesota Law Review 77; at note 426, the article cites Rebuhn as an example of how the "variable obscenity" approach would be applied.

5. "The Obscenity Cases: Grapes of Roth", 7 Supreme Court Review, 62-66 (1966).

7. *Ginzburg's* Companions

In passing, the companion cases that came before the Court along with *Ginzburg* deserve some attention. As has been stated, Edward *Mishkin* appealed to the Court for reversal of a conviction for selling obscene material in New York. His material consisted of cheaply-printed books dealing with sado-masochistic activities, and which, strictly speaking, contained comparatively little sex. His conviction was sustained.

Fanny Hill sought reversal of a Massachusetts *in rem* decision *which* would have barred her from the state. *Her* conviction was reversed.

These cases would mean little but for the fact that Mishkin's defense contended that his material appealed only to a special group, and that the "average person" would not find them appealing at all; thus, according to *Roth*, with its "average person" basis, his materials were *not obscene*. The Court, unimpressed, concluded that to appeal to the "prurient" interest of a deviant group was just as illegal as appealing to the "prurient" interest of the "average man." Mishkin was found guilty of "calculated purveyance of filth."[1] No attempt to define "filth," in the manner of defining "obscene" in *Roth*, was provided.

After the latter-day Comstock attitude that runs through *Ginzburg* and *Mishkin*, *Fanny Hill* is a revelation; there, *the justices* went *to extremes to de*clare their approval of the book; all, that is, except Justices Clark, Harlan, and White. Justice Clark objected to the book because he felt is was obscene, as did Justice White. Justice Harlan felt the states should be allowed to control obscenity within their own broundaries, and, therefore, the Court should not overturn a state decision.

The approving justices found *Fanny Hill* worthy of protection under *Roth*, but paused on *the way to w*arn that the book was not *pro*tected in all cases, but that "Evidence that the book was commercially exploited for the sake of prurient appeal... might justify the conclusion that the book was utterly without redeeming social importance."[2] At first glance, the Court might appear to be only repeating its Ginzburg dicta. However, the statement is more that than that: it is one more precedent, for if Ginzburg becomes overworked, Fanny Hill, at page 412, can be cited with equal effect.

The real virtue of Fanny Hill is in Justice Douglas' separate, concurring opinion. Douglas took the opportunity to lecture his brethren on the subject of literature and the law:

> We are judges, not literary experts or historians or philosophers. We are not competent to render an independent judgment as to the worth of this or any other book, except in our capacity as private citizens.[3]

He pointed out that judges in Massachusetts and New York disagreed on whether the book was obscene, and went on to object to circumstantial condemnation of any book, for "However florid its cover, whatever the pitch of its advertisements, the contents remain the same."[4]

Douglas referred to a "flood" of letters, many of them identical and apparently copied by school children, which reached his office every time an obscenity case came before the Court, and noted that many people desired to suppress books, but added that "Happily, we do not bow to them." He went on to give a historical survey of obscenity law, and to point out that Fanny Hill was involved in what must be the first prosecution for obscenity in the United States, in Boston in 1821. He made pointed reference to the fact that no one had proved a causal relationship between reading and antisocial behavior, and that, rather, the perceived correlations had so far been negative. He found, thus, two opportunities to refer to the pertinent article by Cairns, Paul, and Wishner, first in his historical survey, and later in his cause and effect discussion. He thus made quite clear that he felt that his brethren had not read the article, or if they had, that they had ignored it. One can almost envision the dignified Court squirming over Ginzburg and Mishkin while reading Douglas' opinion (unless they merely congratulated themselves on Fanny Hill?).

Douglas made two more telling points: he quoted at length a Universalist minister who contradicted Norman Vincent Peale's opinion of Fanny Hill and repudiated Peale's desire to suppress it. At another point, Douglas cited Judge Bok's famous discussion of whether he would want his daughter to read an allegedly obscene book; Judge Bok, of course, had said that he hoped his daughter would be able to deal emotionally with such a book by the time she was interested in reading it, but that if she were offended, she might close the book at page one. Douglas' opinion did not significantly influence the Court; however he deserves plaudits for thrusting germane questions before the Court, even if such questions are overruled by casuistic logic.

Notes

1. 383 U. S. 512.

2. Ibid., 420; again, a piece of logic difficult to accept, and more difficult to believe that such a presumed intellect as Abe Fortas would actively join in.

3. Ibid., 427.

4. Idem.

8. Post-Ginzburg

The Supreme Court apparently believed that Rebuhn provided "persuasive" authority for Ginzburg, that their logic resolved "all ambiguity and doubt," and that the decision simply "elaborates" the Roth test. However, the legal profession did not share the Court's confidence in the decision. As has been stated earlier, 19 legal commentators rejected the decision outright, four found the decision difficult to justify, and implicitly rejected it, while only one found it unequivocally agreeable.

Of the first category, the objectors, one said:

> It seems the Supreme Court has thoroughly confused an already vague area of the law. This confusion results from a judicial misinterpretation of the first amendment and the assertion by individual Justices of their personal approaches to censorship of obscenity.... If a penal statute embodied all the inherent inconsistences of the Supreme Court opinions, it would unquestionably be declared unconstitutionally vague. [1]

Another, concerned with legal problems, noted:

> ...a highly subjective element has been engrafted onto the Roth test and standards for judging obscenity. This added element will further confuse trial courts -- already embroiled in an area which defies any real delineation -- and add to the Supreme Court's flood of censorship cases.... it will seriously deter freedom of expression and expose this area to the self-appointed 'watch-guards' of the moral fiber of our society. [2]

And another:

> It is submitted that confusion and contradiction reign today because the Court has never offered

> a fully acceptable rationale to support the conclusion that the first amendment permits the censorship of obscenity, and because it has yet to define obscenity in a consistent and rational manner.[3]

And still another:

> Though paying lip service to the Roth test, the Court's new approach all but completely by-passes it.[4]

And one tempered with levity:

> A Board of Censors, after all, customarily agrees on what it is censoring (or not censoring) and why. Such an agreement is notably lacking in the three decisions and fourteen opinions announced on March 21, 1966. On the question of obscenity and the law a more appropriate imagery would liken the Court to the Tower of Babel.[5]

And one summarized the general feeling:

> The Court...has not clarified, but instead compounded, the problem of determining what constitutes obscene material. They have increased the determinative factors that will vary from case to case....it is now unlikely that anyone can know whether particular material is obscene until the Court announces its opinion in the case.[6]

The foregoing comments, and others cited earlier in this study, make abundantly clear that Ginzburg confused an already uncertain area of law. More comments could be quoted, but their value is marginal, since they only add to the accretion of reaction presented thus far. However, the legal profession is not interested in only carping from the sidelines; it is concerned about the effect that Ginzburg can have on prosecutions of presently approved books, on books yet unwritten, and on the forces of suppression which exist in the country. On the one hand, books which have been granted the right to circulate may be suppressed because of "pandering" in the advertising of them; Justice Brennan specifically said as much in the Fanny Hill decision, and the prosecution of Lust Job because of its cover has also been mentioned. Furthermore, a judge in Pennsylvania has held that a state may still declare a book obscene even after the Supreme Court has declared that the book is not.[7] These events produce the following apprehension:

> It is now possible for non-obscene material to be proscribed because of the conduct of the seller or publisher in promoting the material. This could lead to another round of attempts in the lower courts to ban such works as 'Lady Chatterley's Lover' and 'Ulysses,' both of which have been held to be not obscene per se.[8]

And, on Ginzburg as a precedent:

> The extent to which this concept of variable obscenity will dominate future obscenity determinations depends upon whether the courts apply the standards of Roth first and bring Ginzburg to bear only in a 'close case.' In view of the inability of a majority of the Court to concur in the meaning of Roth, this question might produce much litigation and appeal.[9]

And:

> The Court's opinion in these cases may well return obscenity litigation to the confusion existing prior to the Roth test. Every questionable publication which has previously escaped censorship ... is now vulnerable to partial or total suppression if it is being sold in a titillating manner. Moreover, literature which previously had been adjudicated as not obscene is now subject to new censorship litigation....[10]

The fact that the Ginzburg decision met considerable approval among suppression forces (which deplored the Fanny Hill decision) gives credence to the foregoing apprehensions. Individual prosecutors and policemen, and suppression societies and their individual members, are now encouraged to instigate proceedings against any number of booksellers on the basis of advertising, or, possibly, on the basis of the promotion of the books they sell. That is, if a publisher appeals to "prurient" interest in national publicity for such a book as Gore Vidal's recent novel, Myra Breckenridge, the bookseller who sells it could be prosecuted for "pandering." That the book was a national best-seller, and thus not "offensive to community standards," would be no defense, for the conviction would be based on "pandering."

In these possible prosecutions arises the most serious flaw of Ginzburg, a flaw which arises from its general confusion and its specific application of a "pandering" test, and a flaw that Justice Brennan passed over glibly with the assertion that the decision does not "chill their [obscene materials] proper distribution for a proper purpose." Justice Brennan implied that a rash of prosecutions should not follow the decision, but he may have underestimated the vigor of suppression forces. One commentator offers the bookstalls of New York's Times Square as a barometer of the legal climate, and notes:

> Times Square bookstores...responded to the new decisions by rearranging their displays.... Their expectation, and that of the legal profession, was that prosecutors and censors had been given new ammunition which would result in a great increase of prosecutions against publishers.... This was borne out when the New York City Police Department reported that arrests for the sale of distribution of allegedly obscene literature increased 300% within a week of the Court's decision.[11]

Now, if a Supreme Court decision encourages prosecution of booksellers, the booksellers must either bow to the wishes of the prosecutor or face the expense of a protracted legal process, with the knowledge that if they lose they may be imprisoned and fined. A bookseller, then, might reasonably prefer to bow to the wishes of a prosecutor, or even to a private agency which was threatening to file suit against him. Thus, the Supreme Court contributes, unwittingly, or perhaps in spite of Justice Brennan's assurance, to the suppression of printed material. Granted, little serious or eternally valuable literature will likely be suppressed, since vice societies usually aim at such material as Playboy and Evergreen Review, or that which Edward Mishkin sold. However, the battles against Tropic of Cancer and Lady Chatterley's Lover are not far past, and suppression societies have not established a reputation for refined distinctions between literature deserving censure and literature deserving praise. The danger, therefore, remains open and ill-defined; the bookseller still remains the obvious target of official and private censors.

Thus, one commentator warned:

> The careful weighing of constitutional niceties... is not carried out at the administrative level.... Regardless of the careful judicial review given to state or federal obscenity decisions, most cases of literary suppression will never be reviewed at all. The coercive force of threatening a bookseller, drugstore, magazine stand, etc., with a criminal prosecution acts almost as self-executing censorship in many areas. The cost of litigation and appeal leads one to believe that most censorship is sub-surface and is never reflected in reported cases. Too, where official censorship is condoned, the door is opened to informal and extra-legal suppression by private groups whose methods entail no notions of due process or of freedom of speech. Operating through the use of fear and coercion and playing on ignorance, the damage they have done to the intellectual climate in this nation is incalculable.[12]

And another believes:

> The inherent vagueness of the commercial exploitation concept as applied in close cases will undoubtedly discourage some expression which might otherwise have occurred. A finding of obscenity and affirmance of a conviction in a commercial exploitation context would greatly discourage anyone else from distributing the same material.[13]

Thus the major threat arising from Ginzburg is not that an obscenity case at bar becomes uncertain, but that legitimate booksellers may find their right to engage in business circumscribed by the forces of suppression.

The foregoing quotations may sound like the apocryphal Chicken Little, who could create universal tragedy out of slender inspiration. However, the question could be resolved by reference to court transcripts and citations. If many cases are argued with Ginzburg as guiding precedent, then clearly Ginzburg has become a strong precedent, and the above fears are justified; if not, then the above commentators are unnecessarily nervous. The difficulty here is the monumental task of sifting through every court case in which Ginzburg was cited, and of noting how it was applied. Shepard's Citations, the standard source for such research, indicates little about the cases it lists, other than to show that one case was cited in another. The Citations do show that Ginzburg has been cited 112 times since 1966, while Fanny Hill, and thereby Roth, has been cited 124 times. Roth itself was cited about 300 times between 1957 and 1968. The apparent conclusion is that Ginzburg has gone a great way in a short time.

However, since the Citations give no detailed information, they cannot support the above conclusion. The logical source for a clearer view of the matter is West's General Digest,[14] which classifies cases according to standard legal indexing terms, and summarizes virtually every case that came before a high state or a federal court. West's often cites the ruling precedent, and records the gist of the arguments upon which the court based its decision; thus, West's clearly shows whether "exploitation" or "pandering" was a significant feature of a given decision.

In the period from March, 1966 to about August, 1968, West's records 69 cases in the classification of "Obscenity, obscene publications, pictures, and articles." Of the 69 cases, only seven use the Ginzburg elements of either "pandering" or "commercial exploitation of prurient in terest" as a determining factor. Surprisingly, four cases specifically reject the Ginzburg approach; in any event, the 62 cases which do not depend on Ginzburg clearly depend on Roth; hence, Ginzburg has apparently not earned the respect of prosecutors and is largely disreputable and unemployed. However, West's can tell nothing about the extralegal coercion that limits expression and bookselling, nor does it record the great number of cases that come before petit courts. Thus, West's does not give a complete answer to the questions of "How has Ginzburg been used?" and "Has it produced the results some people feared?"

Charles Rembar believes the fears are ungrounded;

he reports, in denial of the fearful:

> For several years prior to the decisions... Comstock Law arrests had averaged between sixty and seventy a month. In the period July 1966 to January 1967, there was an average of thirty-four a month. Moreover, Post Office action to ban books from the mails... has now virtually disappeared.[15]

Rembar's explanation is not satisfactory, either. On the one hand, its time span is too short, and on the other, it limits itself to "Comstock Law" arrests and says nothing of local arrests on state or municipal charges. His point that Post Office banning has almost ceased imputes some liberal attitude to the Post Office but ignores the fact that the Supreme Court slapped the hands of the Postmaster General rather rudely in _Sunshine Book Co. v. Summerfield_[16] and in _Manual Enterprises v. Day._[17] Furthermore, if Ginzburg was correct in assigning to the late Robert F. Kennedy part of the responsibility for his own troubles, the fact that Kennedy ceased to be Attorney General in 1964 could have something to do with the matter. In any case, Rembar's explanation is incomplete, does not categorically answer the questions posed about the effects of _Ginzburg_, and says nothing of the 300 per cent increase in arrests reported by Semanche, _supra_.

An equally unauthoritative statement was made by O. K. Armstrong, in a _Reader's Digest_ article:

> Encouraged by these courtroom triumphs [_Ginzburg_ and _Mishkin_], prosecutors in numerous communities are drawing up new indictments against suspected pornography dealers.... decent citizens can look forward to the time when the blight of pornography is swept from our newstands, theaters, and mail.[18]

Armstrong also reported that "within six weeks of the new rulings, a dozen movies were found obscene" in several states. Surely, then, _Ginzburg_ caused something to happen.

Another commentator, Leon Friedman, fears _Ginzburg_ may provoke more federal government prosecutions under the mailing statutes (18 U. S. C. A. Sec. 1461). He gives a table showing that mailing code convictions rose from 172 in 1955 to 696 in 1965. The increase was fairly well distributed over the years, with the change from 377 convictions in 1961 to 503 in 1962 being the greatest single jump.[19] Friedman says that the reason for the increased vigor in the Post Office is unclear; however, the table of figures recalls Ginzburg's suggestion about the late Robert F. Kennedy and supports Rembar's statements about convictions up to 1966. Friedman concludes that *Ginzburg* will be treated, in the future, as an "aberration," as "the difficulty of administering the rule declared there becomes apparent to the courts."[20] In view of the evidence from *West's*, Friedman's suggestion seems accurate.

The available evidence, then, provides no conclusion about the effects of *Ginzburg*. However, the freedom that permits William Burroughs' *The Naked Lunch* (after an *in-rem* trial in Massachusetts) to be sold, and which permits Scandanavian nudist magazines to circulate, tells nothing of the number of threats to booksellers and drugstores which may yet occur. Nor does a feeling of security erase *Ginzburg* from the books. *Rebuhn* lay dormant for 26 years; *Ginzburg* could do the same, and then arise to confound all.

During the election campaigns of 1968, George Wallace frequently criticized the Supreme Court's defense of obscenity, and over 13 million people voted for him. Likewise, Richard N. Nixon declared his disapproval of Attorney General Ramsay Clark, and promised to appoint someone else to his place. Ramsay Clark is an anthema to the CDL and other suppressive forces, and Nixon's win may be related to the frustration of suppressive elements. Also, the Senate cited Abe Fortas' approval of an obscene movie as partial reason to withhold approval of his appointment as Chief Justice, as has been noted. Thus, despite a current notion that the battle against suppression has been won,[21] as Macbeth said of another contention, "We have scotch'd the snake, not kill'd it." The snake's recuperative powers are shown in the following quotation from news columnist Charles Bartlett:

> A torrent of salacious filth is overflowing the magazine stands and it is depressing to report

> that the indignation here [Washington, D. C.] does not match the outrage being perpetrated against the public.
>
> Within blocks of the White House... the hometown newspapers are being crowded aside to yield room for the pornographic flood. There are shelves for every perversion and proof for every visitor that total depravity can be the end result of unblinking tolerance.
>
> Congress created a commission on obscenity 13 months ago and it has gotten nowhere.... it will be the middle of 1970 before the public can look for any official affirmance of its repugnance at the sordid abuse of a free press.
>
> The commission chairman, Dean William Lockhart ...plans to spend more than $1,000,000, much of it on behavioral studies of the impact of obscenity on young minds.... it is hard to see what the researchers can add to the concern that is felt by any sensible parent....
>
> ...Ramsay Clark has been shockingly laggard in this area. The rate of convictions is less than half of what it was under Robert Kennedy while the number of complaints has more than tripled. ...[last fiscal year] there were 160,000 complaints and 250 convictions....
>
> The impalement of federal authority upon a constitutional dilemma has left it up to local citizens to erect the dams against the flood of filth. They will have to press for prosecutions and count upon local juries to reflect their anger. Eventually the Supreme Court will read their mood as it does the election returns.[22]

Bartlett's logic would do justice to a Brennan opinion, and is equally disturbing in what it forebodes for freedome of the press. While the President's report of the President's Commission on Obscenity and Pornography will, no doubt, clarify matters somewhat, that clarification is not likely to influence minds such as Bartlett's. Indeed,

Bartlett has already concluded that Dean Lockhart's study will affirm his own prejudices: what will be the degree of his frustration if Dean Lockhart's study utterly contradicts him? What is the reaction of a frustrated reactionary?

Therefore, the situation does not allow academics and friends of free expression to relax; rather, they should act more vigorously, simply because the suppressive forces have been provoked and appear to be quietly gathering strength.

Notes

1. D. F. K., "Constitutional Law -- Freedom of Press -- Obscenity Standards," 31 Albany Law Review, 151 (1967).

2. Crocker, "Freedom of Expression," 17 Western Reserve Law Review, 1335 (1966).

3. Rault, "Constitutional Law -- The 1966 Obscenity Cases," 27 Louisiana Law Review, 107 (1966).

4. Semanche, "Definitional and Contextual Obscenity," 13 UCLA Law Review, 1183 (1966).

5. Magrath, op. cit., 77.

6. Crabtree and Kearney, "Case Comments," 19 University of Florida Law Review, 192 (1966).

7. Commonwealth v. Robin, 219 A. 2d. 546 (1966).

8. Wilson, "Constitutional Law -- Obscenity," 40 Connecticut Law Review, 679, (1966).

9. McPheeters, op. cit., 129.

10. Banner, op. cit., 1386.

11. Semanche, Op. cit., 1202.

12. Jones, 21 Southwestern Law Journal, 104-105 (1967); compare Monaghan's comment, op. cit., 157, at note 136: "...the wary bookseller may not be so willing as the legal

observer to indulge in such nice distinctions; for him the cost is far too great."

13. Sebastian, "Obscenity and the Supreme Court: Nine Years of Confusion," 19 Standford Law Review, 184 (1966).

14. West's General Digest (St. Paul: West Publishing Company, 1966 - 1968).

15. Rembar, op. cit., 487.

16. 355 U. S. 372 (1958).

17. 370 U. S. 478 (1962).

18. Armstrong, "A Victory Over the Smut Peddlers [sic]," 90 Reader's Digest (February, 1967), 152.

19. op. cit., 80.

20. Ibid., 91.

21. See, e.g., Rembar's "End of Obscenity" in 93 Library Journal (May 1, 1968), 1868.

22. "Time for Dams Against Filth," Chicago Sun-Times, (November 18, 1968) 40; Bartlett has been popular among those academics who oppose the Viet Nam war, and has made a name for himself partly by his attacks on President Johnson. Will his apostles in academe endorse his opinion here? Note also that Senator Everett Dirksen attempted to add a "rider" to the Gun Control Bill that would have prevented federal review of obscenity judgments handed down by a jury.

9. Roth to Redrup: Ginzburg Rejected

Justice Brennan's opinion in Ginzburg sounds almost embarrassed, as if he realized that no one would believe him but that he was determined to proceed; Justice Douglas' dissenting opinion can almost be read as reproof to a mule-headed Court, a Court which realized from the beginning that the Ginzburg opinion was a bad one. If the Court did not, it soon learned, for the Justices read the law journals and quote them often; they knew they had disappointed many able lawyers, and worse, that they had made themselves look foolish.

Given such circumstances, the Court had two alternatives: to use Ginzburg whenever it could be applied, and by force attempt to give it credibility; or, to ignore it, to pretend it did not exist, and hope the world would forget it. The record of obscenity cases since Ginzburg indicates the Court took the second alternative; they have sought to bury Ginzburg, not to praise it.

At first, the Court seemed to believe in what it did; it denied Ginzburg a rehearing,[1] and cited Ginzburg as controlling precedent in refusing certiorari in Davis v. U. S.,[2] a case involving the mailing of allegedly obscene phonorecords.

However, an opportunity to escape their own handiwork occurred in the Fall, 1966, term of the Court, about six months after Ginzburg and its companion cases. The Court heard arguments for appeal in the case of Redrup v. New York,[3] and handed down its per curiam decision in May, 1967. Included with Redrup in the decision were Austin v. Kentucky and Gent v. Arkansas. All three cases involved state statutes against obscene material. The Court dealt with the cases cursorily; after a summary of the various positions held by the justices on obscenity, it cited the Roth formula as it found expression in Fanny Hill, and reversed the lower court findings of obscenity. (Justices Harlan and Clark dissented, not with the decision, but with its procedure.) Thus, the gross effect of Redrup was to make Fanny Hill the line of transmission of the Roth formula; however, the net effect made Redrup the line of transmission. Thus, the Roth formula is cited from Roth up to Fanny Hill, from Fanny Hill up to Redrup, and from Redrup thereafter, the important point being that citation of Redrup, or Fanny Hill, amounts to a citation of the Roth formula.

Thus, the Court fell back upon Roth, turning its back on the misbegotten Ginzburg, and continued to broaden the limits of what might be protected under the Roth formula. Following Redrup, the Court handed out eleven per curiam reversals in a row, citing Redrup in every case but one; in one of the cases, Justices Warren, Clark, and Brennan dissented with the reversal, and cited Ginzburg.[4] The following season, in November, 1967, the Court handed down four per curiam decisions, citing Redrup each time.[5] Roth, led by Redrup, marches through these cases with the pride of lasting wisdom. The inescapable conclusion, therefore, is that the Court is not proud of Ginzburg.

Redrup possibly serves to lay at rest some of the fears provoked by Ginzburg, unless, perhaps, it only adds new confusion. In Redrup, the Court noted that"... in none [of the cases at bar] was there evidence of the sort of 'pandering' which the Court found significant in Ginzburg ...."[6] The Court did not elaborate on what it meant by "sort" of pandering. Thus, if Redrup involved pandering at all, it was not the "sort of pandering" which was significant in Ginzburg; however, perhaps Redrup involved no pandering at all. The Court does not say, and one would have to go back to the trial records to determine. Most likely, pandering was not an issue at all.

However, pandering was an issue in Books, Inc. v. United States. Books involved the above-mentioned work, Lust Job. The lower court found pandering in the content of the covers of the book, and thereby found the distributor guilty of distributing obscene materials.[7] In reversing, the Court cited Redrup, but failed to indicate whether it did not agree that pandering was present at all, or whether the pandering identified by the lower court was not the "sort" of pandering that was "significant" in Ginzburg. Now, since Books involved a newsstand, the logical conclusion is that the Court found no evidence of advertising which implied the book would appeal to "prurient" interest; that is, the Court would not equate the cover of a book with Ginzburg's expansive advertising campaigns. By this interpretation, Books is not a particularly important case.

However, another commentator believes the Books decision may establish a distinction between the publisher as defendant and the distributor as defendant.[8] If such a distinction is made, the commentator believes, it has the effect of limiting the precedent, Ginzburg, to its specific facts, which therefore means that Ginzburg cannot apply in any case except one in which the facts are substantially similar. Furthermore, since the representations on the cover of Lust Job are substantially similar to the representations in Ginzburg's advertising material, the Books decision suggests that the actual representations, whether in advertising or on a dust jacket, are not important: the distribution of them is, however. Thus, the distributor's actions become more important than what he actually distributes, and if a bookseller does no more than keep books on a shelf, he is not distributing as Ginzburg did. Thus, Books suggests on the one hand that Ginzburg must be limited to its facts, and on the other hand that broadcast distribution of advertising is the "significant" "sort" of pandering the Court identified in Redrup. Either interpretation limits Ginzburg, but neither eliminates it.

One possibility here is that the Court hopes to encourage discretion among distributors of obscenity. Such discretion would disarm the suppressors and save the Court much trouble. However, the Court could make the point clearer, if such were their aim.

Notes

1. 384 U. S. 934 (1966).

2. 384 U. S. 953 (1966).

3. 386 U. S. 767 (1967).

4. The Cases: Keney v. New York, 388 U. S. 440 (1967); Friedman v. New York, 388 U. S. 441 (1967); Ratner v. California, 388 U. S. 442 (1967); Coberts v. New York, 388 U. S. 443 (1967); Sheperd v. New York, 388

U. S. 444 (1967); Avansino v. New York, 388 U. S. 446 (1967); Aday v. United States, 388 U. S. 447 (1967); Books, Inc. v. United States, 388 U. S. 449 (1967); Rosenbloom v. Virginia, 388 U. S. 450 (1967), in which Sunshine Book Co. v. Summerfield, 355 U. S. 372 (1958) is cited as controlling; A Quantity of Books v. Kansas, 388 U. S. 452 (1967); and Schackman v. California, 388 U. S. 454 (1967), in which the minority above cited Ginzburg.

5. Potomac News v. United States, 389 U. S. 47 (1967); Conner v. City of Hammond, 389 U. S. 48 (1967); Central Magazine v. United States, 389 U. S. 50 (1967); and Chance v. California, 389 U. S. 89 (1967).

6. op. cit., 769.

7. 358 F. 2d. 935 (1966).

8. Baughman, 19 Case Western Reserve Law Review 755 (1968).

Postscript

After the Supreme Court upheld Ginzburg's conviction it denied him a rehearing. To his appeal for a new trial the Court held that only the court of original jurisdiction could grant such a retrial, whereupon Ginzburg appealed to that court for a retrial, with no success. He then appealed for a moderation of sentence, and the court agreed to hear his arguments. Ginzburg's basis for appeal was that his sentence would impose an undue hardship on his family. [1] The question was returned to the Third Circuit Court of Appeals, from whence it had originally gone to the Supreme Court. After much legal maneuvering, the original judge, Ralph C. Body, removed himself from the case, and the appeals proceeded.

Thus, for three years, Ginzburg has been free while his various appeals have been filed and acted upon. Presumably, if the courts were absolutely determined that Ginzburg should be jailed, his appeals could have been exhausted in three months; however, the courts have waited long to act upon them, Ginzburg's attorneys have taken long to prepare them, and Ginzburg has continued to publish one kind of material or another, his latest effort being an expensive pictorial-cum-literary review, Avant Garde. Avant Garde was launched in early 1968, amid various advertisements placed in such publications as Evergreen Review and various college newspapers. Avant Garde is not as pretentious as Playboy, nor as prurient as Evergreen. So far, he has not been required to defend his publication in court, and the Post Office has been cooperative. At least, it conveys Avant Garde from New York to Chicago without hindrance.

Ginzburg's continued absence from jail and the generally increasing freedom to sell obscene material bodes well, at the moment, for the friends of freedom. However, penicillin did not eliminate the gonococcus; it provoked penicillin-resistant mutations. Quite possibly, the new freedom may provoke the suppression forces to greater vigor, or greater subtlety; in any case, smug satisfaction would be dangerous for the friends of free speech. No harbinger warned of the late Senator Joseph McCarthy: he just suddenly appeared one day in the Senate, flailing with the jawbone of an ass at imaginary Philistines. Likewise, a few subtle changes in the national attitude could produce another such Polyphemus. Some people fear that a new wave of Comstockery is imminent;[2] an immediate lack of contrary evidence is no proof that freedom of the press has been fully established. Academics, literati, and librarians must, per force, exert themselves to understand the law and its constant mutations. Hopefully, this paper provides some assistance to that understanding.

Notes

1. New York Times, July 4, p. 17, and October 9, p. 44 (1968).

2. Ibid., April 10, 1969, p. 44.

Bibliography

Significant Cases (in chronological order; *per curiam* decisions omitted)

Ulysses v. United States, 5 F. Supp. 184 (1933).

Rebuhn v. United States, 109 F. 2d. 514 (1940).

Butler v. Michigan, 352 U. S. 380 (1956).

Roth v. United States, 354 U. S. 476 (1957).

Kingsley Books v. Brown, 354 U. S. 436 (1957).

Kingsley v. Regents, 360 U. S. 684 (1959).

Smith v. California, 361 U. S. 145 (1959).

Marcus v. Search Warrant, 367 U. S. 717 (1961).

Manual Enterprises v. Day, 370 U. S. 478 (1962).

Bantam Books v. Sullivan, 372 U. S. 58 (1963).

Jacobellis v. Ohio, 378 U. S. 184 (1964).

A Quantity of Books v. Kansas, 378 U. S. 205 (1964).

Grove Press v. Florida, 156 So. 2d. 537 (1963); 378 U. S. 577 (1964).

Klaw v. United States, 350 F. 2d. 155 (1965) (not cited in text).

Memoirs of a Woman of Pleasure v. Massachusetts, 383 U. S. 413 (1966).

Ginzburg v. United States, 383 U. S. 463 (1966).

Mishkin v. New York, 383 U. S. 503 (1966).

Redrup v. New York, 386 U. S. 767 (1967).

Legal Sources

Banner, Tim K. "Constitutional Law -- Criminal Law -- Obscenity." 44 Texas Law Review (1966), 1382-1389.

Baughman, Thomas H. "Obscenity -- Obscene Publications -- Pandering." 19 Case Western Reserve Law Review (1968), 748-756.

Cairns, Robert B.; Paul, James C. N.; and Wishner, Julius. "Sex Censorship: The Assumptions of Anti-Obscenity Laws and the Empirical Evidence." 46 Minnesota Law Review (1962), 1009-1041.

Crabtree, James, and Kearney, David. "Constitutional Law: A Revised Standard of Obscenity." 19 University of Florida Law Review (1966), 185-195.

Crocker, Leslie J. "Ginzburg, et al. -- An Attack on Freedom of Expression." 17 Western Reserve Law Review (1966), 1325-1341.

Day, J. Edward. "Mailing Lists and Pornography." 52 American Bar Association Journal (December, 1966), 1103-1109.

Dyson, Richard B. "Looking-Glass Law: An Analysis of the Ginzburg Case." 28 University of Pittsburgh Law Review (1966), 1-18.

"Freedom of Speech and Association." 80 Harvard Law Review (1966), 186-194.

Gregory, David D. "Substantive Issues of the Supreme Court's Method of Dealing With Obscenity Regulations." 18 Maine Law Review (1967), 284-296.

Greiner, Richard G. "Constitutional Law -- Obscenity." 11 Villanova Law Review (1966), 861-874.

Henkin, Louis. "Morals and the Constitution: The Sin of Obscenity." 63 Columbia Law Review (1963), 391-414.

Jones, Teddy M., jr. "Obscenity Standards in Current Perspective." 21 Southwestern Law Journal (1967), 285-305.

K., D. F. "Constitutional Law -- Freedom of Press -- Obscenity Standards." 31 Albany Law Review (1967), 143-152.

Kalven, Harry, jr. "The Metaphysics of the Law of Obscenity." 1960 Supreme Court Review, 1-45.

Lockhart, William B., and McClure, Robert C. "Obscenity Censorship: The Core Constitutional Issue -- What is Obscene. ?" 7 Utah Law Review (1961), 289-303.

Magrath, C. Peter. "The Obscenity Cases: Grapes of Roth." 1966 Supreme Court Review, 1-77.

McPheeters, Hugh, jr. "Obscenity -- Variable Concept." 32 Missouri Law Review (1967), 125-130.

Monaghan, Henry P. "Obscenity 1966: The Marriage of Obscenity Per Se and Obscenity Per Quod." 76 Yale Law Journal (1966), 127-157.

Peaselee, Amos T. Constitutions of Nations. The Hague: M. Nijhof, 1956.

Petersen, James M. "Constitutional Law -- Freedom of Speech -- Pandering Held Relevant to the Application of the Roth Obscenity Test." 41 Tulane Law Review (1966), 126-131.

Rault, Gerard A. "Constitutional Law -- The 1966 Obscenity Cases." 27 Louisiana Law Review (1966), 100-109.

Ross, Terry D. "Expert Testimony in Obscenity Cases." 18 Hastings Law Review (1966), 161-179.

Schiller, Charles Phillip. "Constitutional Law -- First Amendment -- Evidence of Pandering." 16 American University Law Review (1966), 122-128.

Sebastian, Raymond F. "Obscenity and the Supreme Court: Nine Years of Confusion." 19 Standford Law Review (1966), 156-189.

Semanche, John E. "Definitional and Contextual Obscenity: The Supreme Court's New and Disturbing Accommodation." 13 UCLA Law Review, 1178-1213.

Shepard's Citations. Colorado Springs, Colorado: Shepard's Citations, 1968.

Skrabut, Paul A. "Constitutional Law: Obscenity Evidence." 51 Cornell Law Review (1966), 785-794

West's General Digest. St. Paul, Minnesota: West Publishing Company, 1968.

Wilson, Thomas Buck. "Constitutional Law -- Obscenity -- Formulation of Standards -- Commerical Exploitation." 40 Connecticut Law Review (1966), 670-679.

Non-Legal Sources

Armstrong, O. K. "Landmark Decision in the War on Obscenity." 91 Readers' Digest, (September, 1967), 93-97.

_______. "A Victory Over the Smut Peddlers [sic]." 90 Readers' Digest, (February, 1967), 147-152.

Bartlett, Charles. "Time for Dams Against Filth." Chicago Sun-Times, November 19, 1968, 40.

Epstein, Jason. "The Obscenity Business." 218 Atlantic Monthly, (August, 1966), 65-60.

Falk, Gerhard. "The Roth Decision in the Light of Sociological Knowledge." 54 American Bar Association Journal (1968), 288-292. (Not cited in text).

Friedman, Leon. "The Ginzburg Decision and the Law." 36 American Scholar. (Winter 1966-67), 71-91.

Hutchison, E. R. Tropic of Cancer on Trial. New York: Grove Press, 1968.

Kalven, Harry, jr. "The New York Times Case: A Note on 'The Central Meaning of the First Amendment'." 1964 Supreme Court Review, 191-221.

Molz, Kathleen. "The Public Custody of the Higher Pornography." 36 American Scholar (Winter 1966-67), 93-103.

New York Times. July 4, 1968, 17.

________. October 9, 1968, 44.

________. April 10, 1969, 44.

Playboy. "Interview: Ralph Ginzburg." 13 Playboy, 13, 44 ff.

Rembar, Charles. The End of Obscenity. New York: Random House, 1969.

PART II :

COLLECTED COMMENTARIES

ON OBSCENITY

The following section of this anthology contains articles, reprinted in whole or part and arranged in chronological order by date of writing, which comment upon the more recent of the opinions given in the first section. The first five articles concern the state of obscenity doctrine prior to Ginzburg. They discuss the Roth test, its precedents and development, and comment upon the assumptions underlying obscenity law.

The next series of articles discuss the implications of Ginzburg and its companion cases of 1966. The final two consider cases after Ginzburg, and attempt to clarify the state of the law as it now stands. As will be noted, the legal profession wondered whether Ginzburg indicated a new direction in obscenity law; the final two articles examine that question in view of subsequent U. S. Supreme Court decisions.

The articles are reprinted here with most documentation omitted. Interested readers are invited to examine the original articles if interested in citations of cases and similar references which are not given here. In most instances, a case is clearly identified in context, and will have been identified in the first section of this anthology.

Harry Kalven, Jr., is a Professor of Law in the University of Chicago Law School. In the following article Professor Kalven surveys U. S. Supreme Court opinions up to 1960, and suggests problems which remained at that time. His article provides a thorough and competent analysis of the law up to 1960.

This article is reprinted by permission of the University of Chicago Press and the author, from 1960 Supreme Court Review, 1-45, copyright by University of Chicago Press. Grateful acknowledgment is made to both author and publisher for permission to reprint here.

The Metaphysics of the Law of Obscenity

by Harry Kalven, Jr.

1. The Problem

The United States Supreme Court had no occasion to pass on the constitutionality of legislation making obscenity a crime for more than one hundred and fifty years after the adoption of the First Amendment. Within the last five years, however, the Court has been confronted with and decided most of the principal questions relating to the problem. It has thus defined a body of law which has rich interest for lawyer and layman alike, and has developed constitutional doctrine with major implications transcending the immediate problem. The purpose of this article is to examine some of the Court's recent opinions in order to see how it has resolved the perplexities inherent in the problem of the validity of such legislation and to see what issues, if any, remain to be decided.

Although it has been argued that the utterance of obscenity was a common-law crime, early instances are infrequent and, at best, ambiguous. The publication of obscene matter does not clearly emerge as a crime in England until the passage of Lord Campbell's Act in 1857. American legislation comes a few years later under the crusading impetus of Anthony Comstock. During the early part of the twentieth century there were judicial decisions, principally from Massachusetts, which laconically assumed the constitutionality of such legislation; but most of these decisions antedate the constitutional doctrines of free speech developed by the Supreme Court in the period from Schenck to Yates. Thus, the law of obscenity regulation seems to have had a kind of "sleeper" development, outside the main stream of decisions dealing with the problems of freedom of speech, until recently two distinguished lower court judges were met with the dilemma of reconciling the theories underlying the free-speech cases with the decisions sustaining obscenity regulation. Judge Curtis Bok, in Commonwealth v. Gordon, and Judge Jerome Frank, in United States v. Roth, both found the problem perplexing, and Judge Frank's opinion reads like a personal plea to the Supreme Court to resolve the constitutional difficulties.

The constitutional problems are primarily of two kinds. The first revolves around the ambiguity of the term "obscenity". The lack of precision had in no way been abated by the slow evolution of the test for obscenity, from the measure of the impact of isolated passages on the susceptible-the formula provided by the leading English case of Queen v. Hicklin in 1868-to the standard of the impact of the whole upon the average member of the audience, a doctrine worked out by Judges Woolsey and Learned Hand in Kennerley, Levine, and "Ulysses." At the time the problem came to the Supreme Court it could still be argued with some force that the term was irreducibly vague and that all definitions were circular-a poor predicate for a law inhibiting free speech. It may be possible to distinguish between degrees of explicitness in discussions of sex, but among explicit discussions of sex it is heroic to attempt to distinguish the good from the bad. Nor were the contemporary decisions of the state courts reassuring: Massachusetts, in 1945, held that the fine, compassionate novel by Lillian Smith, Strange Fruit, was obscene; at about the same time, it held that Forever Amber was not. And the New York and Massachusetts courts had reached opposite conclusions about Erskine Caldwell's God's Little Acre.

The second group of constitutional doubts derived from the clear-and-present-danger test. Toward what dangers was obscenity legislation directed? Analysis reveals four possible evils: (1) the incitement to antisocial sexual conduct; (2) psychological excitement resulting from sexual imagery; (3) the arousing of feelings of disgust and revulsion; and (4) the advocacy of improper sexual values. All present difficulties. It is hard to see why the advocacy of improper sexual values should fare differently, as a constitutional matter, from any other exposition in the realm of ideas. Arousing disgust and revulsion in a voluntary audience seems an impossibly trivial base for making speech a crime. The incitement of antisocial conduct evaporates in light of the absence of any evidence to show a connection between the written word and overt sexual behavior. There remains the evil of arousing sexual thoughts short of action. There is no doubt that the written word can excite the imagination. What puzzled Judge Bok and amused Judge Frank was the idea that the law could be so solemnly concerned with the sexual fantasies of the adult population.

The movement of obscenity cases to the Court took an ironic turn in 1947. The New York Court of Appeals held that Edmund Wilson's Memoirs of Hecate County was obscene. Here was an ideal test case, involving a serious book by the country's most distinguished literary critic. The New York Court of Appeals had disposed of the case without opinion and without dissent, stating "That the conviction aforesaid did not violate the right of freedom of speech guaranteed by the Fourteenth Amendment of the Constitution of the United States." It was an arresting commentary on the vitality of the constitutional issue that at that late date the New York high court did not think it serious enough to warrant an opinion. The hope that the Supreme Court would make both law and history in reviewing this case was dissipated when its judgment came down. The Court had divided evenly, thus affirming the conviction. Following tradition in evenly divided decisions, there was no opinion. The possibility of such division had resulted from Mr. Justice Frankfurter's recusation because he was a personal friend of Wilson's. If it revealed nothing else, however, the judgment served notice on the legal world that the constitutional issue was an open question.

II. Butler v. Michigan

In 1956 the Court's first important decision in the obscenity area, Butler v. Michigan, appeared to dig deeper the hole in which the Court would find itself when it faced the constitutional issue directly.... Mr. Justice Frankfurter, speaking for a unanimous Court... read the [Michigan] statute as making it an offense to sell to the general public a book that might have a deleterious influence on the young.

> The State insists that, by thus quarantining the general reading public against books not too rugged for grown men and women in order to shield juvenile innocence, it is exercising its power to promote the general welfare. Surely, this is to burn the house to roast the pig. Indeed, the Solicitor General of Michigan has, with characteristic can-

> dor, advised the Court that Michigan has a statute specifically designed to protect its children against obscene matter 'tending to the corruption of the morals of youth.' But the appellant was not convicted for violating this statute.
>
> We have before us legislation not reasonably restricted to the evil with which it is said to deal. The incidence of this enactment is to reduce the adult population of Michigan to reading only what is fit for children. It thereby arbitrarily curtails one of those liberties of the individual, now enshrined in the Due Process Clause of the Fourteenth Amendment, that history has attested as the indispensable conditions for the maintenance and progress of a free society....

The Butler case thus appeared to do little more than underwrite the shift in the test audience, from the young and vulnerable to the average adult, when the item in question is distributed to the general public. The point had been brilliantly made by Judge Learned Hand more than forty years earlier in United States v. Kennerley when, although following the Hicklin rule, he added the following dissenting dictum:

> I hope it is not improper for me to say that the rule as laid down, however consonant it may be with mid-Victorian morals, does not seem to me to answer to the understanding and morality of the present time, as conveyed by the words, 'obscene, lewd, or lascivious.' I question whether in the end men will regard that as obscene which is honestly relevant to the adequate expression of innocent ideas, and whether they will not believe that truth and beauty are too precious to society at large to be mutilated in the interests of those most likely to pervert them to base uses. Indeed, it seems hardly likely that we are even to-day so lukewarm in our interest in letters or serious discussion as to be content to reduce our treatment of sex to the standard of a child's library in the supposed interest of a salacious few, or that shame will for long prevent us from adequate portrayal of some of the most serious and beautiful sides of

> human nature. That such latitude gives opportunity for its abuse is true enough; there will be, as there are, plenty who will misuse the privilege as a cover for lewdness and a stalking horse from which to strike at purity, but that is true today and only involves us in the same question of fact which we hope that we have the power to answer.
>
> Yet, if the time is not yet when men think innocent all that which is honestly germane to a pure subject, however little it may mince its words, still I scarcely think that they would forbid all which might corrupt the most corruptible, or that society is prepared to accept for its own limitations those which may perhaps be necessary to the weakest of its members. If there be no abstract definition, such as I have suggested, should not the word 'obscene' be allowed to indicate the present critical point in the compromise between candor and shame at which the community may have arrived here and now? If letters must, like other kinds of conduct, be subject to the social sense of what is right, it would seem that a jury should in each case establish the standard much as they do in cases of negligence. To put thought in leash to the average conscience of the time is perhaps tolerable, but to fetter it by the necessities of the lowest and least capable seems a fatal policy.

In fact, however, the Butler case cuts deeper. The court was saying that the average adult is not merely the preferred test audience for materials distributed generally; it is the constitutionally required test audience. Moreover, if the state cannot bar materials generally distributed by using their impact on youth as a criterion of obscenity, it cannot use the young at all as a justification for regulation. That is, the state cannot justify regulation on the ground that the regulated materials might move the young to anti-social conduct, or might excite the sexual imagination of the young, or might make premature disclosure of the "facts of life" to the young in a vulgar and debased form. Admittedly these are serious problems, particularly the last. They may well justify intervention of the state keyed specifically to distributions to children. But so far as distribution of materials to the general public is concerned the impact on the young has now become irrelevant. If general publications not specifically aimed at children are to be banned as obscene, it can only be because of their effect on the adult audience, because of their impact on the average adult who is sexually experienced and mature. The Butler decision thus served to sharpen the constitutional debate that would attend a decision on the constitutionality of general obscenity statutes.

III. Alberts and Roth

The Court finally reached the constitutional issue in 1956 in two cases which were heard and decided together: People v. Alberts and United States v. Roth. In the Alberts case, a conviction was based on a California statute which made the distribution of obscene materials a crime. The Roth case involved a federal statute making criminal the transmission of obscene materials through the mails. The Court, agreeing that this was the first time the constitutional issue had been "squarely presented" to it under either the First or the Fourteenth Amendment, sustained the validity of both the federal and the state regulation. The opinion of the majority was by Mr. Justice Brennan; Mr. Chief Justice Warren filed a separate concurring opinion; Justices Black and Douglas dissented; and Mr. Justice Harlan concurred in Alberts and dissented in Roth.

The majority opinion, although it decisively and unequivocally disposed of doubts as to constitutionality, did so by a route which neatly bypassed all the perplexities raised by Judges Bok and Frank and the commentators. Mr. Justice Brennan began by stating the question in a fashion that clearly foreshadowed the answer: "The dispositive question is whether obscenity is utterance within the area of protected speech and press." The question could be put differently. Mr. Justice Harlan asked whether the particular materials before the Court could constitutionally be subjected to regulation. For Justices Black and Douglas the question was whether the state could use the criminal law to regulate speech and letters to prevent the alleged evils of obscenity. The Court's beginning was thus reminiscent of its strategy in Dennis, where it limited certiorari to the question whether advocating the violent overthrow of government could be constitutionally punished. The difficulty with this approach, as both Mr. Chief Justice Warren and Mr. Justice Harlan were quick to point out, is that the Court was thereby deciding an abstract question cut off from the color and context of particular circumstances. One can only assume that the referents for "obscenity" in the minds of the majority of justices as they dealt with the question were certain well-known four-letter Anglo-Saxon words, or images of "French postcards." Yet the last time the Court had had the question, the referent was Edmund Wilson's Memoirs of Hecate County.

Having thus stated the issue, Mr. Justice Brennan proceeded quickly to its disposition. He first noted that, although it had never passed on the question, the Court had several times previously appeared to assume its constitutionality in dicta. The First Amendment, in light of colonial history, cannot be read as intended to "protect every utterance." This argument is curious. Because thirteen of the fourteen states which ratified the Constitution had laws prohibiting libel, profanity, and blasphemy, he concluded that obscenity is without constitutional protection. There are at least two difficulties here. The Court seems to have assumed that the only argument against the constitutionality of obscenity regulation rests on the broad premise that under the First Amendment no utterances can be prohibited and that if this broad premise were destroyed the argument must collapse. Further, the Court's use of history was so casual as to be alarming in terms of what other propositions might be proved by the same technique. Is it clear, for example, that blasphemy can constitutionally be made a crime today? And what would the Court say to an argument along the same lines appealing to the Sedition Act of 1798 as justification for the truly liberty-defeating crime of seditions libel?

The opinion then proceeded to the crux of the matter. "All ideas having even the slightest redeeming social importance-unorthodox ideas, controversial ideas, even ideas hateful to the prevailing climate of opinion" are protected against governmental restraint. Obscenity on the other hand is "utterly without redeeming social importance." This is clear from the fact that over fifty nations have entered into international agreements for its regulation, and twenty obscenity laws have been enacted by Congress in the last century. The Court then quoted Chaplinsky to the effect that "such utterances are no essential part of any exposition of ideas..." and concluded: "We hold that obscenity is not within the area of constitutionally protected speech or press."

The opinion, however, was not yet finished. The most interesting part was to come. Mr. Justice Brennan turned to meet the challenge that there must be a clear and present danger of something to justify regulation of speech. He is thus on the very threshold of the perplexities which so entranced Judge Frank. He disposed of them with one quick thrust: since obscenity is not in the area of constitutionally protected speech, it is, quoting Beauharnais v. Illinois, "unnecessary either for us or for the state courts to consider the issues behind the phrase 'clear and present danger.'" The Court thus found further use for the two-level free speech theory which made its first appearance in Chaplinsky and was given status as doctrine in Beauharnais. The spectacular dilemma predicted for the Court when it confronted the perplexities of obscenity regulation turned out to have no horns at all. The perplexities may be puzzling but, the Court said, they are simply not relevant.

After putting obscenity so securely beyond the pale of constitutional concern, Mr. Justice Brennan hastened to add a good word on behalf of sex: "Sex and obscenity are not synonymous." Then followed what must be the least controversial utterance in the Court's history: "Sex, a great and mysterious motive force in human life, has indisputably been a subject of absorbing interest to mankind through the ages." But obscene discussions of sex are not entitled to the protection afforded fundamental freedoms. "It is therefore vital that the standards for judging obscenity safeguard the protection of freedom of speech and press for material which does not treat sex in a manner appealing to prurient interests."

The Brennan opinion invites three lines of consideration. First, is the two-level theory of free speech tolerable as doctrine? Second, is there disclosed a weakness in the preoccupation of free-speech theory with competition in the market place of ideas when we turn to art and belles-lettres, which deal primarily with the imagination and not with ideas in any strict sense? Finally, will the tendency of the Court's decision be to relax or to make more restrictive the enforcement of the obscenity laws?

The two-level speech theory, although it afforded the Court a statesmanlike way around a dilemma, seems difficult to accept as doctrine. It is perhaps understandable in the context of Chaplinsky, where the speech in question is nothing more complex than the utterance "son of a bitch," said rapidly. In connection with libel, as in Beauharnais, or obscenity, as in Roth, however, it seems a strained effort to trap a problem. At one level there are communications which, even though odious to the majority opinion of the day, even though expressive of the thought we hate, are entitled to be measured against the clear-and-present-danger criterion. At another level are communications apparently so worthless as not to require any extensive judicial effort to determine whether they can be prohibited. There is to be freedom for the thought we hate, but not for the candor we deplore. The doctrinal apparatus is thus quite intricate. In determining the constitutionality of any ban on a communication, the first question is whether it belongs to a category that has any social utility. If it does not, it may be banned. If it does, there is a further question of measuring the clarity and proximity and gravity of any danger from it. It is thus apparent that the issue of social utility of a communication has become as crucial a part of our theory as the issue of its danger. Although the Court has not yet made this clear it must be assumed that the Court's concern is with the utility of a category of communication rather than with a particular instance. Thus, to go back to the pamphlet in Gitlow, presumably the question, were the case to arise today, would be about the social utility of revolutionary speech and not the utility of the particular pamphlet which so bored Mr. Justice Holmes. There is, to be sure, no quarrel with the premise that even odious revolutionary speech has value. If a man is seriously enough at odds with society to advocate violent revolution, his speech has utility not because advocating revolution is useful but because such serious criticism should be heard. No one advocates violent overthrow of government without advancing some premises in favor of his conclusion. It is the premises and not the conclusion that are worth protecting. This is in effect what Judge Hand meant in the Dennis case when he spoke of utterances which have a "double aspect: i.e., when persuasion and instigation were inseparably confused." There is thus no contradiction in the concept of speech which presents a clear and present danger but which nevertheless has sufficient social utility to require close constitutional scrutiny. The difficulties are with the other half of the theory, with the categories of speech that have no social utility. Neither in Beauharnais nor in Roth has the Court spoken at any length about the concept of social utility. It has confined itself on each occasion to the historical point that these categories-libel and obscenity-have long been regarded as worthless speech subject to prohibition. But, if history alone is to be the guide, the same inference might better be drawn about the utility of revolutionary speech.

It is at this point that Mr. Justice Brennan's phrasing of "the dispositive question" bears strange fruit. It seems hardly fair to ask: what is the social utility of obscenity? Rather the question is: what is the social utility of excessively candid and explicity discussions of sex? Here too there is the problem of the mixed utterance. The well-known sexual passages in Lady Chatterley's Lover are integral to the possibly strange but indubitably serious view of English postwar life that Lawrence wished to portray. And even if they were not a part of a complex whole-which will be destroyed with them if the novel is held obscene, just as the critical premises of the revolutionary would disappear-they would appear to have some value in their own right as a lyrical view of the potential for warmth, tenderness, and vitality of a fully satisfactory sexual experience. The Court's formula thus seems to have over-simplified the problem. The Court may understand obscenity, but it does not seem to understand sex.

The oversimplification is irritating because the Court appeared unaware, as it could not have been, of the distinguished items that have been held obscene. A legal term gets its meaning from the construction put on it by the courts, and the Court's logic thus appears to lead to the conclusion that, in its view, such books as Lady Chatterley's Lover, Memoirs of Hecate County, and Strange Fruit, all of which have been held obscene by distinguished courts, are in the category of speech which is "utterly without redeeming social importance."

I do not think the Court meant to say this-to say, for example, that Memoirs of Hecate County is worthless. There is an obvious way to avoid the apparent reductio ad absurdum. Presumably, in the future, the Court will take it. For everything now depends on what is meant by obscene. If the Court's formula is to make any sense, it must place a heavy burden on the definition of obscenity. Obscenity must be so defined as to save any serious, complex piece of writing or art, regardless of the unconventionality of its candor. If the obscene is constitutionally subject to ban because it is worthless, it must follow that the obscene can include only that which is worthless. This approach makes sense. So-called hard-core pornography involves discussions of sex which are not integral parts of anything else. In themselves, they are, at best, fantasies of sexual prowess and response unrelated to the serious human concern that moved Lawrence and, at worst, a degrading, hostile, alien view of the sexual experience. If the socially worthless criterion is taken seriously, the Roth opinion may have made a major advance in liberating literature and art from the shadow of the censor.

The Court's approach touches another long-standing puzzle in the law of obscenity. Is there a category of privileged obscenity, using privilege in its technical legal sense? It has long been clear that certain classics-Aristophanes, Rabelais, Boccaccio, Shakespeare, Montaigne, Voltaire, Balzac, and, some would add, the Bible itself-have been immune from obscenity regulation. The Court has never explicitly held that the other values of a work make privileged its obscene parts; but the pattern of decision and prosecution has been clear. The abortive effort of the Postmaster a few years back to bar Lysistrata was greeted with, and defeated by, laughter. Judge Frank argued that the judges had written such a privilege into the law and had thereby given the game away:

> To the argument that such books (and such reproductions of famous paintings and works of sculpture) fall within the statutory ban, the courts have answered that they are 'classics' - books of 'literary distinction' or works which have 'an accepted place in the arts,' including, so this court has held, Ovid's Art of Love and Boccaccio's Decameron. There is a 'curious dilemma' involved in this answer that the statute condemns 'only books which are dull and without merit,' that in no event will the statute be applied to the 'classics,' i.e., books 'of literary distinction.' The courts have

> not explained how they escape that dilemma, but instead seem to have gone to sleep (although rather uncomfortably) on its horns.
>
> This dilemma would seem to show up the basic constitutional flaw in the statute: No one can reconcile the currently accepted test of obscenity with the immunity of such 'classics' as e.g., Aristophanes' Lysistrata, Chaucer's Canterbury Tales, Rabelais' Gargantua and Pantagruel, Shakespear's Venus and Adonis, Fielding's Tom Jones, or Balzac's Droll Stories. For such 'obscene' writings, just because of their greater artistry and charm, will presumably have far greater influence on readers than dull inartistic writings.
>
> ....
>
> The truth is that the courts have excepted the 'classics' from the federal obscenity statute, since otherwise most Americans would be deprived of access to many masterpieces of literature and the pictorial arts, and a statute yielding such deprivation would not only be laughably absurb but would squarely oppose the intention of the cultivated men who framed and adopted the First Amendment.
>
> This exception-nowhere to be found in the statute -is a judge-made device invented to avoid that absurdity. The fact that the judges have felt the necessity of seeking that avoidance, serves to suggest forcibly that the statute, in its attempt to control what our citizens may read and see, violates the First Amendment. For no one can rationally justify the judge-made exception....

While the unperplexed blandness of the Court's majority opinion in Roth is disconcerting in the teeth of so vigorous and engaging a commentary in the court below, it is probably true that the Court has solved Judge Frank's dilemma. On the two-level theory, the classics do not need a special privilege; they fall automatically into speech on the first level, and hence automatically outside the realm of the constitutionally obscene. To put this another way, the Court is giving a constitutional privilege to all communication that has some social value. And Judge Frank's pointed query as to why obscenity embedded in a classic was less dangerous than obscenity in a book without literary distinction is not so pointed now, since the latter is banned not because it is dangerous but because it is worthless.

The Brennan opinion, however, remains curious on two grounds. The Court did not make its own best point but defined obscenity substantially in the words of the American Law Institute's model penal code: "Whether to the average person, applying contemporary community standards, the dominant theme of the material taken as a whole appeals to prurient interest." This definition has certain advantages over its predecessors. It insists on the <u>average</u> person, on the material considered <u>as a whole</u>, and on the <u>dominant</u> theme. But it shares the central weakness of all prior legal definitions of obscenity: the word is still defined in terms of itself. The key word "prurient" is defined by one dictionary in terms of "lascivious longings" and "lewd." The obscene, then, is that which appeals to an interest in the obscene. In the process of defining obscenity the Court said nothing about social worthlessness. The opinion thus failed to break sharply enough with prior definitions of obscenity, to narrow them sufficiently, to make plausible its assumption that the obscene cannot include materials of some social utility.

Moreover, it is unclear how the formula will help a future court faced with the question whether a particular item can be banned constitutionally. Everything now depends on the classification. If the item is obscene it can be banned without regard to its danger. But in any close case a court, in order to determine whether the item is "obscene enough," will have to decide first whether it can be banned. The Court's formula offers no guidance on the constitutional issue.

I suggest that the difficulties in working out the implications of the new free-speech doctrine also reflect a difficulty with the older forms of that doctrine. The classic defense of John Stuart Mill and the modern defense of Alexander Meiklejohn do not help much when the question is why the novel, the poem, the painting, the drama, or the piece of sculpture falls within the protection of the First Amendment. Nor do the famous opinions of Hand, Holmes, and Brandeis. The emphasis is all on truth winning out in a fair fight between competing ideas. The emphasis is clearest in Meiklejohn's argument that free speech is indispensable to the informed citizenry required to make democratic self-government work. The people need free speech because they vote. As a result his argument distinguishes sharply between public and private speech. Not all communications are relevant to the political process. The people do not need novels or dramas or paintings or poems because they will be called upon to vote. Art and belles-lettres do not deal in such ideas-at least not good art or belles-lettres-and it makes little sense here to talk, as Mr. Justice Brandeis did in his great opinion in Whitney, of whether there is still time for counter-speech. Thus there seems to be a hiatus in our basic free-speech theory.

I am not suggesting that the Court will have any hesitation in recognizing, not, as Keats would have it, that truth and beauty are one, but that beauty has constitutional status too, and that the life of the imagination is as important to the human adult as the life of the intellect. I do not think that the Court would find it difficult to protect Shakespeare, even though it is hard to enumerate the important ideas in the plays and poems. I am only suggesting that Mr. Justice Brennan might not have found it so easy to dismiss obscenity because it lacked socially useful ideas if he had recognized that as to this point, at least, obscenity is in the same position as all art and literature.

So much for the Court's response to the clear-and-present-danger dilemma. What did it do with the objection about vagueness? The Court was either disingenuous about, or indifferent to, the prior record of difficulties with the term, its own recent experience with Hecate County, and the difficulties which become apparent upon any introspective examination. Admittedly, Mr. Justice Brennan argued, the terms of obscenity statutes "are not precise." But, citing and quoting the Petrillo case, he asserted: "All that is required is that the language 'conveys sufficiently definite warning as to the proscribed conduct when measured by common understanding and practices.'" And the obscenity standards meet this test. The Roth case involved a felony for which a five-year sentence could be imposed along with a $5,000 fine. Yet, even for so serious a crime, the Court saw no difficulty.

Once again it was the Court's failure to break more sharply with prior definitions of obscenity that makes its opinion unsatisfactory. Although the whole approach seems to rest on a notion of hard-core pornography, as Mr. Justice Harlan suggested, the Court chose not to make a fresh start by attempting a definition of pornography. Perhaps most troublesome is the fact that the Court, despite Mr. Justice Harlan's dissent, could see no connection between the workability of its two-level theory and the objections about vagueness.

In the end, although the majority opinion in Roth has made several major contributions to the law and should replace Queen v. Hicklin as the key case in the field, it is unsatisfactory because in the teeth of Judge Frank's stimulating opinion below and of Mr. Justice Harlan's stimulating dissent in the Court, it appeared to find no difficulties. It is unsatisfactory, too, because in an effort to solve the small problem of obscenity, it gave a major endorsement to the two-level theory that may have unhappy repercussions on the protection of free speech generally.

The other opinions in the Roth case deserve comment as an index to the unpersuasive quality of the majority opinion and to the full complexity of the issue as it is presented to the Court. The Chief Justice filed a brief concurrence, full of caution as to the scope of what had been decided. "I agree," he said, "with the result reached by the Court in these cases, but, because we are operating in a field of expression and because broad language used here may eventually be applied to the arts and sciences and freedom of communication generally, I would limit our decision to the facts before us and to the validity of the statutes in question as applied." He thought that both defendants were "plainly engaged in the commercial exploitation of the morbid and shameful craving for materials with prurient effect." He concluded: "I believe the State and Federal Governments can constitutionally punish such conduct. That is all that these cases present to us, and that is all that we need to decide." Mr. Chief Justice Warren thus concurs only in two points: there is some material within the category of the obscene which can be prohibited constitutionally both at the state and federal level, and whatever it was that Roth and Alberts were distributing, it was bad enough to fall within this category. Presumably

Mr. Chief Justice Warren was not indorsing the two-level theory or the revised definition of obscenity. In some future case he could decide consistently with his opinion that some material, although obscene within the new definition, could not be barred constitutionally. It is clear that the majority opinion had not put to rest for him the perplexities of the theme.

As might have been anticipated, the First Amendment difficulties which Mr. Justice Brennan so carefully muted exploded in the dissent of Mr. Justice Douglas, with whom Mr. Justice Black concurred. First, Mr. Justice Douglas noted that the tests used by the trial judges and the revised test announced by the Court require only the arousing of sexual thoughts; this he vigorously rejected as a sufficient predicate for government regulation. Second, he regarded the fact that the trial judge in Roth used offensiveness to "the common conscience of the community" as a test, as "more inimical still to freedom of expression." He argued that such a standard would surely be unconstitutional "if religion, economics, politics, or philosophy were involved. How does it become a constitutional standard when literature treating with sex is concerned?"[1]

It is thus apparent that the effectiveness of Mr. Justice Douglas' dissent turned on his rejection of the two-level theory. He argued for a single unified doctrine of free speech that would cover both obscenity and political speech. On that interpretation his argument is irresistible, since the regulation of speech in other areas on the ground that it aroused improper thoughts, or that it offended the common conscience of the community, would surely fall.

Mr. Justice Douglas met the two-level theory squarely. The issue, he said, cannot be avoided by saying that obscenity is not protected by the First Amendment. The question remains, "What is the constitutional test of obscenity?" With the exception of Beauharnais, none of the Court's prior cases have resolved free-speech issues by placing "any form of expression beyond the pale" of the First Amendment. And, unlike Beauharnais, there is "no special historical evidence" that literature dealing with sex was intended to be treated in a special manner. The first American obscenity decision did not come until 1821. More important, he challenged the basic idea of weighing the social utility of speech: "The First Amendment...was designed to preclude courts as well as legislatures from weighing the values of speech against silence." I think he put his finger firmly on the fundamental difficulty of the two-level theory. It is to be hoped that the force of his dissent will prevent the Court from adding any new categories of speech that are "without redeeming social importance." It is thus clear that Justices Douglas and Black, like Judges Frank and Bok, would favor unifying free-speech theory by requiring that there be evidence of clear danger of action resulting from material dealing with sex before they would permit it to be banned. As between the competing embarrassments of invalidating obscenity legislation or complicating free-speech theory, their choice is clear.

The most complex and interesting of the separate opinions is that of Mr. Justice Harlan. It is apparent from his opening sentence that the Court's opinion had not dispelled his doubts: "I find lurking beneath its disarming generalizations a number of problems which...leave me with serious misgivings as to the future effect of today's decisions."

Mr. Justice Harlan's first point went to the abstract way in which the Court put the "dispositive question." "This sweeping formula appears to me to beg the very question before us. The Court seems to assure that 'obscenity' is a peculiar genus of 'speech and press,' which is as distinct, recognizable, and classifiable as poison ivy is among other plants. On this basis the <u>constitutional</u> question before us simply becomes, as the Court says, whether 'obscenity,' as an abstraction, is protected by the First and Fourteenth Amendments, and the question whether a <u>particular</u> book may be suppressed becomes a mere matter of classification, of 'fact,' to be entrusted to a fact finder and insulated from independent constitutional judgment." Mr. Justice Harlan thus exposed the central weakness of the majority opinion: the difficulty in using the two-level theory where classification at the first or second level depends on a key term as vague as obscenity. The thrust of his objection, however, went to the implications for judicial review of obscenity judgments. He objected that the classification as obscene, which under the Court's formula is decisive of the constitutional question, will be made by the original trier of fact and deferred to, thus encouraging the state and federal reviewing courts "to rely on easy labelling and jury verdicts as a substitute for facing up to the tough individual problems of constitutional judgment involved in every obscenity case." He asserted that no matter how a jury labelled Ulysses or the Decameron, a conviction for selling those books would raise "the gravest constitutional doubts."

Mr. Justice Harlan thus pointed up an important issue about judicial review in free-speech cases. Is not the issue of clear and present danger, or the issue of obscenity, a constitutional fact which the reviewing court must decide for itself? This has been a troublesome and clouded point in the clear-and-present-danger cases, but the case for such an independent reviewing judgment is stronger with issues of obscenity. It seems to me clear, although the Court did not say so, that obscenity is a constitutional fact. The majority opinion makes sense only so long as the Court will be scrupulous and serious in scrutinizing lower-court judgments as to what is obscene. Otherwise the Court may be trapped into the absurdity of asserting that a work like Ulysses is "utterly without social importance" because some lower court has held that it was obscene.

Roth and Alberts are unfortunate cases from the point of view of clarification of this issue, since the majority of justices appear to have regarded the particular items as obscene beyond doubt. Hence, although Mr. Justice Brennan did not make an independent judgment as to the obscenity of the items in this case, it does not necessarily follow that he would not do so in a more troublesome case. I would predict, therefore, that Mr. Justice Harlan's point as to independent review will triumph as soon as the occasion arises, and that the Roth case will liberalize the enforcement of obscenity statutes because lower courts as well as the Supreme Court will feel the pressure of the requirement that the item be "utterly without social importance," that it be "constitutionally obscene."

As one reads Mr. Justice Harlan's complaint about the abstract way in which the Court put the question, the thought occurs that Roth, too, is perhaps destined, like Dennis, to have its Yates aftermath, with Mr. Justice Harlan writing the majority opinion.

Mr. Justice Harlan's second point is of major interest. It will be recalled that it was not until Gitlow that the Court held that the First Amendment was a restriction on the states. In his dissent in Gitlow, Mr. Justice Holmes noted the possibility that the First Amendment might apply less stringently to the states than to the federal government. Holmes, however, was content merely to note the possibility. The point remained unnoticed until Mr. Justice Jackson took it up vigorously in Beauharnais. He marshaled several arguments for his conclusion that the power of the states to regulate speech is subject to different and lesser constitutional restrictions than the power of the federal government. First, he argued from the important differences in wording in the First and Fourteenth amendments that "liberty" in the Fourteenth incorporates only the general notion of such restraints as are essential to the concept of the "ordered liberty" of Palko. Second, he was properly concerned lest the Court in Beauharnais be taken to imply that federal seditions libel laws would be constitutional-a result which, he felt, has long been rejected by the Court and by American political practice. Third, he was impressed with the number of states which had criminal libel laws on their books then and at the time the Fourteenth Amendment was adopted. Fourth, he thought the functions of the state and federal governments are sufficiently different to warrant the use of different standards. The states should be allowed to experiment; libel is primarily a local concern; the interest of the federal government is highly attenuated. Hence he saw a dilemma if we must either limit the states to what is permissible for the federal government in the regulation of speech or permit the federal government what is permissible to the states. He would eliminate the dilemma by applying differential constitutional standards.

It is extraordinary that the distinction between the First and Fourteenth should have been stressed only in the two cases, Beauharnais and Roth, in which the Court seriously employed the two-level theory. Is this just coincidence or is there a relationship? Mr. Justice Jackson seemed concerned to avoid the need for a two-level theory by distinguishing between state and federal power. Since he could accommodate the prevalence of state criminal libel laws by allowing more constitutional leeway at the state level, he had no need for a two-level theory to achieve the same purpose.

Mr. Justice Harlan, however, faced certain difficulties that did not confront his predecessor. He did not reject outright the two-level theory-and therefore left open the problem of what the two levels are at the state tier and what they are at the federal tier. Doctrinal niceties thus appear to be proliferating at a dizzy rate. Mr. Justice Harlan made a determined effort to apply his separate state and federal criteria to the materials before the Court. He concurred in Alberts because, constitutionally, the state should be permitted to regulate obscenity on the ground that such material might influence action either immediately or over a long period of time. This is especially true since the point is one of scientific controversy. "Nothing in the Constitution requires California to accept as truth the most advanced and sophisticated psychiatric opinion. It seems to me clear that it is not irrational, in our present state of knowledge, to consider that pornography can induce a type of sexual conduct which a state may deem obnoxious to the moral fabric of society." There are two implications in this passage. First, in Mr. Justice Harlan's view the state can regulate obscenity, not because if falls within a lower category of speech, but because the state has broader powers. Second, the limit of the state's power is the familiar one, that the legislative judgment not be "irrational." In the Roth case, the problem is quite different. If a state bans a book, the ban holds only for that state, whereas if the federal government does it, the ban holds for the entire country. Then, too, the federal government has only an attentuated interest in obscenity. Mr. Justice Harlan then made an interesting switch in premises: the trial judge's charge would allow conviction for stirring up sexual thoughts; the limited federal interest is not a basis for the regulation of mere thoughts. Therefore, the conviction of Roth was unconstitutional. He did not tell us whether the state can reach mere thoughts, since he read the federal statute as turning on the stirring up of sexual impulse and the state statute as turning on influencing conduct.

In dealing with the federal half of the question, Mr. Justice Harlan did seem to reject the application of the two-level theory of the majority. He would not agree that a book which stirs sexual impulses is necessarily "without redeeming social importance." "It is no answer to say, as the Court does, that obscenity is not protected speech. The point is that this statute, as here construed, defines obscenity so widely that it encompasses matters which might very well be protected speech. I do not think that the federal statute can be constitutionally construed to reach other than what the Government has termed as 'hard-core' pornography." It is regrettable that Mr. Justice Harlan was unable to persuade the Court to shift to the new and apparently narrower-if still undefined-concept of hard-core pornography.

The Harlan opinion, despite its elegance and apparent subtlety, is full of unresolved difficulties. If he did not reject the two-level theory, he applied it at neither the state nor the federal level. The test of state power over speech is apparently that of ordinary substantive due process. The test of federal power is obscure, since there is no discussion of clear and present danger. If the federal government cannot regulate mere thoughts in this area, it may, nevertheless, reach hard-core pornography, which arguably does no more than stir sexual fantasy. Apparently the federal government cannot reach action, as can the states, on the doubtful ground of a connection between speech and action.

The combination of the Brennan and Harlan opinions has thus created more free-speech doctrine than can be used sensibly. It would seem to me monstrously complex to have a four-level speech theory. And it would seem to me "burning the house to roast the pig" to solve the obscenity problem at the price of reducing the constitutional control over the states to mere substantive due process, although Mr. Justice Frankfurter, to be sure, has long and ably argued for this result in the political speech cases. Further, if Mr. Justice Harlan meant to reject the two-level theory, there is still the puzzle of balancing the government's interest against the freedom involved. That balance would be quite different for political speech than for obscenity. Moreover, it is difficult, and I would add unwise, to read Palko as meaning that only some of the basic notion of free speech is integral to "ordered liberty." It has been difficult enough for the Court to decide which of the Bill of Rights are incorporated in the Fourteenth Amendment; it should not assume the further burden of deciding how much of each is incorporated. In any event, it is abundantly clear that the effort of the Court to deal with obscenity within its committment to free speech has opened issues about free speech which transcend in importance the limited problem of obscenity. Even more than the two-level theory of the Brennan opinion, the split-level First Amendment theory of the Harlan opinion advances a doctrine which could have the most profound impact on freedom of speech. It is unfortunate that the collision of complex analyses in the Brennan and Harlan opinions could not have been carried to more explicit resolution.

The third of Mr. Justice Harlan's basic objections to the majority opinion was that the Court had ignored differences between the two statutes involved and, moreover, differences between the statutory standards and the Court's definition of obscenity. It is partly these differences which permitted him to reach different conclusions in the state and in the federal cases. Yet the distinction drawn here, like those in his opinions in Yates, Barenblatt, and Lerner, reveal a capacity to find satisfying distinctions that seem too fine for the ordinary mind. His proposition that the state statute defines obscenity in terms of affecting conduct and the federal statute in terms of affecting thoughts is based on no significant difference in the wording of the two statutes. Both statutes are confined to flat prohibitions of "the obscene." Nor can reliance be placed on the constructions given by the California court and by the trial judge's charge in Roth. The California test is whether the material has a tendency to corrupt by exciting "lascivious thoughts or arousing lustful desires." The charge to the jury in Roth spoke of whether the material would arouse sexual desires or impure sexual thoughts in the average person. I frankly do not see the difference. Both definitions emphasize impact on thoughts, and the California court's reference to "the tendency to corrupt," I suggest, is tautological; the court meant that the arousing of lascivious thoughts necessarily corrupts. The elaborate structure of the Harlan opinion collapses at this point: the neat symmetry is illusory. He did not need the distinction between state and federal power to decide the issues actually before him. Yet he ducked the interesting issue, in his terms, of whether the state has the power to reach thoughts. He put a strained interpretation on the two cases in order to have occasion to sponsor a view of the constitutional inhibitions against regulation of speech generally which may have grave consequences at the state level.

His second distinction between the definitions in the two cases and the Court's "prurient test" seems more solid. The Court avowedly borrowed its definition from the

American Law Institute's proposed model penal code. Mr. Justice Harlan pointed out that the draftsmen explicitly rejected "the prevailing test of tendency to arouse lustful thoughts or desires." Unfortunately, he did not pursue this point-pursuit which might have led to an analysis of that curious term, "prurient interest." It is not easy to see any difference between "arousing lascivious thoughts" and having "an appeal to prurient, that is lascivious interests." Further, although the A. L. I. draftsmen rejected the traditional test because they thought it "unrealistically broad" for our society, Mr. Justice Harlan is silent on whether the "prevailing test" is constitutionally permissible as a test for the states.

The Harlan critique does, however, expose another difficulty with the majority opinion. Is the prurient test to be taken as the constitutional test of obscenity so that any substantial deviations from it must raise a constitutional doubt? If so-and it would appear to be so-Mr. Justice Harlan's suggestion that the tests used in Roth and Alberts are not the same as the prurient test raised a serious issue for the majority as to the validity, in their own terms, of the two convictions. For if the prevailing tests, which were employed in both cases, are different from the prurient-interest test, as the A. L. I. spokesmen argued, then both defendants were convicted under tests of obscenity that were broader and presumably more vague than the constitutional test. It is a serious weakness of the Brennan opinion that it is not more directly responsive to his point.

Whatever else might be said about Roth and Alberts, it is clear that they will have a major effect, not only of future obscenity regulation, but, for better or worse, on general free-speech doctrine as well.

IV. Kingsley Pictures Corp. v. Regents

In the 1958 Term, the Court added another major decision on obscenity [Kingsley Pictures Corp. v. Regents, 360 U. S. 684 (1959)]. It will be recalled that one possible evil was "thematic obscenity," that is, the advocacy of improper sexual ethics.[2] In People v. Friede thirty years earlier, a New York court found Radclyffe Hall's The Well of Loneliness obscene. The court found the book well-written and compassionate, and in no sense vulgar or offensive in its imagery, but too favorable toward homo-sexuality. The notion that there could be obscene ideas as well as obscene images had seemed particularly hard to square with developing free-speech doctrine. In Kingsley, the issue came before the court. Ironically, the Kingsley case involved that most celebrated of obscenity causes, Lady Chatterley's Lover, but in the form of a motion picture rather than a book.

The New York Board of Regents had refused to license the picture. The Supreme Court unanimously found this action unconstitutional. The unanimity, however, ended with the decision. There were six separate opinions. The proliferation of individual opinions in this case, indicative of the continued difficulties of regulation of obscenity after Roth, is the kind of thing that the layman finds dismaying--not, it must ruefully be admitted, without cause.

Kingsley involved another major problem of obscenity: the validity of prior restraints. This is one of the major unresolved issues affecting not only motion picture censorship but postal censorship and possibly censorship of books as well. It is clear that censorship in advance of publication labors both under a bad name historically as well as some special constitutional inhibition. It is clear also that the Court is not prepared to say that all prior restraints are invalid. For several years, the Court has studiously avoided deciding whether such restraints are bad when related to obscenity. Kingsley afforded one more opportunity to pass on the issue; but only Justices Black and Douglas accepted the invitation. In separate concurring opinions each argued that the action of the Regents was bad because the entire New York movie censorship scheme was an unconstitutional prior restraint.

The other opinions invalidated the Regent's action on the narrower grounds which will be considered here. The opinion of the Court was delivered by Mr. Justice Stewart. The New York statute under which the Regents had acted permitted the refusal of a license if the picture was "immoral." A recent amendment had amplified the definition of immoral to include the presentation of "acts of sexual immorality... expressly or impliedly... as desirable, acceptable or proper patterns of behavior." Mr. Justice Stewart read the Regents' action as based on the ground that the picture presented "adultery as proper behavior...under certain circumstances." Accepting this as the definitive construction of the statute, he was faced squarely with the issue of thematic obscenity and held squarely that the statute was unconstitutional. He said:

> It is contended that the State's action was justified because the motion picture attractively portrays a relationship which is contrary to the moral standards, the religious precepts, and the legal code of its citizenry. This argument misconceives what it is that the Constitution protects. Its guarantee is not confined to the expression of ideas that are conventional or shared by a majority. It protects advocacy of the opinion that adultery may sometimes be proper,[3] no less than advocacy of socialism or the single tax. And in the realm of ideas it protects expression which is eloquent no less than that which is unconvincing.

This ranks as one of the Court's clearest and most impressive utterances about free speech in general. Specifically, it means that one of the possible target evils of obscenity regulation, the obscene theme, has now been declared an unconstitutional predicate for government intervention.

The Stewart opinion is also notably courageous in its apparent willingness to allow those who would do so to put in a good word for adultery. It is not without interest that the Court is willing to expose itself to public criticism and embarrassment on this point but is unwilling to do so on behalf of obscenity. The other justices, who felt compelled to concur separately, do not appear to disagree with this view or with the result.

Mr. Justice Clark agreed with the majority reading of the New York statute but chose to put his decision on the ground he had advanced in the Burstyn case, that the criterion of "immorality" as defined by the amendment was "too vague."

> The only limits (sic) on the censor's discretion is is his understanding of what is included within the term "desirable, acceptable or proper." This is nothing less than a roving commission in which

> individual impressions become the yardstick of action, and result in regulation in accordance with the beliefs of the individual censor rather than regulation by law.

Thus Mr. Justice Clark, like Mr. Justice Stewart, found the statute unconstitutional on its face.

Justices Frankfurter and Harlan each filed opinions with different points of departure. They had in common two objections. First, that the Court should not have found the statute bad on its face but only in this particular application. Second, that the Court misread the construction of the statute by the New York Court of Appeals. Mr. Justice Frankfurter's opinion has familiar echoes of his earlier opinions on free speech. After references to D. H. Lawrence's views on obscenity and to a recent debate in Parliament, he proceeded to his main point:

> Unless I misread the opinion of the Court, it strikes down the New York legislation in order to escape the task of deciding whether a particular picture is entitled to the protection of expression under the Fourteenth Amendment. Such an exercise of the judicial function, however, onerous or ungrateful, inheres in the very nature of the judicial enforcement of the Due Process Clause. We cannot escape such instance-by-instance, case-by-case application of the clause in all varieties of situations that come before this Court.

He then analogized the task at hand to that found in the confession cases, the right-to-counsel cases, and the church-and-state cases. Such careful balancing is inherent in the concept of due process. "The task is onerous and exacting, demanding as it does the utmost discipline in objectivity, the severest control of personal predilections. But it cannot be escaped, not even by disavowing that such is the nature of our task."

However one may feel about the evils of doctrinaire liberalism against which Mr. Justice Frankfurter has so valiantly fought, one cannot, I think, be happy with this opinion. Justices Stewart and Clark and Black and Douglas made valid general points about which Mr. Justice Frankfurter chose to remain silent. Is thematic obscenity constitutionally subject to state control? Is the two-level theory of Roth operative here, where ideas about sexual morality are involved? Is the New York statute too vague? Moreover, is Mr. Justice Frankfurter adopting Mr. Justice Harlan's view in Roth, that the First Amendment has a different impact on the states, or is he arguing, as his Dennis opinion suggested, that the problem reduces to the idea of substantive due process at both the state and federal levels? Are prior restraints keyed to obscenity valid? With so many important and pressing general questions in view, it is difficult to accept the ideal of judicial self-restraint which would avoid passing on any of them in order to praise the difficult process of marginal inclusion and exclusion under the Due Process Clause. In his desire to avoid broad libertarian generalizations, Mr. Justice Frankfurter generalized too little. He is clear that the motion picture cannot be banned constitutionally, but he tells us almost nothing about the criteria that dictate his judgment about this particular. The preoccupation with balancing values in free-speech cases, although it steers clear of the doctrinaire, comes precariously close to the opposite evil of the intuitive, particularized judgment which offers no guidance for the future.

Certainly Mr. Justice Frankfurter's colleagues were not happy about his opinion. It struck angry sparks in the opinions of Justices Douglas, Black, and Clark. The first commented on the irrelevance of the references to England, which has no written Constitution and has different assumptions about the roles of court and legislature. The second (who, unlike his colleagues, refused to see the picture) spoke wryly of the Court's becoming the Supreme Board of Censors, adding: "My belief is that this Court is about the most inappropriate Supreme Board of Censors that could be found." He added an animadversion to the reference to D. H. Lawrence's view on obscenity. And Mr. Justice Clark noted that fifteen times in a fourteen-page opinion Chief Judge Conway had said that the picture was proscribed because of its espousal of sexual immorality-a remark aimed directly at Mr. Justice Frankfurter's complaint about "culling a phrase here and there" in misconstruing the decisions of the New York Court of Appeals.

The sixth and last opinion in Kingsley is that of Mr. Justice Harlan, in which Justices Frankfurter and Whittaker joined. It followed closely the argument of the Frankfurter opinion but made more evident what it was they found embarrassing in the holding that the New York statute was unconstitutional on its face. A few years earlier the Court had dealt with another case involving La Ronde, to which the Regents had denied a license on the ground that it was "immoral." The Court, in a one-line per curiam decision, had held the Regents' action unconstitutional, citing the Burstyn case. New York had then tried to remedy the vagueness of the term "immorality" by the amendment defining it more fully. Mr. Justice Frankfurter in his opinion had made the familiar point that it is not the province of the Supreme Court to meet the "recalcitrant problems of legislative drafting. Ours is the vital but very limited task of scrutinizing the work of the draftsmen in order to determine whether they have kept within the narrow limits of the kind of censorship which even D. H. Lawrence deemed necessary." Yet it is clear that both he and Mr. Justice Harlan were embarrassed at the idea of the Court's once more sending the statute back to New York for redrafting. The point is not so well taken in this instance, however, since the Court was not rejecting the statute, as Mr. Justice Clark would have done, because it was to vague. It rejected it on grounds that give ample advice to the draftsmen. Mr. Justice Harlan agreed that the "abstract" advocacy of adultery (which is certainly an interesting concept) may not be constitutionally prohibited but insisted that the Court was misconstruing the New York interpretation of its statute. He understood the New York Court of Appeals to have sustained a ban on the espousal of adultery, either by "obscene portrayal or by actual incitement," and found that statute, so construed, not unconstitutional on its face.

Turning to the question of this application of the statute, Mr. Justice Harlan then affirmed his position in Roth, that the states have wider latitude than the federal government. But even that latitutde did not permit them to bar this picture. Lady Chatterley's Lover was nothing more than a "somewhat unusual, and rather pathetic 'love triangle,' lacking in anything that could properly be termed obscene or corruptive of the public morals by inciting the commission of adultery." Presumably, then, even the states cannot regulate ideas about sexual behavior unless they are imbedded in obscene imagery or unless they amount to direct incitement. In short, ideas about sexual behavior have the same constitutional status as ideas about anything else-which was precisely Mr. Justice Stewart's point.

Mr. Justice Harlan, however, added a remarkable sentence, perhaps in an effort to dissociate himself from the self-righteous tone of Mr. Justice Frankfurter on the question of making difficult individual judgments. "Giving descriptive expression to what in matters of this kind are in the last analysis bound to be but individual subjective impressions, objectively as one may try to discharge his duty as a judge, is not apt to be repaying." The candor is commendable, but the remark plays directly into the hands of Mr. Justice Black, who complained that Justices Harlan and Frankfurter were substituting personal subjective judgment for constitutional rule.

The Kingsley case, then, if it added to the law on obscenity, also disclosed even more explicitly than did Roth a major tension in free-speech doctrine between those judges who favor a clear statement of ruling principle and those who favor a particularized balancing that is inevitably personal. Once again an obscenity case opened up basic issues transcending the problems of obscenity.

V. Smith v. California

The most recent important decision on obscenity is Smith v. California, [361 U. S. 147 (1959)] decided in the 1959 Term. It provides a fitting conclusion to the Court's recent work and may prove to be the most important decision on the subject yet rendered. The case was concerned with a Los Angeles ordinance making it a crime for anyone to have in his possession for sale any obscene or indecent writing or book. The Court was unanimous in holding the ordinance unconstitutional, but once again there was a proliferation of separate opinions-this time five. The defendant urged a series of arguments which had varied appeal for the different justices. He asserted that the ordinance was bad because it did not require scienter. He complained that the trial judge had excluded the testimony of experts as well as other evidence on the contemporary literary and moral standards of the community. And he urged that the material in question was not obscene. None of the justices reached the third point. They reacted differently to the other two. The *Smith* case highlights two further important issues in the regulation of obscenity: (1) The problem of the disseminator or bookseller who, as a practical matter, is far more likely than the author or publisher to be the target of prosecution; (2) the relevance of external evidence of community standards to the delicate judgments of obscenity and constitutionality.

The majority opinion by Mr. Justice Brennan effectuated his promise in *Roth* to be vigilant in the scrutiny of obscenity prosecutions. For him the fatal flaw in the ordinance was the absence of a requirement of *scienter*. As Mr. Justice Brennan read the ordinance, a bookseller could be convicted although legitimately unaware of the contents of the book. Because the Court had already upheld drug legislation imposing absolute criminal liability without *scienter*, Mr. Justice Brennan did not find the ordinance bad because it was unfair to the bookseller. Rather, he argued that if the seller were absolutely liable there would be a serious clog in the free flow of communications, for the seller would deal only in material with which he was acquainted and which he regarded as safe. The result would be "a censorship by booksellers" of non-obscene items. Thus the ordinance would effect an unconstitutional interference with free speech and press. The case thus posed a dilemma. If the state must prove that the seller knows that the book is obscene, the state will have an impossible burden to meet and the practical enforcement of obscenity laws will collapse. On the other hand, if the presence of the book in the store is sufficient, the seller will, as Mr. Justice Brennan reasoned, censor the books he offers for sale.

Mr. Justice Brennan relented enough to suggest, in passing, that something less than full *scienter* might suffice. But, following the tradition of Mr. Justice Frankfurter, he carefully noted: "We need not and most definitely do not pass today on what sort of mental element is requisite to a constitutionally permissible prosecution of a bookseller for carrying an obscene book in stock." It is sufficient that today the Court is considering a statute "which goes to the extent of eliminating all mental elements from the crime."

Two points in the majority opinion clamor for attention. First, it is striking that the Court found a First Amendment violation because of the indirect consequences of the ordinance. Normally restraints have been direct, in the form of criminal penalty or refusal to license; no conjecture has been necessary as to whether the free flow of communication will be affected. The very purpose of such regulation is avowedly to ban circulation of the item. But the purpose of the Los Angeles ordinance was not to turn booksellers into censors of non-obscene items. To find that it would have this effect, the Court must have speculated as to a chain of human behavior. In the attacks on congressional investigating committees and the federal loyalty program, a principal point has been that they would have the effect of discouraging free speech and free association by making people unduly cautious of what they said and what organizations they joined, *i. e.*, by turning them into censors of their own speech and choice of associates. Although this argument of restraint by consequence won some minority judicial support, the courts have steadfastly rejected it as a basis for finding a First Amendment flaw in the procedures of the congressional investigating committee or the loyalty program. It is, therefore, of no small interest that the Court accepted such reasoning here, though admittedly the bookseller is a more strategic link in the flow of public communication than the ordinary witness before a committee or the ordinary government employee.

Second, the dilemma about *scienter* sharpens on reflection. The Court was concerned primarily with the bookseller's knowledge of the contents of the book, but Mr. Justice Brennan noted explicitly the possibility "of honest mistake as to whether its contents in fact constituted obscenity." If the Court were to require knowledge that the book is obscene, it would indeed be difficult for the prosecution ever to succeed: the defendant can always, with some plausibility, argue that he did not think the item was obscene and is astonished that others so view it. The objection as to the vagueness of "obscenity" which Mr. Justice Brennan dismissed so cavalierly in *Roth* had risen again to haunt the Court. The vagueness argument may have lost the battle but won the war, since the vagueness of obscenity may so bedevil the effort to prove *scienter* that the effective enforcement of regulation against the dissemination of obscene matter will collapse at the prosecution of the bookseller, the key link in the chain of distribution. It is difficult, however, to see why the seller should receive more protection than the author or publisher. The latter have to take the risk that the Court's judgment of what is obscene will not agree with their own. This is precisely what the constitutional objection to vagueness means-that the law is so unclear that one cannot tell whether he is committing a crime or not. Having once rejected this point in Roth, the Court is not likely to accept it in the guise of the scienter requirement in future prosecutions of booksellers.

The separate concurrences of Justices Black and Douglas were hardly a surprise. They continued to advance their dissenting view in Roth, that the regulation of obscenity by criminal sanction is unconstitutional. Hence the bookseller could not be validly prosecuted for the dissemination of the obscene material because this is an unconstitutional predicate for a crime. In their view, the ordinance would be equally unconstitutional however it handled the scienter requirement.

As in the Kingsley case, Justices Harlan and Frankfurter concurred in the result only. Mr. Justice Frankfurter hesitated either to accept or to reject the Court's concern with scienter. He recognized that the food and drug cases were no precedent for the issue here: "There is an important difference in the scope of the power of a State to regulate what feeds the belly and what feeds the brain." But he also felt that the consequential impact of such ordinances on the non-obscene "cannot be of a nature to nullify for all practical purposes the power of the State to deal with obscenity." Having thus posed for himself the dilemma that the Smith case raises, he neatly avoided it by finding the critical flaw not in the wording of the ordinance but in the exclusion by the trial judge of expert testimony on community standards.

In the course of his discussion Mr. Justice Frankfurter made two interesting points. First, in an unusual turnabout, he complained that the majority opinion had not given sufficient guidance to the state as to how to draft a valid scienter requirement. "Invalidating a statute because a State dispenses altogether with the requirement of scienter does require some indication of the scope and quality of scienter that is required." Although he could be quoted against himself at length on the narrow but vital function of the Court in scrutinizing the work of legislative draftsmen, he scored a good point against the Brennan opinion. It would indeed be difficult to draft an ordinance which would be practically useful and yet would comply with the scienter requirement. The moral I draw is that there are serious weaknesses in Mr. Justice Frankfurter's favorite doctrine of judicial economy.

Second, in his emphasis on the utility of expert testimony he was directly responsive to the criticism that Mr. Justice Black made of his views in the Kingsley case. Unless the testimony of such experts can come in, the judicial judgment of obscenity, and hence of constitutionality, will be "merely a subjective reflection of the taste or moral outlook of individual jurors or individual judges." Thus it is the ascertainment of community standards that is to give the obscenity judgment an objective referent. Mr. Justice Frankfurter would thus add an important gloss to the constitutional definition of obscenity in Roth: whether the dominant appeal is to prurient interest measured by prevailing community standards is to be determined in part by expert testimony. It is, therefore, unconstitutional to bar such testimony. This view is strongly indorsed by Mr. Justice Harlan, and the English have recently adopted it. There is nothing in the other opinions inconsistent with it. Although I am inclined to applaud this development, I cannot refrain from suggesting a few doubts. The experts apparently are to testify to literary standards and to community moral standards rather than to psychological connections between words and actions, or to psychiatric views of the harm that may be caused by exposure to the obscene. Presumably, there are people who know enough about literature to inform the Court of the status of Ulysses or Hecate County or Lady Chatterley. But this the Court already knows. When it comes to the prevailing moral standards, to the community view of what is obscene, it is not at all clear what expertise is available. The Court appears to be inviting the well-publicized difficulty of the Court of Appeals for the Second Circuit in the Repouille case, when it puzzled over the meaning of the "good moral character" requirement in the naturalization law in a most sympathetic case of euthanasia.

I suggest that heavy reliance on expert testimony to objectivize the obscenity judgment indicates once again how powerful the argument is that obscenity is a fatally ambiguous concept. And I would echo Mr. Justice Douglas' dismay in Roth that shock to the community conscience is the test of permissible speech. Finally, I wonder whether the only experts on the issue at hand are not the jury, as Judge Learned Hand suggested years ago, and whether the logic of Mr. Justice Frankfurter does not lead to the conclusion that the jury is the proper constitutional arbiter of obscenity.

Mr. Justice Harlan's opinion is not on all fours with that of Mr. Justice Frankfurter. He found a broader error in the trial. He objected not only to the refusal to permit expert testimony but also to the refusal to permit more amateurish efforts by the defendant to "compare the contents of the work with that of other allegedly similar publications which were openly published, sold and purchased, and which received wide general acceptance." The admission of this evidence, like that of the experts, is a constitutional requirement in the Harlan view.

The implications of the Harlan and Frankfurter opinions in Smith for the conduct of obscenity defenses should not be minimized. Until now an obscenity trial has been a rather pedestrain affair, with not much more than the material itself as the evidence. Defense counsel have been champing at the bit to introduce other evidence. If the Frankfurter-Harlan position is given effect, the trial of an obscenity case will not only be enlivened by a battle of experts but also by content analysis of lingerie advertisements, of bathing-suit photographs, of the hidden and not so hidden sexual symbolism of all advertising, and perhaps even of the content of ordinary speech and off-color jokes. In brief, Life and Saturday Evening Post will be called upon to rescue Playboy and Esquire.

One final detail of the Harlan opinion remains to be noted. Once again the Justice repeated his thesis of Roth, that the First Amendment applies less stringently to the states. Once again, none of the other justices paid any attention to the point. And once again, as in Kingsley, the distinction did not seem to guide Mr. Justice Harlan's own opinion, since he found that the state had exceeded its constitutional power.

VI. Conclusion

This article began by noting four possible target evils of obscenity regulation. What has the Court said of them in the cases we have examined? The majority in Roth used the two-level theory to avoid saying anything. Mr. Justice Douglas dissented on the ground that government could not control speech in an effort to control thoughts, sexual or otherwise. Mr. Justice Harlan, on the other hand, held that the state could regulate obscenity only on theory that it affected conduct, but that the federal government could not regulate it on the theory that it affected thoughts. Hence the twin evils of arousing sexual behavior and of arousing sexual thoughts receive an interesting pattern of rejection in the opinions. In the Kingsley case, the third possible evil, thematic obscenity, was held by the majority to be an unconstitutional basis for regulation in the name of obscenity.

There is left then only the fourth possible evil, the arousing of revulsion and disgust in a non-captive adult audience. Thus far the Court has had no occasion to speak to this point. The issue appears to have been available in Roth since the federal statute uses the word "filthy" along with "obscene, lewd, lascivious," and the trial judge had defined "filthy" in his charge to the jury. The defendant had suggested the point in the Court of Appeals, resting his argument on vagueness. Chief Judge Clark, quoting Learned Hand, found, however, that the trial judge's definition was adequate: "'Filthy' pertains to that sort of treatment of sexual matters in such a vulgar and indecent way, so that it tends to arouse a feeling of disgust and revulsion." In any event, the defendant had waived objections to the trial judge's charge.

The point, however, is not that "filthy" is vague but that it points to an evil of obscenity which is the exact opposite of that usually recognized: the obscene is bad because it is revolting, not because it is alluring.[4] Since it cannot be both at the same time for the same audience, it would be well to have more explicit guidance as to which objection controls. I suggest that the evil of arousing revulsion in adults who are a non-captive audience is simply too trivial a predicate for constitutional regulation. It is probable, especially since "filthy" is still in the federal statute, that a case will arise when "arousing revulsion" is part of the court's charge to a jury and the Court will yet be faced with the issue and invited to fill this hiatus in its coverage of the obscenity issues.

This account of the Court's encounter with obscenity would not be complete without some reference to a series of three _per curiam_ decisions that followed _Roth_. Ordinarily a _per curiam_ decision makes thin reading, but these three cases serve to mark, more distinctly than the facts in either _Kingsley_ or _Smith_ permitted, how the Court will interpret the definition of obscenity advanced in _Roth_. They serve, too, as the basis for a hypothesis which Thurman Arnold has voiced in a recent brief to the Supreme Court of Vermont as to what the Court's strategy will be in future obscenity cases.

The three _per curiam_ cases are _One, Inc. v. Olesen_, _Sunshine Book Co. v. Summerfield_, and _Times Film Corp. v. Chicago_. The first two cases involved magazines and the third a motion picture. In _One, Inc._, the Court of Appeals for the Ninth Circuit held a magazine with a homosexual slant to be clearly obscene, saying that it was "offensive to the moral senses, morally depraving and debasing, and that it is designed for persons having lecherous and salacious proclivities." In the _Sunshine Book_ case, the Court of Appeals for the District of Columbia affirmed, not without dissent, the trial judge's finding, based on a meticulous examination of each photograph, that the pictures in a nudist magazine were obscene. And in the _Times Film_ case the Court of Appeals for the Seventh Circuit, after seeing the motion picture, found "that, from beginning to end, the thread of the story is supercharged with a current of lewdness generated by a series of illicit sexual intimacies and acts.... The narrative is graphically pictured with nothing omitted except those sexual consummations which are plainly suggested but meaningfully omitted and thus, by the very fact of omission, emphasized." It held that the motion picture was clearly obscene. The Supreme Court granted certiorari in all three cases. In each case in reversed _per curiam_, citing only the _Roth_ case. These three decisions, coupled with the citation of _Roth_, point unmistakably in one direction: the Court is feeling the pressure generated by the two-level theory to restrict obscenity to the worthless and hence to something akin to hard-core pornography. Thus the three decisions appear to add an important gloss to the *Roth* definition. And the prophecy that *Roth* would serve to narrow the range of obscenity regulation appears fulfilled.

It is at this point that Mr. Arnold enters with the appropriate last word. Having been engaged as counsel for the defense in a prosecution in Vermont for the sale of an allegedly obscene magazine, he submitted a brief to the Vermont Supreme Court which must rank as one of the more extraordinary briefs ever filed. The main point is advice to the Vermont court on how to handle the issue before it sensibly and diplomatically. Mr. Arnold purports to get his rule of judicial prudence from the United States Supreme Court. The rule is simple: the court should hold the items before it not obscene unless they amount to hard-core pornography, and should, after rendering a decision, shut up. In Mr. Arnold's view, any fool can quickly recognize hard-core pornography, but it is a fatal trap for judicial decorum and judicial sanity to attempt thereafter to write an opinion explaining why:

> Ordinarily when the Supreme Court grants certiorari and reverses *per curiam* without argument or submission of briefs it means that the law was clear without argument. But it cannot be said of these three cases that previous decisions compelled their results. There must be a different reason for the Court's silence. We think that reason becomes apparent from a reading of the hundreds of cases where the courts have tried to analyze the concepts of obscenity and which we have refrained from citing because no more unedifying section or judicial literature exists. Vermont has indeed been fortunate in escaping it. The spectacle of a judge poring over the picture of some nude, trying to ascertain the extent to which she arouses prurient interests, and then attempting to write an opinion which explains the difference between that nude and some other nude has elements of low comedy. Justice is supposed to be a blind Goddess. The task of explaining why the words 'sexual relations' are decent and some other word with the same meaning is indecent is not one for which judicial techniques are adapted.

> It is our belief, therefore, that the Supreme Court's refusal to write opinions in these three cases was exceedingly wise. No one can reason why anything is or is not obscene.... What the Supreme Court is saying to the lower court judges is that ... if the material is bad enough they can leave the case to a jury. If it isn't the indictment should be dismissed or a verdict directed. This decision may be made at a glance. Studying the material for hours doesn't tell a judge any more about its obscene character than he knew when he first looked at it.
>
> While it is apparent that the Supreme Court has adopted the 'hard core' pornography as a Constitutional test its use of the per curiam opinion neatly avoided the trap of defining what 'hard core' pornography is. Such an attempt would have started the futile and desperate game of definition all over again. As William James, the great psychologist, said: 'Such discussions are tedious-not as hard subjects like physics or mathematics are tedious, but as throwing feathers endlessly hour after hour is tedious.'

Mr. Arnold may well be right as to the Court's strategy. Like Judge Frank and Judge Hand, he has a rich appreciation of the comic aspects of judicial review of obscenity; and the Court, although it has been notably solemn in its dealing with the theme, may have come to see his point. "The Court evidently concluded that its actions must speak for themselves in this field. This may be an unconventional way of making law, but in the field of pornography it is certainly sound judicial common sense." The Arnold advice has a familiar ring-all the Court can do in these cases is to make the difficult individual judgment; it can add little by way of generalization as to why. This is very close indeed to the position of Justices Frankfurter and Harlan. Obscenity, too, makes strange bedfellows.

I cannot leave the Court's efforts in this field without a word about the extraordinary difficulty of its task. The difficulties have, I think, three main strands. First, there is the specific topic of obscenity itself, a topic freighted with all the anxieties and hypocrisies of society's attitude toward sex. I think it not unlikely that none of the justices takes the evils of obscenity very seriously. Yet, as responsibly placed men, understandably they cannot follow Judge Frank and say so. There are few topics on which the public and the private views of a person are so likely to diverge. And the justices are compelled by their roles to express a sober public view of the matter. Second, when they pass on the constitutionality of obscenity they come close to major doctrine about free speech and free press. They cannot handle obscenity issues, which they may not care much about, insulated from the implications their decisions may have for free-speech issues about which they do care. Finally, they perform their roles in an institutional context that necessarily raises issues about federalism, about judicial review, about holding statutes unconstitutional on their face or only in their application, about *de novo* review of constitutional fact, about whether they should ever decide any more issues than they are compelled to, and about whether they are obliged to give legislative draftsmen advice on how to cure the defects the Court may find in their work. In brief, the most impressive aspect of their task is that any decision must treat so many variables. The rest of us are fortunate indeed that our job is so much easier and less responsible.

Notes

1. Some years ago I participated in a seminar on obscenity to which scholars from various disciplines were invited. I particularly remember the point made by the representative from Philosophy, Professor Charner M. Perry of the University of Chicago. He wondered how we would feel about restrictions on literature describing other vices such as greed, cowardice, or gluttony in the same way that obscenity may be said to be related to sexual intemperance.

2. Recognition of this category of thematic obscenity is not inconsistent with my view that belles-lettres properly do not deal in ideas. Thematic obscenity refers primarily to novels in which sexually unconventional conduct does not meet with punishment. Thus, *Lady Chatterley's Lover* is not an argument in favor of adultery but a story in which the author is sympathetic to the illicit lovers and in which the plot does not show, as compared, for example, with *Madame Bovary* or *Anna Karenina*, that "adultery does not pay."

3. Mr. Justice Stewart did not note that Aristotle would disagree; "Not every action or feeling however admits of the observance of a due mean. Indeed the very names of some essentially denote evil.... All these and similar actions and feelings are blamed as being bad in themselves.... It is impossible therefore ever to go right in regard to them -- one must always be wrong; nor does right or wrong in their case depend on the circumstances, for instance, whether one commits adultery with the right woman, at the right time, and in the right manner...." Nicomachean Ethics II, vi, 18-19 (Loeb Classical Library ed. 1926).

4. Judge Frank did not ignore this difficulty: "If the argument be sound that the legislature may constitutionally provide punishment for the obscene because, anti-socially, it arouses sexual desires by making sex attractive, then it follows that whatever makes sex disgusting is socially beneficial -- and thus not the subject of valid legislation which punishes the mailing of 'filthy' matter."

Professors William B. Lockhart and Robert C. McClure have become noted for their studies of obscenity law. The following article is reprinted from 7 Utah Law Review (1961), with the kind permission of the Utah Law Review, the Minnesota Law Review, and the authors; grateful acknowledgment is made to all the permission to reprint.

This article is the text of an address delivered March 3, 1961 at the University of Utah by Dean Lockhart as part of the University's Advancement of Learning Lecture Series arranged in recognition of graduate instruction, research, and service at the University of Utah during the post-war years, 1946-1961. Documentation is not provided in this article as full citations may be found in two earlier articles: Lockhart and McClure, Literature, The Law of Obscenity and the Constitution, 38 Minn. L. Rev. 295 (1954); Lockhart and McClure, Censorship of Obscenity: The Developing Constitutional Standards, 45 Minn. L. Rev. 5 (1960). Acknowledgment is made to the Minnesota Law Review for permission to republish these materials in the present form.

Miss Leslie J. Crocker, writing in 17 [Case] Western Reserve Law Review, p. 1335 ff. (1966), suggests that the U. S. Supreme Court relied heavily on the work of Professors Lockhart and McClure in reaching its decision in Ginzburg, since Ginzburg implies a "variable" approach to obscenity. Miss Crocker's article appears in this anthology.

William B. Lockhart is Dean and Professor of Law, University of Minnesota.

Robert C. McClure is Professor of Law, University of Minnesota.

Obscenity Censorship: The Core Constitutional Issue -- What is Obscene?

by William B. Lockhart and Robert C. McClure

I. Introduction

In 1948 the United States Supreme Court considered for the first time the claim that literature attacked as obscene is entitled to constitutional protection. The occasion was an appeal from New York's censorship of Edmund Wilson's Memoirs of Hecate County -- a work of high literary quality by a distinguished author and critic. But after what must have been a most interesting debate in conference the Court wrote no opinion and gave us no guidance, because it was equally divided. And the Memoirs remained censored in New York.

In 1954 my colleague, Professor Robert McClure, and I explored this unresolved problem in an article published in the Minnesota Law Review. We recognized that not all material posing as literature or art is entitled to constitutional protection for freedom of expression. But we took the position that literature attacked as "obscene" should be judged by constitutional standards that would give appropriate weight to social and literary values and adequate protection to the basic rights of free expression and freedom to read.

Three years later in 1957 the Supreme Court, with Justices Black and Douglas dissenting, upheld the constitutionality of federal and state obscenity laws in the Roth case, declaring that obscenity is "not within the area of constitutionally protected speech and press." The exponents of censorship hailed the decision, apparently seeing in it an end to this foolishness about constitutional protection for material relating to sex.

Yet in 1960 and 1961 we find Memoirs of Hecate County published without apparent fear of censorship, of all places in Boston, long a stronghold of censorship forces. And we find Lady Chatterley's Lover, unexpurgated, published freely in competing editions, after the Department of Justice declined to appeal to the Supreme Court a Court of Appeals ruling that the Postmaster General could not constitutionally censor Lady Chatterley as obscene.

The explanation for this turn of events is found in careful analysis of the Roth opinion and six other Supreme Court decisions between 1957 and 1960 -- in three of which no opinions were written. Professor McClure and I have just published a second article in the November 1960 Minnesota Law Review in which we analyze the developing constitutional requirements for censorship of obscenity as reflected in these decisions, and point out how we believe these standards should evolve in the future.

My objective [here] is not to summarize the essence of all Professor McClure and I have written in two long articles. Instead, I will only seek to provide some understanding of the direction that constitutional developments have taken thus far, and to present my views on the key problem in obscenity censorship under a constitution that protects freedom of expression.

It is quite apparent that the Roth decision in 1957 and its progeny in 1958-1960 have resulted in a high degree of constitutional protection for literature and other materials of a type frequently censored under obscenity laws in the 1930's and 40's and 50's. Since 1957 state and federal courts have been increasingly reluctant to enforce censorship. Even the prosecuting authorities have recognized that they must have much stronger cases than formerly. Primarily they are now concentrating on hard-core pornography and material bordering on pornography -- pure trash or worse.

The initial explanation for this marked shift narrowing the scope of censorship can be found in portions of the Roth opinion that were overlooked at first by the proponents of censorship. What they noted and hailed was the ruling that obscenity statutes are not unconstitutional, that "obscenity is not within the area of constitutionally protected speech or press" because "obscenity" is "utterly without redeeming social importance." What they overlooked -- at first -- was the more important statement in the majority opinion that "sex and obscenity are not synonymous" and that the "portrayal of sex, e.g., in art, literature and scientific works" is entitled to constitutional protection, so long as it falls short of "obscenity." Indeed, the opinion stressed the importance of sex as a "subject of absorbing interest to mankind through the ages" and one of the "vital problems of human interest and concern." In the Court's view, it was, therefore "vital" that the "standards for judging obscenity safeguard the protection of freedom of speech and press for material which does not treat sex in a manner appealing to the prurient interest."

Just what does this mean? What the Court seems to have said in Roth is that "obscenity" is not entitled to constitutional protection, but treatment of sex in literature and art is entitled to constitutional protection if it is not obscene. In other words, some treatments of sex are constitutionally protected from censorship and others are not, and the court attaches the label "obscene" to material that it finds not entitled to constitutional protection. Then the Court sought in Roth to state a standard for determining what is "obscene" and hence outside the constitutional protection for freedom of expression. Obscene material, the Court said, "is material that deals with sex in a manner appealing to the prurient interest." Material is subject to censorship if "to the average person, applying contemporary community standards, the dominant theme of the material taken as a whole appeals to prurient interest." And in the opinion, the Court equates "average person" with "normal person."

This formula, announced in Roth as the standard for judging obscenity for constitutional purposes, has been repeated over and over again by the lower courts since 1957 -- with precious little effort to probe its true meaning and its ambiguities. It has been affirmatively useful in protecting freedom of expression by giving constitutional status to the average or normal person requirement and to the requirement that material be judged as a whole, not by its isolated parts. It has raised some difficult problems by its ambiguous reference to "contemporary community standards." Professor McClure and I consider these and other collateral problems in our recent article. But the formula provides no real guidance to the solution of the core problem of obscenity -- the determination of what is "obscene" under the constitutional ruling in Roth that portrayal of sex is constitutionally protected except when "obscene."

[Here] I address myself only to that core problem.

II. The Core Problem: What is "obscene"

A. What the Court has said

I suggest, first, that the Court's definition of obscenity as "material that deals with sex in a manner appealing to the prurient interest" gets us nowhere. It simply pushes the core question back one notch and makes us inquire: what is the appeal to the prurient interest that makes sexual matter obscene?

"Appeal to the prurient interest" does not have an established meaning in law. The expression was rare in obscenity law until Roth, and though it has frequently been repeated by the lower courts since Roth, the repetition has not added to its meaning or our understanding of it. Even the word "prurient" is not in common usage, and when used is ordinarily used to describe a type of abnormal person, a meaning inconsistent with the Court's ruling that material is to be judged by its effect upon the normal person.

The Court borrowed the phrase "appeal to the prurient interest" from a tentative draft of the American Law Institute's Model Penal Code, but the Court and the Institute did not agree upon what the phrase meant. The Institute, which most of us know as the ALI, resorted to the phrase in its model obscenity statute in an effort to escape the prevailing unsatisfactory tests for obscenity. It rejected the test of "tendency to arouse lustful thoughts or desires because it is unduly broad for a society that plainly tolerates a great deal of erotic interest in literature, in advertising, and art." And it rejected the test of "tendency to corrupt or deprave" because of the lack of evidence of any connection between obscenity and misconduct. Instead, the ALI used the expression "appeal to the prurient interest" to focus on the nature of the appeal of the material -- "the kind of appetite to which the purveyor is pandering." This, ALI pointed out, is "quite different from an inquiry as to the effect of a book upon the reader's thoughts, desire, or action." And the Institute defined prurient interest as a "shameful or morbid interest in nudity, sex, or excretion" -- as "an exacerbated, morbid, or perverted interest growing out of the conflict between the universal sexual drive of the individual and equally universal social controls of sexual activity."

That ALI standard might be hard to apply; but the Court spared us the necessity of applying it for constitutional law. For while the Court borrowed the ALI expression -- "appeal to the prurient interest" -- it did not accept the limited meaning ALI gave that phrase. For in Roth the Court said that "material which deals with sex in a manner appealing to the prurient interest" is "material having a tendency to excite lustful thoughts" and went on to say "we perceive no significant difference between the meaning of obscenity developed in the case law and the definition of the ALI Model Penal Code." At this point the Court cited the very page where ALI explicitly rejected the prevailing case law tests for obscenity -- including the test of "tendency to excite lustful thoughts" -- and where it differentiated its "prurient interest" test from all the others. And in a separate concurring opinion in Roth, Mr. Justice Harlan pointed out this contradiction between the ALI explanation of its prurient interest test and the use of that expression in the Roth majority opinion. In Roth the Court could not have failed to be fully aware that it was not accepting as a constitutional test for obscenity the ALI approach to obscenity. Instead, when the Court said it saw no "significant difference" between the definitions of obscenity prevailing in the case law and the ALI definition, it must have meant that their differences were without constitutional significance.

So what the Court really said in Roth was that in the constitutional sense "obscenity" is "material that deals with sex in a manner appealing to the prurient interest," but that this includes the prevailing tests in the case law -- the "tendency to arouse lustful thoughts or desires" and the "tendency to corrupt and deprave" as well as the ALI test of "appeal to the prurient interest" in the sense of a "shameful or morbid interest" as spelled out in more detail in the ALI notes. This really means that the nicely turned phrases that the lower courts are now quoting as the verbal formula for testing obscenity for constitutional purposes is not a single formula at all but one that embraces all the current definitions of obscenity, including the ALI definition.

Any one of these verbal formulas may be constitutionally acceptable as a definition of obscenity, provided it meets the other requirements that the material be judged as a whole instead of by its parts, and by its appeal to or effect upon the normal person, instead of the weak and susceptible -- and provided the definiton is only applied to material that the Court considers obscene. For what really counts is not definitions or verbal formulas but the kind of material the Court views as obscene.

Perhaps I should not have taken so long to arrive nowhere, for we end up with the conclusion that as a constitutional test for obscenity "appeal to the prurient interest" really adds nothing by way of guidance to what the Court is willing to classify as "obscene" and hence censorable. Yet because of the repeated reference to this formula, both in judicial decisions and in commentaries, it seemed necessary to point out that it does lead precisely nowhere. So we must look elsewhere for guidance on the core problem -- what is "obscene" in the constitutional sense.

B. What the Court has done

The most dependable guide to the Court's thinking is to be found in what the Court has actually done, not what it has said. Just because the verbal formula gives us little or no guidance does not mean that the Justices are without any personal concept of obscenity. On several occasions since Roth the Justices have ruled, either as a Court or in separate opinions, that certain material is not obscene and hence not censorable, but with no explanation of how they reached that result.

In three per curiam decisions in the term immediately following Roth the Court unanimously reversed without opinion three U. S. Court of Appeals decisions that had upheld censorship of material found "obscene" by the trial court. It did not send the cases back for a new trial or for reconsideration. It flatly "reversed" the judgment, citing Roth for authority, and ended the censorship then and there. The record in these cases, and the issues raised on appeal, make it reasonably clear that the only ground upon which the reversal could have been based was the Court's conclusion that the material censored was not "obscene" under the constitutional requirements. Also, in

1959, Justices Harlan, Frankfurter and Whittaker in a separate concurring opinion gave as one reason for reversing New York's censorship of the motion picture version of Lady Chatterley's Lover their unexplained conclusion that the picture was not "obscene."

These per curiam and unexplained conclusions that the material under attack was not obscene are significant on two scores. First, they support by actual decision the statement in Roth that the constitutional right to free expression protects material attacked as obscene because of its treatment of sex -- so long as the Court finds it is not "obscene" for constitutional purposes. Second, they give us some light on the kind of material that the Court considers not obscene, which is perhaps as important as knowing what the Court considers obscene.

In our recent article Professor McClure and I have described the nature of the material in the three per curiam decisions. It is sufficient for present purposes to note that the material held not obscene -- but without opinion -- included the following:

> (1) The first was a French motion picture, "The Game of Love," which starts with an episode in which a sixteen-year-old boy is shown completely nude on a bathing beach in the presence of a group of younger girls as a result of a boating accident, and proceeds to depict a series of illicit sexual relations, both with an older woman and a girl of his own age. The Court of Appeals, in finding the picture obscene, concluded: "The narrative is graphically pictured with nothing omitted except those sexual consummations which are plainly suggested but meaningfully omitted and thus, by the very fact of omission, emphasized."
>
> (2) The second was a magazine for homosexuals entitled One-The Homosexual Magazine, which was definitely not a scientific or critical magazine, but appears to have been written to appeal to the tastes and interests of homosexuals.
>
> (3) The third was Sunshine and Health, a nudist magazine that the lower court had found obscene

> because of photographs showing quite distinctly male and female genital organs and public areas.

In each of these cases the lower court found the material obscene and the Supreme Court reversed on the authority of Roth, thus terminating the censorship proceedings apparently on the ground that these materials were not "obscene" within the constitutional requirements for censorship.

Similarly in 1959 when the Court reversed New York's censorship of the motion picture Lady Chatterley's Lover on the ground that New York could not make in unlawful to portray acts of sexual immorality as "desirable, acceptable or proper patterns of behavior," Justices Harlan, Frankfurter and Whittaker wrote a separate concurring opinion in which they concluded that the New York decision was based also upon "actual scenes of a suggestive and obscene nature." Included were scenes which showed the gamekeeper-lover help Lady Chatterley unbutton her blouse and unzip her dress, reach with his hand under her dress to note that she had come to him with no undergarments and caress her buttocks, and which showed them lying in bed in an apparent state of undress before and after consummation of their love. The three Justices concluded that the motion picture was not obscene and hence not censorable, but did not explain their conclusion, or make any attempt to spell out their concept of obscenity.

I am not sure what kind of conclusions we can draw from these unexplained decisions except that the Supreme Court's concepts of obscenity is a very narrow one. Is it significant that the two motion pictures stop short of depicting sexual intercourse itself? Is it significant that the Lady Chatterley motion picture had something important to say about the social order? Is it significant that the publishers of the nudist magazine and the homosexual magazine both purported to be seeking to create an understanding of a way of life, unorthodox though it be? These questions I leave for you to ponder as we move on to consider another basis for understanding what the Court's concept of obscenity may be.

Before doing so, I would like to say that I think the Court was wise in not seeking to explain its decisions in these early cases. The Court has just now moved into an area in which no court yet has satisfactorily explained the basis for its obscenity decisions. It is charting a new course in a very difficult and treacherous area. It is more likely to chart a true course that will avoid dangerous shoals in the future if it gains substantial experience in dealing with difficult cases before it makes an effort to verbalize its standards for determining what is obscene. In time it must do so in order to provide adequate guidance to lower courts -- and to publishers -- but presently I think it has been wise to limit its explanations to problems on the periphery and simply to decide without explanation when it has faced the core problem of what is obscene.

But while the Court is wisely and discreetly silent, commentators need be neither discreet nor wise, and perhaps plunging in where the Court sensibly holds back may provide some aid to the Court and to others dealing with these problems.

C. What the Court probably conceives of as obscene

We have noted a few judicial applications of whatever may be the Justices' concept of obscenity. But these applications only tell us what in the Justices' view obscenity is *not*; they do not tell us what they think obscenity *is*. Do we have any basis for judgment as to what the Justices consider obscene in the constitutional sense? I think we do. I believe the underlying concept of obscenity held by the members of the Court is "hard-core pornography," though I doubt that even the Justices know whether they will stop there.

On what do I base that belief? First, on the type of thing the Court has held *not* to be obscene -- which we have already noted indicates a very narrow scope for obscenity, far narrower than most courts have viewed obscenity in the past. Second, there is good reason to believe that when the Court in *Roth* held "obscenity" wholly outside the area of constitutionally protected speech and press, so as not to require appraisal under the usual clear and present danger test, the Justices had "hard-core pornography" uppermost in their minds. Let me explain the reason for this belief.

In *Roth* the question was not whether any particular material could be censored or was obscene. As presented to the Court, the sole question was whether the federal and state obscenity statutes were constitutional in the abstract, independent of any particular application. In this posture the United States Solicitor General contended that the federal statute was essential to prevent the country from being flooded with hard-core pornography, which constituted ninety per cent of the material caught by the statute. He urged that the validity of the statute must be judged "by this mass of 'hard-core' pornography, which...is its main objective and its major catch." He described hard-core pornography as erotic objects, photographs, books, and movies, all depicting men and women in "every conceivable kind of normal and abnormal sexual relations" and "excesses." He pointed out that such material is produced solely for and solely produces erotic effect, that the only "idea in hard-core pornography is that there is pleasure in sexual gratification, whatever the means," and explicitly noted that "the social value of such notions is, of course nil." Then, apparently to make sure that the Court understood the nature of hard-core pornography, the Solicitor-General sent to the Court a carton containing numerous samples of hard-core pornography and in an accompanying letter pointed out their "extremely repulsive nature," again reminding the Court that at least ninety per cent of the convictions under the federal statute were for this kind of material.

In voting to hold obscenity statutes constitutional, the Justices could not fail to have had material of this kind in mind, for hard-core pornography, particularly in pictorial form, is so blantantly shocking and revolting that it would have been impossible for the Justices to put it out of mind. To give free circulation to such repulsive and totally worthless material in the name of constitutional freedom of expression was unthinkable. In this setting -- none of which is apparent in the opinion itself -- the Court's rejection of obscenity as "utterly without redeeming social importance" takes on new and significant meaning. And in this setting it seems probable that the Court's concept of "obscenity" as material "utterly without redeeming social importance" centered on hard-core pornography. But due to the abstract nature of the issue in Roth the Court had no reason to consider the underlying nature of pornography, or to consider whether some types of material may constitutionally be held "obscene" though not pornographic.

III. A Commentator's Analysis of the Core Problem: What is Obscene?

Considering the true nature of pornography, it is my view that the only material that should be considered constitutionally "obscene," and hence free from the usual constitutional protection for freedom of expression, is material treated as hard-core pornography by the manner in which and the primary audience to which it is sold. Censorship of material outside that category would have to be judged by the same standards that apply to other interferences with free expression, including the requirement that there be a clear and present danger of harmful consequences that the state has the right to prevent.

To explain this position, I will try briefly to make clear to you the true nature of pornography as I understand it, the purpose of limiting this to "hard-core," and what I mean by material "treated as hard-core pornography."

1. The nature of hard-core pornography

The term "hard-core pornography" is used freely by many with no attempt to explain what it means, apparently on the assumption that everyone knows just what "hard-core pornography" is. Certainly, much hard-core pornography can be recognized for what it is without a sophisticated understanding of its true nature. But an understanding of the true nature of pornography is, I believe, essential to a reasoned effort to determine what is "obscene" in the constitutional sense.

Dr. Margaret Mead, the noted anthropologist, gives us one of the best explanations of pornography. She says that pornography is "calcualted to stimulate sex feelings independent of the presence of another loved and chosen human being." Its "essential element" is "the daydream as distinct from reality." According to Dr. Mead:

> The material of true pornography is compounded of daydreams themselves, composed without regard for any given reader or looker, to stimulate and titillate. It bears the signature of nonparticipation -- of the dreaming adolescent, the frightened, the impotent, the bored and sated, the sen-

> ile, desperately concentrating on unusualness, on drawing that which is not usually drawn, writing words on a plaster wall, shifting scenes and actors about, to evoke and feed an impulse that has no object: no object either because the adolescent is not yet old enough to seek sexual partners or because the recipient of pornography has lost the precious power of spontaneous sexual feeling.

Margaret Mead's conception of pornography as daydream material calculated to feed the auto-erotic desires of the immature and perverted and senile is supported by the Kronhausen's detailed analysis of pornographic books. They found in pornographic books the same sexual fantasy that Dr. Mead emphasized. Pornographic books are made up of a succession of increasingly erotic scenes without distracting non-erotic passages. The purpose is to stimulate erotic response, never to describe or deal with the basic realities of life.

Many other scholars have noted in pornography its essential daydream quality, designed to feed the erotic fantasies of the sexually immature. D. W. Abse says that pornography "simply encourages people to luxuriate in morbid, regressive, sexual-sadistic phantasy." W. G. Eliasberg speaks of the appeal of pornography to "immature sexuality" which is "the non-genital, not individualized, not-loving, amorphous interest in sex." London and Caprio note that those who are morbidly interested in or collect pornography "have a libido that is fixated at the paraphiliac level" meaning "psychic auto-eroticism." Benjamin Karpman calls indulgence in pornography a form of psychic masturbation.

In their extensive study on pornography and the law, the Kronhausens describe the various types of erotic scenes characteristic of pornography. These are commonly scenes of willing, even anxious seduction, of sadistic defloration in mass orgies, of incestuous relations consummated with little or no sense of guilt, of super-permissive parent figures who initiate and participate in the sexual activities of their children, of super-sexed males and females, or Negroes and Asiatics as sex symbols, of male and particularly female homosexuality, and of flagellation, all described in taboo words. I have given you only the briefest summary; the Kronhausens develop these characteristic types of pornography in much greater detail. While no list of typical pornography could ever be complete, the Kronhausen study provides a guide that helps to give concreteness to the theoretical analysis of pornography as daydream material nourishing erotic fantasies.

One characteristic of pornography is that it appeals only to the sexually abnormal or immature person, because it feeds his craving for erotic stimulation and fantasy. To the normal, sexually mature person pornography is repulsive, not attractive. The normal person may look at it once out of curiosity, but its effect on him is not erotic stimulation; instead he is repelled by it.

So analyzed, pornography as a concept assumes manageable form: Pornography is daydream material, divorced from reality, whose main function is to nourish erotic fantasies of the sexually immature, or as the psychiatrists say, to nourish auto-eroticism. This concept of pornography provides a reasonably satisfactory and workable tool for distinguishing pornographic material from the non-pornographic.

But in order to make pornography a usable tool for testing obscenity we must exclude a type of widely accepted non-literary material that might be thought to nourish erotic fantasies of a sort. I have in mind the type of material illustrated by the pin-up girl, scantily clad but sculpturally perfect, who may appeal to the artistic in some of us but may also provide a dream world of sorts for others, with possibly some minor element of erotic stimulation. Such pictures are accepted fare in our society, never attacked as obscene or pornographic. To except such material, we must add the qualification "black market" or "hard-core" to "pornographic" in order to indicate that to be "obscene" in the constitutional sense, non-literary material must not only nourish erotic fantasies but be grossly shocking as well. So limited, hard-core pornography becomes a useful tool for drawing the line between the constitutionally obscene and non-obscene.

But note I said a "tool," not a test of the litmus paper variety, for hard-core pornography as I have described it necessarily leaves much room for judgment in making the application -- judgment that must be influenced by considerations relating to social value, or lack of social value, of the materials in question, and the importance to society of free expression. For, after all, we must not forget that the most basic freedom in a democracy is at stake in these adjudications, and the reason for ruling that the right to freedom of expression does not protect "obscenity" from censorship is that obscenity is "utterly without social importance." Necessarily, then, the social value of the material in question will influence a close judgment on whether it is obscene.

2. Material treated as hard-core pornography

You will recall that just before describing hard-core pornography I stated that in my judgment the "obscenity" that is free from constitutional protection should be limited to material treated as hard-core pornography. Why did I put it that way, rather than to say simply that obscenity should be limited to hard-core pornography?

Because in my judgment censorship should not depend upon the intrinsic nature of the material independent of its audience and method of marketing. Instead, it should depend upon the manner in which it is marketed and the primary audience to which it is sold. In this way constitutional protection can be given to the occasional legitimate distribution of hard-core pornography for scientific purposes, while at the same time censorship of material that is not intrinsically hard-core pornography can be permitted when the manner of marketing and the primary audience to which it is marketed indicate that it is being treated as hard-core pornography -- that its function in that setting is to nourish erotic fantasies of the sexually immature. For these reasons I believe that obscenity should be a variable concept, depending upon the manner of marketing -- the appeal in the marketing -- and the nature of the primary audience to which the appeal is made.

Let me illustrate. In rare instances hard-core pornography is sold to social scientists or psychiatrists engaged in the study of pornography and its addicts. For example, the Kinsey Institute imported some hard-core pornography for scientific study and a federal district court ruled it was not obscene when marketed in this manner to this class of purchaser. In the *Kinsey* case, hard-core pornography was not treated as pornography -- it was neither marketed nor bought for its appeal to erotic fantasies. In a constitutional sense, it was not "obscene" when sold to the Institute for scientific study because, as the District Court ruled, it did not "appeal to the prurient interest" of the special audience to which it was marketed.

To the other extreme, I would not be surprised to see a case arise in which a news stand near a high school purchases a huge supply of the unexpurgated edition of Lady Chatterley's Lover, and through posters and otherwise makes a special sales pitch to high school students, not emphasizing the novel's high literary quality and its social message but its sexual passages. I am confident that Lawrence's great novel is not obscene when marketed in the normal way to the public at large; this was the unanimous conclusion of the U. S. Court of Appeals, Second Circuit, and the Department of Justice apparently agreed, for it did not appeal. But if Lady Chatterley's Lover is treated as pornography by the manner of marketing and response of the primary audience of sexually immature youngsters to whom it is sold, then as to that seller and that primary audience of buyers the material is hard-core pornography and should be classified as "obscene." Constitutional freedom of expression requires that Lawrence's novel be free from censorship when sold to a primary audience made up of the public at large, consisting largely of mature, adult buyers. But when it is marketed in such a manner as to appeal to a primary audience of sexually immature kids to nourish their craving for erotic fantasy, then the reason for constitutional protection is not present and there is reason for censorship.

In my opinion this approach -- making the finding of "obscenity" depend upon whether the material in question is treated as hard-core pornography by its primary audience, rather than using a constant standard of obscenity without regard to its audience -- serves a triply useful purpose. It permits material needed for scientific purposes to be freely distributed to scientific audiences, regardless of its intrinsic pornographic nature. It takes a narrow view of what is obscene when distribution is to a primary audience of sexually mature adults, thereby protecting the basic freedom both of the artist and the audience. But it gives much wider protection against "obscenity" when the primary audience is made up of the sexually immature, whether adolescents or abnormal adults, and permits control over material marketed to such audiences to nourish their craving for erotic fantasies. In my judgment, this approach would permit control over most, if not all, of the material that could reasonably be thought harmful to youth when marketed to such an audience.

It is, of course, true that when the primary audience is made up of mature adults, an occasional purchase may be made by an adolescent or by a sexually immature adult, who will find nourishment for erotic fantasies in material that is not hard-core pornography nor treated as such by its primary audience -- Lady Chatterley's Lover, for example. But this is one of the prices we must pay in order to avoid limiting adult reading fare to that fit for children. The Supreme Court so ruled in the Butler case in 1957 shortly before the Roth decision when the Court ruled that obscenity must be tested by the average or normal adult, not the susceptible or immature.

This variable obscenity approach requires that in each instance the finding of obscenity be based upon the nature of the primary audience to which the sales appeal is made and the nature of the material's appeal to that audience. In each instance the question should be: With respect to this primary audience is the material treated as hard-core pornography -- to satisfy or nourish erotic fantasies of the sexually immature? This requires that any peripheral audience be disregarded. The Supreme Court has already ruled that this is so when the primary audience is made up of mature adults: the fact that a few children may gain access to the material through this channel cannot justify banning its sale, at least to adults. Similarly, when a hole in the wall specializing in erotica, with a specialized primary audience of the sexually immature, stocks Lady Chatterley's Lover, it is a reasonable conclusion that the novel is offered and sold to such an audience, not for its literary and social values, but as a stimulant to their erotic fantasies. When sold to such a primary audience, Lady Chatterley would be treated as pornography and could reasonably be held obscene, even though an occasional normal, mature adult in the peripheral audience might accidentally see the novel in the window and buy it for its true values.

As I suggested earlier, one advantage of this approach is to permit the judgment on obscenity to be made on the basis of the appeal to the young, the susceptible or the sexually immature when they constitute the primary audience. One of the criticisms aimed at the Supreme Court's handling of this problem thus far is that in Butler and in Roth it seems to say that material must be judged by its appeal to the normal adult, and harmful impact upon the immature cannot be considered. I have adequately indicated my opinion that this position by the Court is sound when applied to sales to a primary audience of sexually mature adults. But when the primary audience is made up of the sexually immature, there is no reason to give constitutional protection to material treated by that audience as hard-core pornography, even though it would not be obscene when offered to an audience of mature adults. To the immature audience, resorting to the material for satisfaction of their hunger for erotic fantasy, the material is treated as pornography and should be subject to the same controls.

Those who have read the Roth opinions might well object to my suggestion that "obscenity" and hence censorship should depend upon the appeal to the sexually immature when they constitute the primary audience. You may ask, "Didn't the Court say in Roth that it was rejecting a test of obscenity based upon the young and susceptible and that obscenity must be judged on the basis of its appeal to the average or normal man?" It is true; the Court did say that. But to this question I have two answers.

First, a test based upon the prurient appeal to the normal sexually mature adult would, if applied rigidly, exclude all control over hard-core pornography. For hard-core pornography has no appeal to the normal, sexually mature adult. As I have indicated, it is repulsive and revolting to him. Hard-core pornography has its appeal only to the sexually immature -- the sexually abnormal adult and some youngsters who have not reached sexual maturity. If, to be obscene, material must appeal to the prurient interest -- whatever that means -- of the normal, sexually mature adult, then hard-core pornography would never be obscene, although it is the one class of material that most certainly is obscene and is not entitled to constitutional protection. Obviously, something is wrong with such a test.

Second, when the Court rejected the test of the effect upon children in Butler it was dealing with the case of a sale to an adult and there was no suggestion that the seller was appealing to a primary audience of adolescents. And when the Court stated in Roth that material must be judged on the basis of its appeal to normal adults, it was rejecting the old Hicklin doctrine that had come to stand for the proposition that sales to all audiences must be judged by the possible harmful impact on the young and susceptible.

In my judgment the Court's formula in Roth used the positive as a means of stating the negative. In this light, the statement that material is to be judged by its effects on or appeal to the average or normal person is simply a way of stating that material disseminated to the public generally must not be judged by its effects on or appeal to the weak or susceptible, for as Mr. Justice Frankfurter said in the Butler case that would be to "burn the house to roast the pig." That reasoning is sound applied to the general situation before the Court in the two cases, but it has no application to the situation in which a seller is directing his sales pitch at a susceptible audience of the sexually immature. In such a case, I think the Constitution and the Supreme Court will permit controls reasonably designed to protect that susceptible audience so long as the constitutional right to sell to a primary audience of sexually mature is not infringed.

And this interpretation makes sense in dealing with hard-core pornography, which is the principal if not the sole occupant of the category "obscene." For it permits control over hard-core pornography, or anything treated as such, without the fiction of pretending that such stuff appeals to the prurient interest of the normal adult in order to make it fit the verbal formula announced in Roth.

I wish to suggest two possible exceptions to my proposal that obscenity censorship should be limited to material treated as hard-core pornography by the manner in which and the primary audience to which it is sold.

The first is not really an exception, but needs explanation to avoid misunderstanding. I would not give constitutional protection to the sale of intrinsically hard-core pornography to a buyer who is apparently a sexually mature adult, absent some showing that he was buying it for scientific study. This is not really an exception to my proposed test, for since hard-core pornography has no appeal to the sexually mature adult, it is never marketed to a primary audience of normal, sexually mature adults, apart from the small special audience of scientific students exemplified by the Kinsey Institute case. Hard-core pornography is under-the-counter stuff, sold clandestinely, usually in out-of-the-way shops that cater to those whose interests are erotic. Therefore, while a normal adult might pick up such material once out of curiosity, he would belong to a small peripheral audience that would not give immunity to the dealer whose primary audience is made up of the sexually immature.

The second is a true exception that might arise in the case of a statute that explicitly forbids the sale of matter that is obscene to adolescents. A problem would arise under that statute if a book dealer catering to a primary audience of normal, sexually mature adults sold a youngster a book that was not "obscene" for adults but whose only appeal to youngsters was an appeal to erotic fantasy. Lady Chatterley's Lover is probably, again, a good illustration. Conceivably the Court might hold that despite the primary audience of adults, a different standard must be applied in the case of a sale to a child. But there are serious questions of practicality here, for the difficulty of guarding against sales to children might well result in the bookseller reducing his entire inventory of books offered to his primary audience in order to avoid any difficulty over sales to children. In that case, the evil the Court sought to avoid in the Butler case would be upon us again in a different form. The ultimate validity of such an "adults only" requirement for part of the stock of a bookseller catering primarily to an adult audience may well depend upon pragmatic experience with efforts to comply with such statutes designed to protect children but to leave adults free to buy sophisticated books.

Though I have already exhausted my audience, I have not exhausted the probelms and questions that could be raised concerning the proposal that obscenity in the constitutional sense be limited to material treated as hard-core pornography by its primary audience. For further discussion of such matters, such as the feasibility of this proposal from the standpoint of enforcement officials, I must refer you to the recent Lockhart-McClure article.

At this point I can only take time to add one final argument in support of my proposal. Some may say that my proposal limiting the constitutionally "obscene" to material treated as hard-core pornography will not adequately protect youth. They may believe that certain materials are harmful in their effect upon children, even though they are not treated as hard-core pornography -- that is, are not used to nourish erotic fantasies. My answer is that such non-pornographic materials are subject to the same constitutional protection for freedom of expression accorded all other communications. That freedom of expression is not absolute. Distribution of "non-obscene" -- non-pornographic -- material thought harmful to youngsters can still be prohibited if the Court is satisfied that there is a "clear and present danger" of a harm the government has the right to prevent. I will not try to expand on "clear and present danger" except to refer you to the 1954 Lockhart-McClure article, and to add that under this approach the Court would weigh the social value of the material under attack, and the importance of free expression with respect to such material, against the seriousness of the harm sought to be prevented and the probability that reading or viewing the material in question will cause such harm.

But my concern [here] is not with such issues. My discussion ... is limited to consideration of where the line should be drawn on material that the Court says is not even subject to the freedom of expression protections -- as to which we do not even get to the "clear and present danger" issues because the material is labeled "obscene." And my proposition is that that line should be drawn at material <u>treated</u> as hard-core pornography by the <u>primary audience</u> to which it is directed.

IV. <u>Conclusion</u>

In conclusion, let me say just a word about the Supreme Court's function in the developing constitutional law relating to censorship of obscenity. You may gather from my discussion of the core problem, "What is obscene," that the Court has provided very little guidance, and that the guidance it has provided needs much refinement. I suppose the Justices themselves would be the first to admit this. But remember the point I made earlier. The Court will do a better job long-range, if it feels its way now in this brand new field of constitutional adjudication, decides only what it has to decide, and says very little while it gets the feel of the problem. Remember that people like McClure and me have spent a large share of time for several years, off and on, studying this problem, whereas the Justices can devote very little time, actually, to resolving each case.

But while the Court has not provided much direction -- yet -- on the core problem of obscenity, it has made a great deal of progress and some very significant law on the collateral problems involved in the administration of obscenity laws. It has established the constitutional requirement that material must be judged by the dominant theme of the material as a whole, not by its isolated parts. It has established the requirement that a bookseller must be chargeable with knowledge of the alleged obscenity in order to be convicted criminally. It has made it clear that the constitutional guarantee protects the right to advocate unconventional ideas and behavior "immoral" by current standards, and do so in effective and dramatic ways, so long as the manner of conveying the idea is not "obscene." And it is becoming increasingly apparent that the Court will not permit a finding of "obscenity" by an administrator or lower court to conclude the matter; independent judicial review of the finding of obscenity seems assured, with review of enough cases in the Supreme Court to keep the other appellate courts in line.

These collateral protections still require refinement, but that will come as appropriate cases arise to permit these refinements to be hammered out in concrete settings. So long as we have independent judicial review, I am satisfied that in the long run freedom of expression will be adequately protected. The Court will occasionally make mistakes -- as I think it did when late in January it upheld five to four the power to require a censor's approval of motion pictures in advance of showing, despite the powerful dissenting opinion by Chief Justice Warren showing the serious abuses of such power, to which commercial interests will often bow as a practical matter rather than challenge the particular abuse as they could do successfully if they appealed to the Courts. But the problem of prior restraint is outside the scope of this discussion. I would only add that independent judicial review of particular exercises of the censor's power in the last year or two has reduced substantially the extent of movie censorship. The impact of the decisions to date has been felt in all forms of communication, where there is much greater freedom of expression than before 1957. I, for one, am satisfied that under the direction of the Supreme Court our state and federal courts will protect frcedom of expression and at the same time permit society to protect the immature against the evils of pornography.

The assumptions underlying obscenity law have rarely been acutely examined. In the following article, two psychologists and a legal scholar examine some of these assumptions in the light of available evidence of effects of obscene material. (The question has been examined by Drs. Phyllis and Eberhard Kronhausen, in Pornography and the Law, New York: Ballantine Books, 1960).

Robert B. Cairns is Assistant Professor, Department of Psychology, Indiana University. James C. N. Paul is Professor of Law, University of Pennsylvania and Director, Institute of Legal Research, Law School, University of Pennsylvania. Julius Wishner is Professor, Department of Psychology, and Professor of Psychology and Law, University of Pennsylvania Law School.

This article is reprinted from 46 Minnesota Law Review, 1009-1041 (1962), with the kind permission of the Minnesota Law Review, to whom grateful acknowledgment is made for permission to report here.

This study was supported by the Institute of Legal Research, University of Pennsylvania Law School. It grew from two other projects: (1) an Institute study by Professor Murray L. Schwartz and Professor James C. N. Paul on Post Office censorship and problems of obscenity control, recently published under the title Federal Censorship: Obscenity in the Mail; and (2) the University of Pennsylvania Law School's program in Law and the Behavioral Sciences. Professor Wishner, for the past several years, has collaborated in several Law School courses on various aspects of law and the social sciences. This particular work grew out of his participation with Professor Paul on a seminar in the field of law and mass communications. Professor Cairns (then at Pennsylvania) was invited to make the initial canvass of relevant literature, which he did during the summer of 1961. Needless to say, all of the authors share joint responsibility for our final digest of the material reported here.

The authors would like to express their thanks to Dr. Wardell B. Pomeroy, Director of Field Research, Institute for Sex Research, Indiana University, and to the Institute's Trustees for permission to use materials in the Institute's library. Professor Paul owes a continuing, happy debt to Professor Murray L. Schwartz for all his past collaboration in developing ideas which are reflected in this paper.

Robert B. Cairns
James C. N. Paul
Julius Wishner

Sex Censorship: The Assumptions of Anti-Obscenity Laws and the Empirical Evidence

by Robert B. Cairns, James C. N. Paul, and Julius Wishner

While concepts of "obscenity" may be very old, albeit ambiguous, most English and American laws on the subject are comparatively recent: they are of Nineteenth Century origin, and they appear to be a by-product of the development of mass literacy and mass communication.... men have come to fear the consequences of permitting any man to read, see and even think about sexual activity, sexual feelings and, sometimes, the nudity of others. The law of obscenity has been fashioned to control mass communication which may produce that result. New laws and new techniques to suppress have been devised to keep pace with new techniques of creation and distribution.

The precise function of these laws has never been too clear. Their value has long been questioned by people who are concerned with their inhibiting effect on thought and expression in a free society. In the last decade courts have struggled, with increasing difficulty, to rationalize their constitutionality. Unquestionably the courts have given men more freedom today than they enjoyed even ten years ago, and perhaps most Americans believe the Constitution should require that tolerance; but the belief that law should still outlaw some depictions of nudity or sexual experience will not down. Quite the contrary, precisely because the law now is more tolerant and uncertain, some writers, publishers, movie producers and others appear to seize the occasion to augment, by design, the "sex" put in works for popular consumption. Because this material seems now to have widespread appeal and circulation, an articulate segment of the public has been stridently demanding stricter law, even as another segment asserts a right to be rid of all restrictions. The disagreements, fears and recriminations generated by this state of affairs may reflect the need for a continuing hard look at the rationale of sex censorship.

Why do we have it? What are the assumptions underlying it?

I.

Some may justify anti-obscenity laws simply on the ground that immodesty of expression in books or pictures is morally wrong no matter what effect the material may have on behavior or personality; thus (the argument may run), when expression becomes patently immoral, according to the tenets of an overwhelming majority, the wrongness of the act of producing or contemplating it becomes so serious that the state is justified in acting to suppress the work and punish those who utter it. Others might argue that obscenity, as legally defined, is so devoid of idea content or other utility as to be worthless to our culture; it is not the kind of communciation protected by the first amendment. Therefore its prohibition should pose no first amendment problems; government, in punishing obscenity, is not restricting "speech."

These arguments have been asserted by the courts, but they hardly seem persuasive, at least in the absence of other justification, to support laws authorizing suppression of communication. With all due deference, there are surely some obscene creations which do have to some members of society idea content or some sort of cultural interest or value as expression. This, it would seem, is clearly demonstrated by the history of anti-obscenity enforcement. Further, the current legal definition of obscenity hardly excludes material which may have some intellectual significance. The free speech issue cannot be dissipated just by insisting that speech -- the communication of thought, feelings, and experience -- is never suppressed by obscenity law enforcement.

Nor is it enough to damn obscenity as immoral. Bad it may be, but badness in the abstract is not the test of speech we may suppress. Whatever the view of earlier times, our government today is not -- cannot be -- concerned <u>simply</u> with enforcing widely held religious precepts which inveigh against portrayal or contemplation in communication of sex stimuli on the ground that, purely as an intellectual abstraction, such stimuli are evil. The consequences of obscenity exposure must entail something more than mere elicitation of a thought which one is not supposed to think.

Those who debate the need for legal controls usually have tacitly accepted the proposition that we must be concerned with the effects of the communication we would outlaw. The issue is commonly framed in terms of whether exposure, or repeated exposure, to obscenity (at least obscenity in some kinds of media, such as movies) causes overt misconduct (at least among some kinds of people) or some other discernible behavior which the state may properly prevent because it is harmful to others, or to vital community interests. While there seems to be much discussion of these questions, there has been surprisingly little effort to synthesize relevant empirical research which may help us to discover the answers.

Our purpose here is to attempt a summary of the <u>empirically demonstrated</u> effects of psychosexual stimuli, to speculate whether this evidence supports any possible justification, and to suggest some areas for further research.

We deal only with sex stimuli -- the portrayal of nudity or sexual activity -- and not with other, possibly analogous and allegedly dangerous communication such as the depiction of physical violence or cruelty. Of course, much material of concern today combines both sex and violence in liberal terms, but the research we have surveyed seems to have focused on material which is mostly just erotic, if it is anything. Nor is it necessary to wrestle with the meaning or lack of meaning in the legal definition of obscenity. A <u>sine qua non</u>, as we have said, is a sex stimulus; the question we ask is whether there is any empirical evidence to support any assumption about the effects of any form of communication of that character, be it legally obscene or not.

Let it be re-emphasized, too, that our self-assigned task here is limited to reviewing findings developed through empirical investigation. We do not consider, let alone catalogue, all the opinions, assumptions, or naked assertions of fact about the effect -- or lack of effect -- of obscene communication. Of course, we do not mean to deprecate the importance of getting the responsible opinions of responsible people. The law in this field, as in many others, is probably going to operate on intuition if it cannot operate on science. Expert conjecture is perhaps the only present way we can secure answers to the critical questions we must ask when we seek justifications for the sex censorship laws which society seems to demand and which the courts, thus far, constitutionally condone. So the opinions of psychiatrists, law enforcement officers and other people who have had contact with some consumers of obscenity may well be a controlling consideration. But there is no substitute for reliable, factual information; the opinions of experts should at least be consistent with what scientific knowledge we have; and understanding the scientific evidence should be a matter of concern to those who would preach on what the law ought to say about sex expression.

II.

We turn then to a survey of the reported behavioral science investigations which seem immediately relevant. To the interested layman and the serious investigator alike, this material is frustrating; the big questions remain unanswered. Indeed, the data stop short just at the point where they suggest new and interesting hypotheses or problems for more research. But a survey of these materials -- an attempt to understand the findings we have -- may show how complex is our subject, and it may supply a lesson in humility to those who are opinionated and to those who demand opinions from others.[1]

Early in the present work it became evident that the effects of sexual stimuli have rarely been studied in adequately controlled experimental investigations. Materials are not totally lacking, however. In the study of other substantive psychological issues (e. g., somatic response patterns, effects of guilt, conflict measured physiologically and cognitive effects of sexual identity), various types of sexual stimuli, usually photographs of nude females have been assessed. In this review we cover a potpourri of sociological, physiological, and psychological research; the common element, for us is the empirical data each yields on the effects of sexual stimuli.

Subjective reports of sexual arousal: Perhpas the simplest method to ascertain the effects of sexual material is to ask people who have observed it to give an introspective account of their immediate, resultant feelings. The techniques of self-report may range from the use of a brief questionnaire to lengthy, intensive interviews. Some limitations of this technique are well known. Distorted results may be caused by conscious dissimulation, or because the technique presumes a self-knowledge on the part of the interviewee that is seldom justified, or because one cannot be confident that the subjective evaluations of interviewees can be equated one with another. Other limitations include interviewer bias, selective forgetting by the interviewee, and unwillingness to cooperate or over-willingness to comply. The last may result in invention, sometimes unconscious, in an attempt to maintain the interest of the interviewer. Some researchers, notably Kinsey and his associates, recognize and attempt to compensate for these limitations. Others, unfortunately, have not.

The early interview studies, though sometimes cited in communications research, tend to be unsophisticated with respect to such issues. Moreover, a variety of moral predilections frequently permeated the research design. Among the results reported in the pioneer work of Blumer and Hauser, in 1933, are the following: "Of a sample of 110 inmates of a penal institution 12 per cent stated that the movies stirred them sexually; 19 per cent indicated that an exciting picture makes them want to make love to a girl; while 35 per cent indicated that the movies have taught them how to attract girls, how to flirt, kiss or make love.... Of a sample of 252 delinquent girls in a state training school, 121, or 48 per cent acknowledge that they usually 'felt like having a man make love to them' after they had seen a passionate love picture...." Twenty-five per cent of females in this sample were siad to have "acknowledged engaging in sexual relations after becoming sexually aroused at a movie."[2]

What can be made of these conclusions? A formidable catalogue of the methodological shortcomings underlying them can be found in Adler's Art and Prudence. The investigators, in the very design of many questions (such as: "how important do you think movies were in getting you into trouble?"), seemed to be inviting negative evaluations of the efforts of motion pictures, and they appeared to attach highly pejorative connotations to being "stirred sexually." No attempt was made to discover whether noninstitutionalized, normal males had similar reactions which might destroy any implication of a causal connection between being stirred sexually and crime or criminals. Cumulatively these criticisms weaken confidence in the authors' data; we cannot rely on them alone.

A similar study by Haines, in 1955, raised similar problems. One hundred inmates of the Cook County (Illinois) prison between the ages of 16 and 21 were interviewed to determine the role that "pornography" plays in the delinquency of juveniles. According to Haines, "each inmate interviewed was told that Senator Kefauver was interested in the effects of television, movies and radio on teenagers, and would like to know his reaction as to the role these mediums played in his committing an offense, or offenses, which resulted in his incarceration." The prisoners all agreed to cooperate, and they were interviewed in private, "out of the hearing of ther inmates." Concerning the type and extent of query, Haines indicates only that "questions were asked regarding television, radio, movies, pornography, and sex." Ninety-four per cent of Haines' sample reported that they had seen "eight pagers" or "sixteen pagers" which depicted sexual acts. Of this group, 14 per cent indicated that they were habitually sexually excited by these materials. (This figure seems rather small compared to results of other investigators.) Haines reports: "Some stated that, after looking at the booklets, they sought sexual relief on the streets, through their girl friends, or through self-abuse." But interestingly, none of the subjects who had been charged with criminal sexual behavior reported that his crime was linked to the viewing of these materials. Nevertheless, Haines concluded that "television, pornography, and movies play a distinct role in the creation of antisocial behavior in susceptible teenagers."[3]

As in the case of Blumer and Hauser's study, the experimental controls were absent. No attempt was made to obtain responses from a matched non-criminal group; whatever safeguards, if any, taken to minimize the operations of experimentar bias are not reported; the statistical analysis is totally inadequate. Furthermore, the explanations given to the subjects about the study (e.g., "Senator Kefauver was interested") might well inspire a distorted subjective report. Again, we must look for more persuasive evidence before we can begin to generalize from these findings.

In view of the public's special interest in the effects of sexual stimuli in mass communication on children and adolescents, studies of these groups were particularly sought for this paper. Unfortunately, only one additional study of relevance to our topic seems worthy of consideration. Ramsey, in 1943, interviewed 280 boys in early (ages 11-14) and late (ages 15-18) adolescence, and administered questionnaires to obtain information about their sexual development.[4] Among other things, Ramsey asked his subjects to rank order 15 "erotic stimuli" in terms of the extent to which each leads to sexual arousal. The results indicate that the younger group considered the following three experiences to have the strongest potential for sexual arousal: "sex conversation," "female nudity," and "obscene pictures" (the type is not given). For the older adolescents, the ordering was: "female nudity," "daydreaming," and "obscene pictures." Least likely to lead to sexual arousal were male nudity, dancing and music for the younger boys; and literature, male nudity and music for the older adolescents. These data suggest that adolescent males often require overt sexual stimuli for sexual arousal to occur. Age changes, at least within the restricted range that Ramsey studied, seem for the most part unimportant. The only age-trend which may be significant is that internal cognitive cues ("daydreaming") play an increasingly important role in the sexual arousal of males.

Without doubt, the most comprehensive and meaningful studies on the subjective effects of sexual stimuli were those undertaken by Kinsey and his associates.

Included in their interview schedule was a set of questions (the exact form was not specified) which dealt with the association between various classes of psychosexual cues and reports of sexual arousal. Reproduced in Table I is a summary of the reported effects of the following stimuli: portrayals of nude figures, genitalia of the opposite sex, commercial motion pictures, burlesque and floor shows, portrayals of sexual action, romantic literary materials, and erotic stories.

Certain trends reported here seem noteworthy. In the first place, a sizeable proportion of the sample, both

Table I

		Sexual Response			
		Definite frequent	Sometimes	Never	N
Portrayals of nudes	male	18%	36%	46%	4191
	female	3%	9%	88%	5698
Observing genitalia	male*	"many"	"many"	"few"	
	female	21%	27%	52%	617
Commercial films	male	6%	30%	64%	3231
	female	9%	39%	52%	5411
Burlesques and floor shows	male	28%	34%	38%	3377
	female	4%	10%	86%	2550
Observing sex acts	male	42%	35%	23%	3868
	female	14%	18%	68%	2242
Reading literary material	male	21%	38%	41%	3952
	female	16%	44%	40%	5699
Reading erotic stories	male	16%	31%	53%	4202
	female	2%	12%	86%	5523

* Percentages not reported

male and female, report that they experience sexual arousal from some form of written or pictorial communication portraying sexual behavior or nudity. The data provided do not permit, however, an estimation of the generality of sexual arousal within a single individual, e.g., whether the person who reports sexual arousal by pictures of nudes also reports that erotic stories have a similar effect.

Second, males and females differ significantly in terms of the materials they report to be sexually arousing. The more direct and unambiguous the sexual cue, the more probable the masculine sex arousal. On the other hand, the indirect, romantic psychosexual cues appear to be an effective source of sexual arousal for females. This difference between the sexes is also reflected in the finding that males develop stronger preferences for particular types of sexual activity, and that they react sexually, in some sense, to a greater variety of objects which have been associated with their sexual activities.

An important consideration in the evaluation of the Kinsey reports is the absence of moral prejudgements in the design of their interview techniques or of sermonizing on the results. These investigators simply set out to discover facts concerning sexual behavior and attitudes. While the general weaknesses attributed to self-report techniques must necessarily apply to Kinsey's work, it continues to be classic of this type of study, and the facts reported merit careful consideration.

Summing up thus far: the self-report method of ascertaining the effect of exposure to psychosexual stimuli is one way, a frontal assault as it were, of investigating the question: does this material affect in any way the thought and behavior of persons who view it? The method is difficult for a number of reasons. Questions can be loaded and answers prejudged. Sampling and statistical procedures are often difficult. In the studies of Blumer and Hauser, Haines and others can be found all these difficulties, and their results therefore lead to no definite conclusions. However, the findings reviewed in this section all tend to support the following generalizations: (1) depictions of nudes and unambiguous descriptions of blatant sexual activity are associated with subjective reports of sexual arousal in most males -- adult and adolescent; (2) romantic, "love" oriented descriptions of human heterosexual behavior are associated with subjective reports of sexual arousal in many females; (3) each of the studies reflects considerable difference among individuals in response to sexually relevant material. Some males fail to report sexual arousal after exposure to the most detailed descriptions of sexual activity; some females report intense sexual arousal by viewing pictures of sexual intercourse as well as by other sets of cues that are even remotely concerned with heterosexual behavior. Above all, the data reviewed in this section point to the existence of a wide range of variation among persons in their reported response to psychosexual cues.

Preference for psychosexual stimuli: Other investigations of possible relevance have explored factors which determine individual preference for viewing sexually related stimuli. Although few studies have provided data on determinants of this preference, the work that has been undertaken leads to some provocative questions.

An unpublished study by Professor A. M. Buchwald indicates that there are marked differences between men and women in their choice of viewing psychosexual materials.[5] In Buchwald's experiment, college students were introduced to procedures which, they were told, assessed extra-sensory perception. The subject's task was to guess whether each successive card of a deck held face down was blank or had a picture on the reverse side; the cards being randomly drawn from a deck that contained an equal number of blank and pictorial cards. If the subject responded "picture," he was shown the reverse side of the card; if the subject responded "blank," he was told whether his response was correct or incorrect but he was not shown the card. Thus, the subject who consistently guessed "picture" would view all the cards; the subject who invariably guessed "blank" would see none of the pictures.

Twelve groups of male and female subjects were tested in Buchwald's study, and each same-sex group viewed a different class of objects on the cards. Depictions of food, children, animals, extreme violence (highway accidents, murder photographs drawn from police files), and nudes (taken from "Playboy" type publications) constituted the five classes of stimuli. The control groups were shown a circus scene produced by a rubber stamp from a child's stamping set. The results indicate that only in a single subgroup, the one in which male subjects observed nude females, did the proportion of "picture" responses exceed that obtained in the control group. Not unsurprisingly, then, college men tended to maximize the likelihood of their viewing nude females while female subjects and men who viewed non-sexual pictures demonstrated no consistent preference for viewing the cards. Reports from other investigations in which subjects had an opportunity to observe clothed male and female models yielded similar results: men show a stronger preference for viewing female models than do women for viewing male models.[6] Further study by Zamansky[7] indicates, however, that all men are not equally attracted to photographs of the opposite sex. Comparing a group of 20 adult homosexual males with a control sample of 20 "normal," heterosexual men, he found that the homosexuals spent a significantly longer time than did the normal subjects in viewing pictures of men in preference to pictures of women, when photographs of both were presented simultaneously. The homosexual subjects, in fact, avoided viewing pictures of females, even when these were paired with neutral pastoral scenes. Since pictures of nude females (or nude males) were not used in this study, Zamansky's findings provide only suggestive evidence for the issues considered in this paper. It seems probable, however, that problems of sexual identity, as reflected in predominant homosexuality or heterosexuality, play an important role in determining an individual's preference for or avoidance of various classes of sexual material.

What occurs when sexually conflicted males are required to view pictures of female nudity? Miller and Swanson devised an experimental situtation where three groups of college men, of varying strengths of masculine identification, were requested to peruse photographs of attractive female nudes. Before and after the presentation of the photographs, each subject completed a set of equivalent incomplete story tests which were designed to assess his ability to solve problems of interpersonal relationships. The results indicated that the less masculine subjects (men in the "effeminate" and "unconsciously feminine" groups) tended to reflect considerable disorganization in their fantasy problem solving behavior following the presentation of the nude pictures. The masculine group, on the other hand, performed as effectively after viewing the photographs as they had prior to the presentation of this material.

One further study, quite early but still relevant to this analysis of preference deserves notice. Two European investigators (Bracken and Schafers)[9] investigated the question: does there exist a relationship between the choice of reading matter and the nature of crime for which a sample of male prisoners had been committed? According to their report, murderers display a preference for high-grade information books and adventure stories; swindlers prefer light novels, thieves tend to choose books on "practical culture," and sexual offenders show a preference for "sex books." The results, however, need to be replicated before confidence can be placed in these findings.

Apart from the proposition, hardly surprising, that men typically demonstrate a strong preference for viewing portrayals of nude members of the opposite sex, the studies discussed in this section suggest the following generalizations: (1) males who have not achieved an adequate masculine identification avoid and, presumably, are threatened by, portrayals of female nudity; (2) non-voluntary exposure to pictures of nude members of the opposite sex leads to measurably cognitive disorganization in sexually conflicted men. The predispositional patterns that determine a strong preference for such portrayals have yet to be studied systematically. Although there is some indication that certain persons are strongly attracted to depictions of nudity the personality and motivational factors that account for this attraction have not been identified reliably.

<u>Fantasy measures of sexual arousal</u>: The studies in this section are concerned with the effects of sexual stimuli of one aspect of an individual's actual behavior. Unlike the self-report technique, these investigators are not interested in what the subject <u>says</u> he does under such and such conditions, <u>which do not exist at the moment</u>; rather, they <u>create</u> a certain condition, <u>e.g.</u>, show pictures of nudes, and then they <u>observe</u> some aspect of the subject's behavior, in this case, a fantasy production.

One technique is to have a subject tell or write a story about the picture he has seen. Another technique is to show the picture and give a Thematic Apperception Test (TAT) which also calls upon the subject to tell a story. Various qualities of the story may be analyzed for content, and this is taken to reflect the current thinking of the subject. These stories may be considered as reactions to the particular qualities of the picture (e. g., female nudity) or they may be a function of environmental conditions before or during the subject's reaction, or, more usually, they may be construed to be the result of an interaction of qualities of the subject, picture, and current situation.

One series of investigations used the analysis of creative stories as a means of assessing the subject's sexual arousal following the presentation of pictures of nude females. Thus, Clark tested the hypothesis that sexual arousal would occur only if the nude pictures were presented in a permissive, guilt-free situation.[10] Reasoning from Conger's notion that guilt is lessened under the influence of alcohol,[11] Clark expected that greater sexual arousal would occur when the subjects were intoxicated than when they were sober. To test this general hypothesis, he presented the nude pictures under two conditions: (1) in a group testing situation in a university classroom, and (2) at a fraternity beer party. Following each condition, a second experimenter administered a group Thematic Apperception Test (TAT) which required each subject to create short stories for eight pictures of relatively ambiguous interpersonal situations. The stories were then scored for the presence of absence of sexual content, and Clark found more sexual content in the stories obtained in the party situation than in the university setting. Indeed, when expermients were made in a formal, classroom setting, there were fewer stories containing a reference to sex following a showing of nudes than were produced following the presentation of ordinary pictures selected for their apparent lack of sexual qualities.

Thus, the conditions under which observations of nude photographs occur seem to affect the extent to which subsequently obtained TAT stories are concerned with sex; but it is not clear that the study has shown that equally strong sexual arousal was not present in both setting. That is, the circumstances of testing in the university might tend to inhibit the expression of sexual content on the TAT, while participation in a beer party might facilitate the production of such stories. Both groups may have been equally aroused by the pictures, but the classroom setting may have inhibited direct sexual expression. Indeed, in a later discussion of this study, Clark adopts this alternative interpretation:

> These results seem to indicate that under normal (non-alcohol) conditions the sexual arousal causes sufficient anxiety to lead to the inhibition of manifest sexual imagery whereas, under the influence of alcohol this anxiety or guilt is sufficiently reduced to permit increased expression of manifest sexuality reflecting directly the heightened state of arousal.[12]

Similar problems of interpretation are apparent in an interesting study by Musseh and Scodel.[13] Following a procedure similar to that of Clark, they studied the effect of varying the formality of the laboratory situation in which the arousal stimuli were presented. Male college students, presumably volunteers, were presented with pictures of nude females and were given instructions to rate each picture on a dimension of attractiveness. The slides were presented to one group by a "formal, professorial, and somewhat stern man in his sixties." A young, informal, permissive graduate student administered the same slides to a second group, and TAT cards were administered to all, immediately following the pictures, by a third experimenter. The results showed that the informal group produced more thematic stories containing direct reference to sex than did the formal group. These results were offered as support for the hypothesis that the arousal of socially disapproved needs in the presence of an authority figure leads to the inhibition of that need.

All this suggests that the potential effect of a sexual stimulus is affected by the situation in which the material is presented, as well as the erotic content of the material observed. In neither study is it clear whether no sexual fantasies were aroused in the non-permissive situations, or whether sexual fantasies were in fact aroused and their report inhibited. The Mussen and Scodel work suggests the latter, but their experiment does not allow exclusion of the former possibility. The distinction between failure to arouse sexual ideation and inhibition of expression may be important to the analysis of the effects of reading or viewing obscene material.

A recent study by Lieman and Epstein[14] provides further clarification of the role of sexual guilt in determining an individual's fantasy responses to sexually relevant stimuli. Sixty unmarried college men were tested as a group with a specially constructed thematic test, and were subsequently given a questionnaire designed to obtain information on guilt over sex. The thematic test pictures were arranged along a dimension of "sexual relevance," e.g., one picture depicted a man lying on a bed, embracing a woman and being kissed by her as she was leaning over him (high relevance); another picture showed a young man sitting at a desk and writing a letter (low relevance). Included in the sex guilt inventory were such statements as: "I avoid sexy shows when I can"; "It is wrong to indulge in sex strictly for pleasure"; "I feel guilt about my sexual behavior"; "I find discussions about sex slightly annoying." Lieman and Epstein's results indicate, among other things, that subjects who reflect very little guilt on the inventory tend to produce more "thematic sexual responses," i.e., stories which contain direct sexual references, than do the men who indicate considerable sex guilt on the inventory. This difference between "low sex guilt" and "high sex guilt" subjects was greatest on pictures of high sex relevance. Although the generality of these findings to our present study is limited by the fact that even the "high sex relevant" pictures probably could not be considered even mildly obscene, these findings support the results of Clark and of Mussen and Scodel which were obtained in entirely different contexts.

To sum up this section: experimenters have sought to determine the conditions under which men who view pictures of nude women will, shortly thereafter, produce fantasies with sexual themes. Under some circumstances -- in a permissive "guilt-free" setting -- there is evidence that they do produce such fantasies. However, where the environment is formal and stern, these fantasies are not aroused, or at least not verbalized. Similarly, individuals who report that they are generally inhibited in their sexual behavior, and who experience guilt over sexual conduct, fail to produce sexual responses, even in fantasy, in a situation where such a response would be appropriate. Thus, there is some support for the hypothesis that men with considerable sex guilt fail to become aroused by sex stimuli of a type prevalent in obscene communication.

Physiological assessment of sexual arousal: Another group of studies has investigated physiological indices of an individual's response to portrayals of love, nudity and sexual activity. The particular measures utilized ranged from estimates of prostate gland activity to the galvanic skin response (GSR), blood volume, and respiratory rate. It should be noted that these indices are sensitive to any emotional arousal, as well as sexual arousal. Thus, the sexual content of the arousal must be inferred from the stimulus situation to which the subject appears to be responding. Similarly, if the subject experiences strong emotion that has been previously associated with sexual arousal, e.g., guilt or anxiety, these too may be reflected physiologically.

In contrast to the response measures of sexual arousal considered up to this point (self-report, preference, fantasy), somatic response patterns are, for the most part, uninfluenced by the subject's attempts to dissimulate or voluntarily inhibit his behavior. This relative invulnerability to individual control is a desirable attribute which compensates, in part, for some of the problems of interpretation.

The earlier investigations of Dysinger and Ruckmick used GSR as a measure of sexual arousal.[15] Studying groups of children and adults in both a laboratory and a theater situation, Dysinger and Ruckmick related the subjects' GSR to scenes during a motion picture at which the most extreme responses occurred. Although subjects observed three types of films (comedy, adventure, and "love/erotic"), the findings most pertinent to the present paper are those which were obtained with films containing mild sex stimuli. The results suggest that the various age groups respond in markedly different ways to different scenes. Thus the authors state: "In scenes of love and in scenes suggestive of sex, the greatest... reaction was produced in the group near 16 years of age; adults gave an average response that was less intense; children under 12 years of age gave less... responses than adults." Female subjects, as a group, tended to register somewhat higher GSR's than males during the love and romance situations, whereas the males as a group responded most intensely to the danger and adventure scenes. However, all the differences were slight and tests of statistical significance were not provided in the report. It is therefore uncertain whether these trends can be accepted as reliable.

Driserens and Woods[16] investigated the effects of mildly erotic literature on respiration rate and blood volume. The subjects were instructed to read "First Night," the saga of a timid bridegroom drawn from the magazine (apparently commercial, "over the counter"), Honeymoon Tales. During the reading, the pulse rate and inspiration/expiration ratio (measure of respiratory functioning) were recorded for each subject. Even though a total of only 10 male (college and graduate) students were studied, the subjects were separated into three groups of constitutional types on the basis of their responses to the physiological measures. The authors assert several "tentatively made" conclusions: "Individuals who represent in high degree the physiologically active type are most frequently and easily influenced by sex literature"; "the abstract thinking type of individual is not readily influenced by sex literature." However, the reported data provide little support for these conclusions, with no statistical tests of significance reported.

Probably the most adequate exploration of somatic response patterns elicited by sexually relevant cues was that of Davis and Buchwald.[17] To investigate the question, "Is it possible to produce different kinds of somatic (i.e., autonomic and skeletal muscle) response in the same individual by administering qualitatively different stimuli?", male and female subjects were presented with pictures of various objects and situations. The stimuli ranged from depictions of nude females, to a "photograph of a smiling Japanese decapitating an Australian prisoner," and to cartoons. By recording a number of somatic response measures simultaneously with the presentation of the pictures, it was possible to compare the effects of the different stimuli, and to explore the differential response patterns of the two sexes. A total of 12 somatic response variables were recorded, including measures of GSR, respiratory rate, and several circulatory system indices.

Davis and Buchwald's results indicate that the male subjects did, in fact, produce different response patterns as they observed the various pictures; e.g., the somatic responses of the men during the viewing of nudes was discernibly different from the responses elicited by the geometrical figures. Female subjects did not show a similar differentiation in their responses. Furthermore, Davis and Buchwald note that the stimuli in which nudes are depicted, as compared to the other stimuli, elicit the most intense somatic responses in the male subjects. A similar but statistically nonsignificant trend was found in the analyses of the female sample. In summary, Davis and Buchwald have presented some persuasive evidence that: (1) male college students show consistent and strong somatic responses when observing pictures of nudes; (2) male responses to sexual stimuli are discernibly different from responses to other scenes; (3) female response to the nudes is not unlike their response to other scenes.

In one of the few studies whose purpose was to investigate effects of "pornography," Clark and Triechler[18] investigated the influence of sexual films on the activity of the prostate gland, which secretes the hormone acid phosphatase during sexual arousal. Five males and two females watched "two or three short 'pornographic' movies and one 'non-sexual' stress," in individual sessions. Urine samples collected before, during and after the motion pictures, were analyzed for quantity of acid phosphatase. Of the seven subjects who took part in the study, four men showed increased acid secretion directly following the observations of the films. Both females, and one of the five males studied, showed a decrease in acid phosphatase activity. According to the investigators, the one male reported that he was "quite embarrassed, almost repulsed, by the movies."

The Clark-Triechler results, however, must be interpreted with caution since the index of prostate activity used, acid phosphatase in the urine, is influenced by the operation of other glands as well. Furthermore, prostatic fluid is secreted at times other than during sexual arousal. In this latter regard the data reported indicate that the subject who decreased in acid phosphatase during presentation of the sexual stimuli also showed a decrease during the non-sexual stress situation. Also, two of the subjects who were placed in a non-sexual stress situation showed an increase in acid phosphatase in "very much the way as they responded to the pornographic movies." Thus, it does not necessarily follow that the sexual material caused the decrease. Finally, there was considerable variability in the measures used, even in the limited sample that was studied. Since statistical evaluation of the data were not reported in the paper, it seems most appropriate, at present, to consider these results to be only suggestive of a relationship, and deserving of further study. The results are, however, consistent with Kinsey's findings on sex arousal and with the studies indicating that sexual guilt tends to inhibit arousal and with the other reports considered in this section.

To sum up the study of somatic response patterns, it seems clear that strong, measurable somatic responses occur when some men are presented with sexual stimuli such as pictures of nude females. Women tend not to be as reactive, or at least, do not produce somatic responses of the same general pattern as do male subjects. Men who report that (1) they are not affected by the stimuli or that (2) they are repulsed by the depictions of sexual behavior, appear to produce somatic responses that are consistent with these subjective reports. In fact, many of the findings that have been reviewed here seem highly consistent with those of the self-report studies, notably the results of Kinsey and his associates. The determinants of somatic response to sexual stimuli by males have yet to be systematically explored. However, preliminary data suggest that such variables as masculinity and age may prove to be highly relevant for the process of sexual arousal.

III.

It is possible to synthesize most of this material, to formulate some generalizations, and to speculate about some further, unproven hypotheses which might justify some controls on the dissemination of communication freighted with sex stimuli.

Despite the inadequacies of some of the investigations, we believe the results are consistent enough to suggest the following -- which are offered, not as empirical laws, but as propositions which, thus far, appear to emerge from the evidence:

1. A significant proportion of our society is sexually aroused to some extent by some form of sex stimuli in pictures and probably in books.

2. Portrayals of female nudity and of sexual activity lead to sexual arousal in many males -- adolescents as well as adults. These materials arouse females far less

frequently.

3. Females, on the other hand, are more frequently sexually aroused than men by complex stimuli which portray "romantic" or "love" relationships and which constitute, in general, less direct sexual cues.

4. Males differ among each other in terms of preference for and response to various types of sex stimuli. Factors which account for different preferences among males for viewing sexually relevant materials include: adequacy of masculine sexual identity, strong guilt with respect to sexual behavior, physical maturity and intellectual ability.

5. The environmental circumstances under which the sex stimuli are viewed may influence the extent to which the viewers will show evidence of sexual arousal. It is not clear, however, whether the failure to observe evidence of sexual arousal is due to the fact that no arousal occurred or that the overt expression of the arousal was inhibited.

6. Exposure to certain types of sex stimuli is, for some persons, both males and females, a distinctly aversive experience. Sexual guilt appears to be an important determinant of the extent to which viewing sexually relevant material will be considered an unpleasant event.

Put in more "lay" terms, we think the studies show that exposure to certain kinds of erotic materials may often cause "arousal" in many people. Females are probably more often aroused by less direct, more subtle depictions -- material which we do not call "obscene," which no free society presumably could legally condemn. Many men are more likely aroused, or at least more aroused, by material depicting nudity or sexual relations -- material which is more likely to be "obscene" in the legal sense. Possibly, the more obscene the material (at least up to a point), the more its arousal potential for most men. But men may differ in their reactions to various kinds of sex stimuli. Some stimuli may be both attractive and arousing to some while perhaps unattractive and neutral in effect on others. We know only a little about what may account for these differences.

Arousal is a condition with both psychological and physiological concomitants. It may occur in many contexts.

The strength of the psychological and physiological concomitants may vary. We, of course, are speaking of the condition in a sexual context. In the sense used here, the condition of arousal may include an increase in emotional tone, an intensification of concentration, an increase in thoughts, fantasies, perhaps desires of a sexual nature, an increase in blood pressure, palmar sweating and perhaps prostate gland activity. But all of these things may occur in varying degrees of intensity.

While the phenomena may often occur when males view nude females, (and probably when males view or read about sexual activity between males and females) there are a number of qualifying factors. The setting -- the environment -- of the viewing may be quite important. Where the individual feels inhibited by his surroundings, he may try to avoid the stimulus, or he may try to suppress -- to the extent he can -- his feelings, or at least any outward expression of them. Conversely, where the setting is thought to be "permissive" the conditions of arousal seem expressed in a more overt way. Alcohol probably reduces inhibitions and may augment expression of arousal. Again, the physiological and psychological makeup of the subject may be an important variable. Persons who feel strong guilt about sex, or about the experience of being stimulated by viewing erotic material may seek to avoid the experience or seek to repress the feelings evoked. Homosexuals may, in fact, experience feelings of disgust or revulsion when they view stimuli seen as erotic by heterosexuals. But homosexuals may experience erotic arousal from other types of materials. There is thus a complex of factors -- and we have only given examples of some -- which may determine whether arousal will result and which may affect the strength and perhaps the consequences of that stimulation.

Many discussions of sex censorship seem to assume that obscenity evokes a direct, immediate response of the individual reflected in a state of heightened sexual arousal. But many also assume, or speculate, about a second kind of effect. That is, in contrast to the immediate effects of stimulation, it has frequently been suggested that exposure to obscene materials also influences the individual in more enduring ways and in a fashion that is not immediately observable, i. e., that his attitudes, values and habits relevant to sexual behavior are altered. The distinction between the immediate and long-term effects of stimuli in communciation has been suggested by psychological theorists in other contexts. The studies reviewed here have yielded information primarily about the first class of effects -- the immediate, transient responses of the individual to various stimuli. The second class of effects has hardly been studied; the data is only suggestive.

Unfortunately, most justifications for censorship laws are predicated upon the presumed influence of obscenity on the subsequent sexual behavior and morals of the viewer. Thus, granting that many obscene materials do arouse under many circumstances, we need to know more. We need to know how long the conditions of arousal last and how this stimulation might affect overt behavior, attitudes governing behavior and mental health.

We cannot offer empirical evidence to answer such questions because no such evidence exists. The data simply stops short at the critical point. Yet is is possible, and perhaps helpful, to speculate on some hypotheses which may be relevant to the law.

IV.

It may be well to emphasize again a point which sometimes seems obscured in the theorizing and argument about the possible harmful consequences of obscenity. The point is simply that these materials may affect different people in different ways, and the effect, if any, may also vary with the circumstances under which exposure took place. There possibly are many variables and thus it may be that many seemingly conflicting hypotheses can eventually be demonstrated by empirical investigation. We turn then to some of the possibilities.

Obscenity as a cause of sexual misbehavior or crime: One possible rationale for censorship laws is based on the assumption that persons who view obscene materials will be instigated to perform sexual acts which the state can or does legitimately prohibit. This assumption seems to involve two subsidiary propositions: sexual cues elicit sexual thoughts and emotions, and the direction of expression of such arousal will be similar to the cues observed. While there is strong support in the empirical literature for the first proposition, we have located no research that has provided a direct test of the second. Investigations that have dealt with this process in terms of another behavior system, *i.e.*, aggression, indicate that, under particular, rather narrowly defined experimental conditions, identification with observed behavior can be demonstrated.[19] Obviously it would be hazardous to apply these results to the issue of sexual stimulation. It may be possible to test the proposition that, under some circumstances, some persons modify some aspects of their sexual behavior. But until the phenomenon is reliably demonstrated, we can hardly assume that the observation of illicit sex practices will lead to *criminal* sexual behavior. Indeed, common experience contradicts this hypothesis for most people.

Further, it has been speculated that the observation of obscene material leads to the performance of criminal acts that are not necessarily sexual in nature. This speculation seems to assume that the state of sexual arousal created by the pornographic materials is relieved by non-sexual, antisocial behavior. Again, there is no evidence to confirm or deny this proposition. Indeed, because of the multidimensionality of the concept "antisocial behavior," this would be an exceedingly difficult proposition to test experimentally.[20]

Other propositions to support sex censorship are similarly speculative. Possibly some sex stimuli may have more of an impact on some immature males, at least adolescents who lack well-developed internalized controls, and thus may be more influential on their behavior; but even among this group there is no satisfactory empirical evidence. Perhaps obscene materials influence some persons who are already prone to sexual misbehavior. But even without an "obscenity" stimulus it may well be that these people -- or some of them -- would engage in illegal actions; they might find their stimulus in some other permissible form of sex expression. And, with the empirical evidence we do have, a quite different thesis is also possible; obscene materials provide a way of releasing strong sexual urges without doing harm to others. Intuitively, all these propositions -- contradictory though they appear -- may seem to have some merit; and for all we know, all, some or none of them could be true.

Obscenity and "Psychosexual Tension": Recently the draftsmen of the American Law Institute's Model Penal Code suggested that the viewing of obscene materials may create undesirable "psychosexual" or "emotional" "tensions." To the extent that the results obtained from the study of persons who reflect considerable sexual guilt and sexual-identification problems are pertinent, it seems clear that the presentation of sexual materials, for some persons, is an aversive or disruptive experience. The extent and generality of this description has yet to be explored systematically. On the other hand, it may also be that other persons who do not evidence strong sexual guilt and who are otherwise "normally" adjusted in terms of sexual behavior may experience considerable relief by observing sexual material. Thus, the same stimulus may have directly contrasting effects, according to the response predispositions of the viewer, and even in the same viewer at different times.

Obscenity as an "obsession": One might also speculate that some of those who are most aroused by whatever form of erotic material operates most effectively to stimulate them may consume more of this material than other people. There is some suggestion in the research reviewed (and it seems to be supported (1) by evidence reflecting the marketing of obscene material in the mails, and (2) by communication research in other fields) that some people may spend considerably more time, energy and money to secure the chance to read or view erotic depictions. It may be that the obscene material is simply used in place of other material to satisfy a desire for sexual stimulation -- a desire which will be fulfilled in any event. Thus, it may be that with some of these people obscenity operates as a safety valve for release of feelings. But the evidence hardly negates other possibilities as well -- including the hypothesis that the obscene material is both an artifact and a causative influence creating, in some, a stronger desire to view more obscenity. If, in fact, the seeking for obscenity becomes a "compulsive" activity to some, this behavior may affect the individual's personality or his values and his attitudes towards sexual conduct or his health, happiness or efficiency. As yet, we cannot evaluate these hypotheses adequately. The data we have merely suggest that this may be an important and researchable area of investigation.

Obscenity in the formation and change of attitudes: Regrettably the research reviewed here has been concerned primarily with the immediate emotional effects of psychosexual stimuli. But what of the impact on articulated attitudes, beliefs and moral values of communication freighted with portrayals of nudity of sex action? Does exposure or repeated exposure change one's concept of desirable sexual relationships and sexual conduct?

Paradoxically, it may be that at heart most men fear obscenity more for what it will do to norms of morality than for any other reason. The earlier cases, insofar as they argue any rationale for anti-obscenity law, seem to urge this thinking. The Supreme Court once wrote:

> The foundation of a republic is the virtue of its citizens. They are at once sovereigns and subjects. As the foundation is undermined, the structure is weakened. When it is destroyed, the fabric must fall. Such is the voice of universal history.[21]

In 1957, the United States Government, defending the constitutionality of its power to punish use of the mails to disseminate obscene communication, quoted this statement and argued at great length the general proposition that "public morality would be seriously affected by the distribution of obscene material" and declared:

> The distribution of obscenity creates a substantial risk of inducing immoral sexual conduct over a period of time by breaking down the concept of morality as well as moral standards.
>
> The common circulation of such material could hardly help but induce many to believe that their moral code was out of date and that they should do what, they suppose, others are doing.
>
> The conduct with which we are concerned need not be that which would immediately follow the reading of one book, the seeing of one pornographic moving picture, or the study of a set of photographs. Just as in the Dennis case, the feared conduct may be the result of repeated indoctrination.... Once moral standards have been

> corrupted, one's conduct is no longer guided by them. It requires little judicial notice to know that one whose morals have been corrupted is likely to engage in sex conduct which society has a right to prohibit. In this slower, but no less serious way, obscenity brings about immoral conduct.
>
> The collective public conscience pushes the individual in the direction of being honest, fair, law-abiding, and decent. While separate elements may sometimes be singled out, public morality is really indivisible, in the sense that one aspect of it cannot be corrupted and leave the rest unaffected.
>
> The man who finds that the Government will or can do nothing to stop the distribution of pornography to his family will be less willing to abide by society's demands on him, whether it be as to gambling, distribution of narcotics, or the candor with which he fills out his income tax. Similarly, the corruption of moral standards in the realm of sexual conduct cannot help but corrupt other aspects of moral life. Morality, like morale, cannot be undercut at one point without affecting all conduct.[22]

This line of argument, we repeat, is frequently asserted -- particularly in legislative forums. The old analogy, whether based on fiction or fact, to the decline of Rome is invoked; and, it is implied that obscenity, for some reason, exerts some undefined yet powerful appeal and insidious influence on those who contemplate it, and this influence apparently cannot be counteracted by ordinary appeals to reason. Thus, for purposes of defining freedom, expressions reflecting moral heresy cannot be treated as expressions of political heresy. The latter can be routed by argument, the former apparently cannot, and therefore, such expressions must be quelled by the state.

Plausible research to undergird such views is yet to be developed -- indeed, the precise questions for investigation are probably yet to be formulated. The most usual effect of communication in such fields as politics, so the research indicates, is to reinforce or to modify slightly existing attitudes and values, rather than to invoke new beliefs or produce sudden change. Research in other, possibly analogous fields -- the effect on children of exposure to crime and violence in the media, the effects on adults and children of "escapist" TV and radio programs -- suggests that ordinarily those kinds of communication do not act like "hypodermics" to inject forthwith some new belief or motivation in the audience. It may well be that the frequent exposure to various forms of portrayed sexual activity would lead to significant changes in some viewer's attitudes regarding this behavior. This does not indicate, however, that the change would necessarily be toward greater acceptance of the behavior depicted. On the contrary, the shift in attitude might be in the direction of greater rejection or of greater acceptance, according to the nature and the strength of the pre-existing attitudes that the viewer holds. Where no strong sexual attitudes exist a priori, either because of a person's youth or his sexual naivete, one would expect that the exposure to sexual stimuli would have its strongest effect. Furthermore, some children may be more susceptible than others to sexual stimuli. There are indications in the empirical literature that certain children, namely those functioning at a borderline intellectual level, and those who present signs of behavioral maladjustment, show adverse effects after repeated exposure to "escapist communication" or to depictions of violence. By analogy, some kinds of obscenity might strengthen a socially undesirable orientation towards sex and sexual relationships. But these speculations have to be submitted to direct empirical test.

V.

If one insisted on supporting empirical evidence it would be hard to find a rationale for our anti-obscenity laws which squares with first amendment theory. But proponents of controls have never accepted this burden. Nor is it clear they must. Legislative committees have accepted opinions, including opinions concerning facts and, sometimes unfortunately, opinions couched in extreme and therefore doubtful terms or opinions which are not carefully labeled as opinions. In more recent times, the courts have usually eschewed discussion of these treacherous questions (what is it that is supposed to make obscenity bad, and how do we know that this is so?). The Supreme Court in its recent first amendment forays has thus far been able (to the satisfaction of most of the Justices) to avoid such issues by treating them as more or less irrelevant. Unfortunately the questions cannot be so neatly turned away. We should continue to seek the answers. If the social sciences cannot give us ulitmate answers, at least, given systematic, inter-disciplinary efforts they can move us closer to a more certain knowledge.

Many more pages could be written to attempt to group and synthesize some of the clinical observations and opinion-type assertions which have been set forth to support or refute the need for obscenity laws. But, whatever the value of the exercise, it is not our present purpose. We would caution, however, that claims based on empirical knowledge must be modest: the temptation to generalize from the data is dangerous. While experts in behavior have every right to speak, they do disservice if they confuse personal theory with scientific fact.

The behavioral science side of our joint-author team does not feel it their province to render judgment. The lawyer-author, after mulling the meagre data and its implications, is willing to stick, for the time being, to guns he mounted in other publications with another co-author.[23]

The gist of that thought is: obscenity (as legally defined -- and circumscribed -- by recent Supreme Court decisions) is quite often (but of course, not always) qualitatively different from other "speech"; its idea-content is different and often of negligible intellectual value (though not always and not to all men). Obscenity <u>may</u> (we do not know) exert a peculiarly strong and socially undesirable influence (in terms of inducing a strong immediate response, or in terms of influencing overt conduct, personality, attitudes, or all of these) on some people, perhaps notably, people who are in some ways sexually immature. Quite possibly this is not a large group percentage-wise, but numerically it may still be of significant size. Obscenity also seems to be an outrage to some people. They rebel not simply at its open availability but at commercial efforts to exploit it and to foster its wide circulation among youths and others; and the strength of these feelings -- especially among parents -- must be accommodated to some extent as a matter of Realpolitik. For these and other reasons, and until we know more, perhaps we should accept legal controls which seek to prevent that kind of commercial distribution which in essence multiplies the risks we may incur when obscenity falls frequently and easily into the hands of the immature. Thus, we might condemn commercial distribution which exploits obscenity and which is either intentionally aimed at youth (and perhaps others with an obvious obsessive interest) or which is carried on with reckless disregard of the quality of the audience whose patronage is solicited. Controls of this kind have been discussed elsewhere. They seem to have some basis in reality, yet they hardly impinge on any man's freedom to read or create.

Notes

1. First, a note regarding the procedure followed in the review of the empirical studies seems relevant. Our initial step was a search of the volumes of the Psychological Abstracts from 1925 to June 1961. The Psychological Abstracts provide a brief resume of scientific reports relevant to the study of behavior. The coverage is excellent: in 1960, 564 journals, foreign and domestic, were reviewed regularly. It is important to emphasize again that only a few of the studies which we found and discussed were designed to investigate the effects of "obscenity"; thus, in many, the subject was not told that he was being assessed for arousal upon viewing erotic or obscene materials. There may be a lot in a label. Perhaps if subjects are told that they are viewing "obscene" or "sexy" pictures, their responses would be stronger.

From this preliminary survey approximately 250 articles were selected for further study. The bibliographies of these articles were perused to locate additional research reports. After this material had been collected, we searched the files of the library of the Institute for Sex Research, one of the most extensive repositories of literature related to sex. Finally, we made contact with some other investigators who have been recently active in research in the areas of study covered by this article.

2. Blumer & Hauser, Movies, Delinquency and Crime 73-74, 83, 86 (1933). See also Blumer, Movies and Conduct (1933).

3. Haines, "Juvenile Delinquency and TV," 1 J. Social Therapy (1955).

4. Ramsey, "The Sexual Development of Boys," 56 Amer. J. Psychology 217 (1943). Another study, Lorang, "The Effect of Reading on Moral Conduct and Emotional Experience," Studies in Psychology and Psychiatry, March, 1945, appears to compound some of the errors of the interview studies already considered in the context of a rather naive experimental design.

5. Personal communication with Dr. A. M. Buchwald of Indiana University.

6. Brandt, "Your Eyes Reveal the Secrets of Your Interests," 51 Iowa Academy of Science Proceedings 361 (1944); Maccoby, Wilson & Burton, "Differential Movie-Viewing Behavior of Male and Female Viewers," 26 J. Personality 259 (1958).

7. Zamansky, "A Technique for Assessing Homosexual Tendencies," 24 J. Personality 436 (1956).

8. Miller & Swantson, Inner Conflict and Defense (1960).

9. Von Bracken & Schafers, "Ueber die Haltung von Strafgenfangenen zur Literature," 49 Zeitschrift Fur Angewandte Psychologie 169 (1935).

10. Clark, "The Projective Measurement of Experimentally Induced Levels of Sexual Motivation, 12 J. Exp. Psychology 44 (1952).

11. Conger, "The Effects of Alcohol on Conflict Behavior in the Albino Rat," 12 Q. J. Studies on Alcohol 1 (1951).

12. Clark, "The Effects of Sexual Motivation on Phantasy," in Studies in Motivation 44, 48 (McClelland, ed. 1955).

13. Mussen & Scodel, "The Effects of Sexual Stimulation Under Varying Conditions on TAT Sexual Responsiveness," 19 J. Consulting Psychology 90 (1955).

14. Lieman & Epstein, "Thematic Sexual Responses as Related to Sexual Drive and Guilt," 63 J. Abnormal & Social Psychology 169 (1961).

15. Dysinger & Ruckmick, The Emotional Responses of Children To The Motion Picture Situation (1933).

16. Diserens & Wood, "Psychophysiological Behavior Under Various Types of Literature," 30 J. Abnormal & Social Psychology 484 (1936).

17. Davis & Buchwald, "An Exploration of Somatic Response Patterns: Stimulus and Sex Differences," 50 J. Comparative & Physiological Psychology 44 (1957). The authors express certain reservations in the interpretation of their results:

> [O]ne may be tempted to name the pictures fear, horror, sex, etc., and enumerate the somatic consequences of each, but we feel the temptation ought to be resisted. Although the psychological intermediates would then be defined only by the pictures, they would seem to speak of all the common incidents which people call by such names. Incidents and situations which people have come to call by the same name need not share an essence, and the wisdom of the ages provides untrustworthy landmarks for scientific categories.

Id. at 52. Obviously we have succumbed to the temptation. However, the comments by Davis and Buchwald are highly relevant here in that they suggest one of the fallacies inherent in arbitrarily choosing such a concept as "pornography" or "obscenity" as the basis for categorizing stimuli.

18. Clark & Triechler, "Psychic Stimulation of Prostatic Secretion," 12 Psychosomatic Medicine 261 (1950). [The source of acid phosphatase in the female subjects (prostate gland?) is not reported.]

19. Cf. Bandura & Ross, "Imitation of Film-Mediated Agressive Models," 1962 (unpublished manuscript).

20. Compare the difficulties encompassed in studies of the etiological roots of delinquency, such as Glueck & Glueck, Unraveling Juvenile Delinquency (1950); Bandura

& Walters, Adolescent Agression: A Study of the Influence of Child-Training Practices and Family Interrelationships (1959). These studies have been cited to contradict the proposition that obscenity is a causal factor. But obscenity is probably not discussed in these studies because the investigators were primarily concerned with other more discrenible causative factors. In general, these studies show how a complex of determinants influence the development of delinquency. But they can hardly be cited to rule out obscenity as one possible influence.

21. Trist v. Child, 88 U. S. (21 Wall.) 441, 450 (1874).

22. Brief for United States, pp. 59, 60, 64-65, Roth v. United States, 354 U. S. 476 (1957).

23. Paul & Schwartz, Federal Censorship: Obscenity in the Mail, 191-220 (1961).

Professor Louis Henkin, in the following article, presents a fresh view of the social motives for obscenity legislation. The article is reprinted from 63 Columbia Law Review, 390-414 (1963), with the kind permission of the editors of the Columbia Law Review and the author; grateful acknowledgment is made for permission to report here.

Louis Henkin is Professor of Law and of International Law and Diplomacy, Columbia University.

Professor Henry Monaghan, writing in 76 Yale Law Journal 136ff. (1966), offers some objections to Professor Henkin's thesis (see p. 227, this anthology)

Morals and the Constitution: The Sin of Obscenity

by Louis Henkin

The several cases in which the Supreme Court of the United States has examined obscenity legislation under the light of the Constitution have unloosed a torrent of writing -- official, legal, psychological, and lay. The many words have reflected and evoked passion; they have not brought clarity, to the constitutional questions or to the social questions. They have not spoken to a common effect; they have not joined issue. The Supreme Court itself has split and splintered in variegated opinions and doctrines. Students of the Court's work have cast stones at some Justices, or at all of them. Those who make the obscenity laws and those who enforce them, and others who vigilantly support their hands, have welcomed the Court's decisions with a spate of metaphor about the poison of obscenity and its fearful consequences for man and child. "Libertarians" have deplored another breach in the constitutional bulwark against repression.

At risk of adding yet another tongue to Babel, I venture a few pages with modest purpose. I wish to focus on a small point, but one of constitutional consequence. To me it seems that the unusual confusion -- more prevalent than in discussions of other attempts of government to regulate forms of expression -- is due in large measure to misapprehension of the concern and the interest that inspire government to regulate obscenity. Specifically, I believe, despite common assumptions and occasional rationalizations, that obscenity laws are not principally motivated by any conviction that obscene materials inspire sexual offenses. Obscenity laws, rather, are based on traditional notions, rooted in this country's religious antecedents, of governmental responsibility for communal and individual "decency" and "morality."

If I am correct about the origins and purposes of obscenity legislation, much of the constitutional discussion about the control of obscenity seems out of focus. Concentration on whether obscenity may -- or may not -- incite to unlawful acts aims beside the mark. The question, rather, is whether the state may suppress expression it deems immoral, may protect adults as well as children from voluntary exposure to that which may "corrupt" them, may preserve the community from public, rampant "immorality." This different question may receive the same or a different answer; clearly, the path and the guide posts, the facts sought, the issues considered, and the doctrine applied may be very different. Indeed, this inquiry might today command attention even to a question that must have appeared insubstantial earlier in the history of the Constitution: the authority of government under the Constitution to adopt "morals legislation," to suppress private, individual indulgence which does no harm to others, in the name of traditional notions of morality.

The proper issues of obscenity regulation, I believe, do not lead constitutional lawyers deep into the penumbra in which speech moves toward unlawful action; they demand, rather, forthright and sophisticated exploration of the claims of "unsophisticated" morality and of the community's authority to maintain standards of "decency" and to prevent the corruption of individual character and morals. We may glance at Schenck and Dennis. More relevantly, we might look instead at innumerable unquestioned assertions in cases like Stone v. Mississippi and Mugler v. Kansas.

I. The Purpose of Obscenity Regulation

One cannot, of course, demonstrate beyond doubt a single aim of obscenity regulation. Motives and purposes for legislation are notoriously elusive, ambiguous, and multifarious. The fear that obscenity may induce crime is one occasional reason or rationalization for regulation. Perhaps some legislators...have this reason in mind. At bottom, there are other, authentic motives for obscenity laws.

Clearly, "obscenity," and other concepts to which it is frequently joined in legislation, include at least some expressions that do not relate at all to "incitement" to illegal action. For one instance -- too often concealed by the emphasis on sex in discussions of obscenity -- the accepted definition of obscenity includes not only the sexual but the scatological. Surely the latter does not lead to any unlawful act: it may be emetic; it is not aphrodisiac.

"Sexual obscenity," too, is regulated for purposes unrelated to fear that it may lead to "sex crimes." Obscenity -- sexual or scatological -- is forbidden, in large part, not because it incites but because it offends. A state forbids obscenity -- and nudity, "indecent exposure," graffiti -- as it forbids public fornication and public excretion, because it is offensive to others. The state seeks to suppress or abate these noxious emanations on grounds akin to traditional notions of "nuisance." While "nuisance" may here be a metaphor -- and metaphor has tended to obscure rather than clarify constitutional analysis -- this kind of obscenity legislation has a social purpose to protect others from impact of acts or expressions offensive to them.

Let it be admitted immediately that control of scatological obscenity or of sexual "nuisance" obscenity does not raise the difficult questions. Socially, as well as constitutionally, troublesome issues derive from a large and important area of regulation aimed at sexual materials addressed to willing adults who would not be subject to this "obscenity" if they did not wish to be and who, if they stumbled upon it innocently, might quickly and effectively avoid it. The forms of regulation, too, are not designed and limited to protect the unwitting and unwilling, or to render obscenity private. Regulation frequently aims to prevent even the eager from obtaining the materials or from regarding them, however clandestinely; government seeks to destroy the materials and to prevent and to deter their production.

No doubt many who support such regulation of private voluntary indulgence in obscenity have said or felt that this obscenity may incite the person exposed to it to unlawful sexual action. Today, psychologists are examining and debating whether some obscenity may inspire "psychosexual" tension possibly harmful to mental health. They strive to determine, too, whether different kinds of "obscenity" in different circumstances might influence behavior: whether it may sublimate and deflect from sexual activity, or whether, in some cases at least, obscenity may incite an "abnormal" person to commit unlawful sexual acts. Greater psychological knowledge may some day provide an intelligent basis for evaluating the impact of obscenity on behavior. Even then, but surely now, conclusions as to whether such materials incite to unlawful action may not determine the constitutionality of laws regulating obscenity. For, it seems clear, obscenity legislation has had other purposes and motivations. The accepted definition of obscenity, as that which "appeal(s)...to prurient interest," makes no assumption that it will incite to any action. The history of obscenity legislation points, rather, to origins in aspirations to holiness and propriety. Laws against obscenity have appeared conjoined and cognate to laws against sacrilege and blasphemy, suggesting concern for the spiritual welfare of the person exposed to it and for the moral well-being of the community. Metaphors of "poison" and "filth" also emphasize concern for the welfare of the one exposed and for the atmosphere of the community. A "decent" community does not tolerate obscenity. A "decent" man does not indulge himself with obscene materials.

The moral concern of the community may consist of several different strands frequently entangled beyond separation. Obscenity is immoral, an individual should not indulge it, and the community should not tolerate it. In addition, obscenity, like other immoral acts and expressions, has a deleterious effect on the individual from which the community should protect him. Obscenity is bad for a man, and the concern is not for his "psyche," his mental health. Obscenity is bad for character. It "corrupts" morals, it corrupts character. Character, of course, bears on behavior, but the corruption feared, it should be emphasized, has a very unclear, very remote, and problematic relation to a likelihood that he will commit any particular unlawful act or indeed any unlawful act at all, immediately or in the future.

This concern of the state for the "character" and "morals" of the person exposed is particularly evident in the plethora of laws designed to prevent the "corruption of youth." Among other evil influences, obscenity, it is assumed, may "corrupt" a child. The state assists parents who seek to prevent this corruption, or may even act in loco of those parents who are remiss in protecting their own children. The Supreme Court built constitutional doctrine on these assumptions when it held that Michigan could not "reduce the adult population of Michigan to reading only what is fit for children." Again, the corruption of youth by obscenity is deemed to have some immeasurable effect on character and personality; it is not believed to "incite" to any particular actions now or in the future. While in regard to youth it has always been assumed that government has special responsibility and authority, laws adopted for their protection reflect assumptions and attitudes about obscenity not inapplicable to the regulation of obscenity for adults.

Society intervenes because it is immoral for a person to indulge in obscenity and because obscenity corrupts morals and character of man or child. Either purpose is aimed at saving the "user" from his own indulgence, however private and discreet. But if indulgence in obscenity is prevalent, the prevalence becomes notorious, and the immoral activity takes on a public character and offends "public order." The state may seek to eradicate even isolated, clandestine obscenity; it is concerned in particular to suppress commercial exploitation in order to reduce the public disorder, as well as to protect individuals from their own moral weakness by preventing the spread of the moral infection.

Communities believe, and act on the belief, that obscenity is immoral, is wrong for the individual, and has no place in a decent society. They believe, too, that adults as well as children are corruptible in morals and character, and that obscenity is a source of corruption that should be eliminated. Obscenity is not suppressed primarily for the protection of others. Much of it is suppressed for the purity of the community and for the salvation and welfare of the "consumer." Obscenity, at bottom, is not crime. Obscenity is sin.

II. Obscenity Regulation: The Relevant Constitutional Inquiry.

If obscenity laws are seen primarily as "morals legislation"... constitutional discussion of such laws would seem to deserve emphasis different from that which has preoccupied the judges and the writers.

Immediately, we would move aside... the assumption that "unlawful action" incited by obscene materials is the "evil" at which obscenity laws are directed. These writings bear the mark of the particular time in the history of constitutional adjudication when the obscenity cases made their way up to the Supreme Court. For the principal cases raising the issue of freedom of communication in recent years have involved "speech" found to be part of a pattern of subversive action believed to endanger the safety of the nation. In this context, the Supreme Court struggled to establish lines between theoretical speech and "incitement" to unlawful action. It accepted a test akin to "clear and present danger" (though somewhat diluted) to distinguish immune speech from that which was linked to unlawful action. The Court's opinions emphasized that speech may blend into and become action, and may then be controlled or suppressed to avoid the violent overthrow of government -- a clearly evil consequence that government could clearly prevent.

...this preoccupation with the relation between speech ...and undeniably unlawful consequences, led lawyers as well as Justices carelessly to impose this context upon... obscenity when it finally forced itself upon the Supreme Court's attention. If in fact the state's concern with obscenity has little to do with incitement to action, constitutional discussion based on the link between obscenity and unlawful action seems far beside the point. If unlawful action is not the evil at which the state aims...a "clear and present" danger...is not the relevant concern. The evils at which the state aims are not unlawful action, but indecency and corruption of morals. Of these evils, the dangers assumed are clear and immediate. The impact of "nuisance" obscenity on others is indubitable and immediate. The immorality of indulgence even in private obscenity, the state may believe, is clear; the consequences of widespread indulgence and commercial exploitation on prevailing "decency" are present and certain.

Clear and present danger of unlawful action is a relevant inquiry on only one view -- that the state cannot suppress obscene materials for the "moral" purposes we have suggested, that it can regulate forms of expression, including those falling within the definition of the obscene, only if they are "brigaded with action," only if they incite, say, to rape or other violence, or perhaps to adultery or fornication. This seems to be the view of Mr. Justice Black, and others have supported him. It is constitutional doctrine at which one may arrive; surely one cannot begin -- and end -- there.

One cannot dismiss, without consideration, what appears to be the principal basis of obscenity laws. One cannot assume, without consideration, that the Constitution forbids society to hold the view societies have held and continue to hold -- that obscenity is immoral, that it corrupts morals and character of the persons exposed and the moral tone of a community, and should be suppressed to prevent such corruption.

If minority views have mistaken the moral purposes of obscenity legislation...prevailing views too have failed to attend to moral foundations of obscenity laws in framing issues and building doctrine. To the majority of the Supreme Court in Roth v. United States, the purpose of the legislation was apparently irrelevant. The Court asserted that "obscenity is not within the area of constitutionally protected speech or press." It seemed to reach that conclusion by reading "freedom of speech" in the first amendment as having an important qualification: the speech protected by the Constitution is only that which has some "redeeming social importance." Obscenity, the Court said, has none. The Court supported this reading of the Constitution by reference to history: obscenity was not intended to be included in the freedom of speech protected by the first amendment and in the liberty which the states could not deny without due process of law. Since the constitutional language does not protect obscenity...there is no need to ask what is the purpose of obscenity legislation or whether it has any purpose at all. "Clear and present" danger, of unlawful action or of some other evil consequence, is also irrelevant. So is, presumably, any consideration of "preferred" freedom, or the weight to be given to the interest of the speaker, or the interest of society in his freedom to speak or in his particular speech.

That the Supreme Court's approach leaves too much to be desired has been suggested by others, beginning with the Justices who did not join the Court's opinion. Critics have questioned the Court's reading of constitutional language and of history. They have thought to trace circles in the Court's reasoning, and to identify questions that it seemed to beg. Some of the criticism might be met by reducing the reference to "redeeming social importance" from doctrine to rationalization, from a constitutional standard to an explanation of a historical exception. Roth, then, does not limit the protection of the first amendment to speech having social importance; Roth asserts simply that as a matter of historic interpretation the general phrases of the first and fourteenth amendments did not purpose to deny to government the authority to suppress that which is obscene. Those to whom history is not a whole answer may support the decision by suggesting that it reflects the attitude of a majority of the Court in other "speech cases"; the Court, invoking history, is asserting that expression is not ipso facto immune to regulation for social ends, that obscenity is a proper object of social regulation, that in the balance of freedom and authority under the scrutiny of the Constitution the public's interest in suppressing obscenity outweights the exponent's freedom of expression.

These restatements of the Roth doctrine may provide more respectable doctrine; they do not justify disregard of the special character of obscenity laws as "morals legislation." The claims of history, generally, are subject to the caveat that laws and practices accepted as valid when a constitutional provision was adopted may yet be found invalid in the light of later readings of an organic, creative Constitution. In regard to "morals Laws," in particular, one may ask that the Court consider whether moral assumptions and assertions of a past day necessarily survive as exceptions to freedom today. The Court accepts "appeal to prurient interest" as the test for permissible limitations of obscene materials under the Constitution. If this is asserted as the traditional meaning of obscenity, the Court does not appear to re-examine its continuing validity as a constitutional standard. If it is a new test, the Court does not distinguish it from past notions of obscenity and justify it as presently valid to effect purposes presently permissible to the community. Should not the Court ask why may the state today outlaw obscenity? What governmental purposes, valid today, are these laws designed to effectuate? Are the means proper to these purposes? History, surely, does not foreclose argument that in new light old laws reveal no reasonable foundations, or are based on irrational or false assumptions.

If, history apart, we are to balance conflicting claims of liberty and authority, the balances of 1789 ought not to be determinative; one might urge that a court consider that not all of an ancient morality remains equally vital, that changing values may have dissipated notions once deemed fundamental to morality, and that countervailing values of freedom, growing in potency, may now outweigh these values in the constitutional scale. In Roth, the Court, again, does not examine the nature of the public interest in regulation, and the relation to this interest of the means used, to determine the weight to be given to authority. Since the Court -- like most statutes -- does not distinguish between proscription of the most private indulgence in obscenity and social attack on public obscenity or organized commercial exploitation, the claims of authority appear to rest strictly on the historic concern for private morality. The nonrational, nonutilitarian aims of "morals legislation," like obscenity laws, might well have weight quite different from other historically accepted regulations of speech that have a social, utilitarian purpose, e.g., libel laws. On the other balance, the Court dismisses obscenity as utterly without "redeeming social importance." It does not consider that there may be "social importance" to expressions or words even if they do appeal predominantly to prurient interest. It does not ask: whether regulation of obscenity may have a deterrent and limiting effect on other expressions not themselves obscene; whether there are social values in leaving all individuals free to express, others free to receive, without external limitations and without the shadow of the censor and the vigil of the heirs of Comstock; whether, like other attempts to regulate "the morals" of adults and to save them from themselves (e.g., Prohibition), efforts to deal with obscenity by law may produce greater evils, and may even aggravate the very evils at which these laws are directed.

The need for facing the questions here suggested may be emphasized by reference to a unanimous decision of the Supreme Court that does not deal with obscenity at all. In Kingsley Int'l Pictures Corp. v. Regents of the Univ. of the State of N.Y., the state had refused to license the film "Lady Chatterley's Lover" on the ground that it was "immoral," or "of such a character that its exhibition would tend to corrupt morals." The legislature had defined these terms to apply to any film "which portrays acts of sexual immorality...or which...presents such acts as desirable, acceptable or proper patterns of behavior." The New York courts affirmed the denial of a license for the film "because its subject matter is adultery presented as being right and desirable for certain people under certain circumstances."

The Supreme Court of the United States was agreed in reversing the state's judgment below, though hardly in the reasons for doing so. The majority recognized...that this was not an obscenity case...that the case could not be decided on the basis of some special exception to the freedom of speech enjoyed by "obscenity laws." Yet the Court's opinion, too, did not wrestle with what, I believe, is the real issue. It did not consider that while this was not an obscenity case, it was a "morals" case. The Court stated that New York was censoring the advocacy of an idea, whereas the Constitution, the opinion said, guarantees freedom to advocate ideas. "It protects advocacy of the opinion that adultery may sometimes be proper, no less than advocacy of socialism or the single tax." But ideas promoting adultery -- unlike those urging the single tax -- impinge on traditional morality. The state, indeed, did not claim that the film incited to adultery; it found the film to be immoral and tending to corrupt morals. Incitement to action, one might urge, is as irrelevant here as it is to obscenity cases in which, in effect, the state bars the obscene because it is immoral and tends to corrupt morals.

Recognition that laws against "obscenity" and laws against "immorality" are equally "morals" legislation would have required a very different opinion from the Court, if not a different result. The Court would have had to recognize that legislation against the "immoral" had historical credentials similar to, if not better than, obscenity laws, that the common obscenity statute indeed also forbade the "immoral"; legislation against the "immoral," then, might have as good a claim as obscenity legislation to historical exception from the freedom of speech. The result in the case could have been reached only by distinguishing, in some relevant way, this "morals legislation" from obscenity laws. An acceptable distinction does not readily appear. Somehow, the Court seemed to be denying to the state the assumption that ideas can be immoral or can corrupt morals, even though it had permitted to the state, in effect, the assumption that obscenity is immoral or can corrupt morals. (Would the Court hold that a child also is deprived of his liberty without due process of law if the state keeps from him materials expressing ideas that may "corrupt morals" without inciting to action?) Or did the Court silently measure and conclude that freedom for "ideas," any ideas, inevitably outweighs the state's interest in preventing "immorality by idea" or corruption of morals by ideas?

The confusion remains. Nothing we have said suggests that any of the obscenity cases before the Court was wrongly decided, or that the dissenters, pursuing the analysis urged, could not again find themselves in dissent. The questions suggested may well reconfirm a majority in the conclusion that "obscenity is not within the area of constitutionally protected speech or press." Dissenting Justices may yet conclude that although a state may legislate against certain acts on the ground that they are immoral, it cannot constitutionally suppress expression on the ground that it is immoral or that it corrupts morals. On any view, the recognition of the moral foundations of obscenity laws may suggest that proper differentiation might bring different constitutional results in different cases. It may be that the Constitution regards state concern with private morality privately indulged differently from state protection of the sensibilities of others against offensive public display, or state prohibition of commercial exploitation and promotion of obscenity. It may be that however much one questions the authority of the state to impose morals, even on children, our society recognizes the authority of parents to educate their children, and the state may protect and support the right of parents to impose their morality on their children.

Courts and lawyers, it seems to me, must face the problem of obscenity on the terms in which society has framed it. Laws against obscenity are rooted in traditional notions of morality and decency; the moral foundations of these laws cannot be disregarded in re-assessing their constitutional validity today. It should not be assumed, without re-examination, that the morality of an older day remains a legitimate aim of government with social import outweighing growing claims of individual freedom.

III. The Constitutional Claims of Private "Immoralities"

It has been suggested that the Supreme Court has read obscenity out of the protection for expression in the first and fourteenth amendments without asking whether the "moral" character of obscenity laws continues to justify that historical exception today, or whether the moral aims of these laws may properly outweigh the freedoms suppressed. I venture now to suggest that the moral purpose and motive of obscenity legislation -- and of other prevalent laws aimed at private indulgence in "immoral" activity -- may invite inquiry of yet a different, fundamental order.

We lay aside now claims of freedom to communicate, even the obscene; we are concerned, instead, with claims of the "consumer" to freedom and privacy to indulge in what others may deem immoral. The authority of the state, under the Constitution, to enact "morals legislation" -- laws reflecting some traditional morality having no authentic social purpose to protect other persons or property -- has always been assumed; it has deep roots, and it has seemed obvious and beyond question. It may now be respectable to ask whether indeed the state may adopt any "morals legislation." And if it be concluded that morals legislation is not ipso facto beyond the state's power, can one avoid asking: what morality the state may enforce; what limitations there are on what the state may deem immoral; how these limitations are to be determined?

In doctrinal terms, one may present these as several constitutional questions, not wholly discrete. For the sake of clarity, I declare them as hypotheses to be examined:

First: even if the "freedom of speech" protected by the first and fourteenth amendments does not include a freedom to communicate obscene speech, suppression of obscenity is still a deprivation of liberty or property -- of the person who would indulge in it, at least -- which requires due process of law. Due process of law demands that legislation have a proper public purpose; only an apparent, rational, utilitarian social purpose satisfies due process. A state may not legislate merely to preserve some traditional or prevailing view of private morality.

Second: due process requires, as well, that means be reasonably related to proper public ends. Legislation cannot be based on unfounded hypotheses and assumptions about character and its corruption.

Third: morals legislation is a relic in the law of our religious heritage; the Constitution forbids such establishment of religion.

The inquiry urged can only be suggested here. I would attempt to state the principal issues. I would underscore the complexity of the questions involved. I would urge, too, that the questions suggested are not clearly insubstantial.

A. Morals as a Legislative Concern -- The Requirements of Due Process

The relation of law to morals has been a favored preoccupation of legal philosophers for a thousand years; in the history of American law the relevance of that relation to constitutional limitations has lain unexamined behind discussions of the scope and the limits of government. That morals were the concern of government was assumed, not explored, in discussions of the reaches of the "police power" limited by substantive "due process of law."

May the state, under our Constitution, legislate in support of "morals"? The question may take us back to another: What are the purposes for which the state may legislate under the Constitution? That question, in other contexts, once deeply troubled the Supreme Court. Not too many years ago the Court seemed to assume that by the law of nature and by social contract government was given limited powers for limited purposes. Freedom was the rule; government had to justify itself, and the justifications had to satisfy the Constitution. The state could, of course, legislate to protect one from his neighbor. Perhaps the whole function of government was to assure that, in regard to one's liberty as well as one's property, *sic utere tuo ut alienum non laedas.* But government also had other purposes, among them the regulation of morality. "Whatever differences of opinion may exist as to the extent and boundaries of the police power, and however difficult it may be to render a satisfactory definition of it, there seems to be no doubt that it does extend to...the preservation of good order and the public morals." Even when *laissez faire* had the strongest constitutional credentials, the Supreme Court agreed that the police power of the states might deal with matters that "relate to the...morals...of the public." Later definitions, abandoning prejudgments against governmental "interference," and recognizing new goals of "general welfare" which the state might pursue, accepted that the police powers "are nothing more or less than the powers of government...." But the newer doctrine was recognizing additional purposes for which government might legislate; it did not, of course, deny the traditional concerns of government, among them "morality."

No one seemed disposed to doubt that the legitimate purposes of government included the preservation of morals, public or private. All law indeed may have appeared as an implementation of accepted morality; no one seriously suggested that laws for the preservation of "morals" might not have the clear justification which is obvious in laws having a social purpose of protecting the person or property of others. Morals legislation, like social legislation, might have appeared equally rooted in "the law of nature," which had respectable credentials in the history of American law. It was obvious that the state could forbid persons to enter into a usurious contract, to gamble, to drink intoxicating liquors, to be a prostitute, to visit a prostitute, to commit fornication or adultery with another willing adult, to enter into a polygamous marriage, to utter obscenity, profanity, immorality in act or word. Clearly, too, the state could declare the morality that determined "public policy," relied on in various contexts to frustrate consensual arrangements.

If the challenge had been seriously pressed, some utilitarian reason for these laws might have been found. But they would have been rationalizations and might have been recognized as such. In truth, the legislation reflected traditional morality, and the preservation of this morality was an unquestionable and unquestioned purpose of government. If the Supreme Court glanced at the authority of the state to enact such legislation, it blended moral and utilitarian bases for the legislation in indisputable justification.

Today, a court would probably not begin with the assumption that government has defined purposes and corresponding "inherent," "natural" limitations. The only limitations on the state, a court might say, are the prohibitions of the Constitution -- specific, like those few in the original Constitution, or more general, like those in the Civil War amendments. If one would today examine embedded assumptions about morals legislation, the question, then, is not whether legislation for decency and morality is within the accepted powers of government; we must ask, rather, whether such legislation deprives one to whom it applies of "liberty or property" without due process of law. But if that question looks very different from the one that might have been asked in the nineteenth century, it may be less different that it looks. For some of the "inherent" limitations on the police power may still be with us in notions that the state may legislate only for a "public purpose." And "due process" still requires some link in reason between purpose and the means selected by the legislature to achieve that purpose. We may state the question, then, as whether morality legislation deprives one of liberty or property without due process of law. The subsidiary questions may still be: Is the state's purpose in "morality legislation" a proper public purpose? Are the means used to achieve it "reasonable"?

Emphasis on "public purpose" has usually been intended to exclude legislation for the special interest of some private person or group. Morals legislation presumably does not serve a strictly "private purpose," even if some groups seem more concerned about morals legislation than is the community at large. The beneficiaries of this legislation, it is assumed, are each citizen and the whole community. But is every "nonprivate" purpose a proper public purpose of government? Can the state legislate, not to protect the person or property of others or to promote general economic or social welfare, but to protect and promote "morals," particularly morals reflected -- or violated -- in private activity?

Perhaps the question can have no provable answer. Supporters of legislation like obscenity laws may urge that government has always legislated in support of accepted morality, and may challenge those who would deny the authority of government to find anything in the Constitution that would take it away. But supporters of the past do not have the only word. Others will stress that the due process clause has intervened, and that it requires government to be reasonable, in purpose as well as in means to achieve the purpose. One may even accept the right of the state to impose restrictions on the individual for his own good -- by preventing his suicide, or forcing medical aid, or compelling education; in the context of society, these are "rational" ends, reasonably achieved. But how can "morals," a nonutilitarian, nonrational purpose, be "reasonable"? Could government conjure up some new (or old), nonsocial principle of morality and impose it by law? Could a state forbid me to go to an astrologer -- or require me to go to one or abide by his conclusions? And if history is invoked, does the fact that some behavior has been deemed "immoral" in the past -- by some, even a violation of "natural law" -- render it forever a proper object of legislative prohibition?

Is it sufficient to justify legislation that such acts continue to be regarded as "immoral," "sinful," "offensive" by large segments of the community? Or does the due process clause, in this context too, serve to protect individuals from the irrationalities of the majority and of its representatives?

One may ask, it is suggested, whether any nonutilitarian morality can be a reasonable public purpose of legislation. But purpose aside, due process requires also that the means to achieve that purpose be not unreasonable. Of course, means and purposes are not discrete categories, and purposes may themselves be means to other purposes. But assuming that the preservation of private morals continues to be a proper purpose of government, obscenity legislation, in particular, raises the further question whether suppression of obscenity is reasonably related to the morality that the state seeks to preserve.

The question may be clarified if one compares obscenity laws to other morals legislation, e. g., laws against incest. Incestual relations have indubitably been deemed "immoral," at least since Biblical times. If the state may suppress what is immoral, there can be no doubt about the validity of laws against incest. Exposure to obscenity, on the other hand, is at most a derivative, secondary "immorality." In itself, it has no ancient roots; presumably, it would have been condemned, or frowned on, as inconsistent with admonitions to be holy and to avoid pagan abominations. In modern time, obscenity has been condemned in large part because it corrupts morals or character. Since, I have said, corruption of morals or character has no clear relation to any unlawful acts, or even acts that could be made unlawful, what evidence is required of the state, or what assumptions permitted to it, to support the conclusion that obscenity corrupts morals? What are these "morals" and this "character," and what does their corruption mean? And if we accept the concept of "morals" as well as their corruption, how does one decide whether the state is reasonable in its conclusion that indulgence in obscenity does or does not effect this "corruption" of these "morals"?

The Constitution does not enact legal positivism; it does not enact natural law. Due process, I hypothesize, requires that the state deal with the area of the reasonable and deal with it reasonably. It is proper to ask whether the preservation of a nonsocial morality is within the realm of the reasonable, whether concepts like "private morality" and its corruption are subject to logic and proof inherent in reasonableness and rationality. These, of course, are not merely technical requirements of constitutional jurisprudence. They suggest that the Constitution renders unto government the rational governance of the affairs of man in relation to his neighbor; only if government is kept within this domain can it be limited government, subject to constitutional requirements of rational, reasonable action administered by an impartial judiciary. It is only by confining government to what is reasonable that the Constitution and the courts can protect the individual against the unreasonable. Private "morals," and their "corruption," and what "corrupts" them, as differently conceived, have profound significance in the life of a nation and of its citizens. But they are not in the realm of reason and cannot be judged by standards of reasonableness; they ought not, perhaps, to be in the domain of government.

Civilized societies, including ours, have increased the area of government responsibility to protect one against his neighbor. The authority of government to protect us from ourselves is less clearly recognized today, except when injury to ourselves may in turn have undesirable social consequences; although, we have suggested, one may justify -- within the limits of the "rational" -- governmental efforts to prevent suicide, or compel health measures, "for the individual's own good." When we deal not with physical injury to ourselves but with "sin," respectable and authoritative voices are increasingly heard that there exists " a realm of private morality and immorality which is, in brief and crude terms, not the law's business." Should not the Supreme Court today, or tomorrow, consider whether under the Constitution some morality, at least, may be not the law's business and not appropriate support for legislation consistent with due process of law?

B. The Religious Origins of Morals Legislation

I have suggested the need to examine, in the light of the due process clause, the power of the state to deprive a person of liberty or property for the purpose of preserving "morality" serving no social, utilitarian purpose. Contemporary constitutional doctrine may suggest yet another, related difficulty about obscenity and other morality laws. For the morality that these laws would protect can trace a discernible path back to origins in religious authority. Can government, which may not establish religion, or interfere with the free exercise of religion and non-religion, enforce a morality rooted in religion? Is legislation, the sole or chief purpose of which is the preservation of a quasi-religious morality, consistent with the separation of Church and State now recognized as the law of the Constitution?

Here, history may again appear to claim constitutional immunity for old laws, but here the Supreme Court has already made it clear that history does not say the last word. The prohibitions of the first amendment in regard to religion have only in recent decades been declared applicable to the states by the fourteenth amendment. And for both state and federal government, careful separation of Church from State is doctrine not long articulated and applied. These doctrines have been applied not only to new practices but also to laws that have been with us since before the Constitution. In 1961, for a major example, the Supreme Court re-examined, carefully and at length, the Sunday Blue Laws dating from colonial days. These laws, in origin, were designed to foster and promote religious observance; they were also "morals" legislation, reflecting the attitude that work on the Sabbath was immoral, sinful. The Court upheld the laws, despite rather than because of their history. The Court seemed unanimous that such laws reflecting religious doctrine and serving a religious function would be a forbidden establishment of religion. They could be upheld only because, the majority concluded, the laws had shed their religious origins and purposes and now served primarily an independent, secular, utilitarian, social function.

The Court's opinion in the "Blue Laws" cases is highly relevant to the inquiry we suggest into the validity of "morals legislation" rooted in religion. Immediately, it helps put the inquiry into narrower focus. Of course, the Justices recognized, some morality underlies all law and our morality and our laws can be followed back to roots in the Bible. Surely, the fact that the mass of our traditional laws reflects a morality rooted in religion, or once identified with religion, raises no constitutional question either serious or substantial. The growth of the secular state -- even on Erastian principles -- and notions of strict separation of Church and State could not have signified any general rejection of this traditional morality. The morality reflected in most of our common laws, moreover, has lost its religious origins and shares with the law of the mass of organized mankind a modern, utilitarian social basis. Laws punishing homicide or theft, though they, too, may have religious roots by way of notions of "natural law" and the Bible (we still refer to them as malum in se), are obviously within the power of the most secular state, subject to the most rigorous constitutional limitations, living by strictest doctrines of limited government.

The constitutional issue begins to stir when we deal with legislation reflecting our particular morality -- when the religious origins are more apparent and persistent, when the law is not common to all civilized nations, when it has no clear utilitarian basis. Some crimes I have mentioned -- polygamy and incest, adultery and fornication, gambling, intoxication, usury -- find their origin in notions of morality rooted in our particular history, the values of the American nation inevitably derived from ancestral voices raised on the moral teachings of the Bible.[1] These laws clearly embody ancient religious attitudes not yet dissipated or diluted although now wearing secular garb. Is it a form of establishment of religion for the state to impose this nonsocial religious morality? Is it, perhaps, an interference with the free exercise of nonreligion by those who do not accept the religious principles and religious authority from which this morality emanates?

The argument need not be taken too far. As to many laws that originate in Biblical morality, it may be urged that, like the Blue Laws, they too have shed their religious origins. The morals of a people are a present reality regardless of their sources. Whatever their roots, whatever their erstwhile function or context in religious observance, laws against incest or polygamy, for example, now reflect mores and institutions -- in particular, the family -- that are the fabric of our society.[2] Moreover, many morals crimes rooted in the Bible -- incest, polygamy, usury, perhaps also adultery -- may find some secular rationalization or justification, some valid governmental purpose even in a secular state, some concern defined in terms of categorical imperative, of avoiding injury to others, of achieving some social aim. That other morals crimes, however, retain heavy traces of their religious origin is evidenced, in part, by the fact that they are not universally punished as crimes and cannot be credibly rationalized. What secular purpose based on injury to others, or to the group, can justify laws against private homosexuality between willing adults? Against other forms of private sodomy? Against various practices of the conjugal bed, including contraception? Against "profanity," "sacrilege," "immorality," "obscenity"? In these cases, one may argue, the religious elements are clear and predominant. Most would accept that it would be a forbidden establishment of religion, or interference with freedom of religion, if the state sought to prohibit taking the name of the Lord in vain or making graven images; why may the state constitutionally forbid homosexuality? The state could not, probably, prohibit private blasphemy or sacrilege; why may it prohibit obscenity?

Different elements in traditional morality may retain different residues of religious origin. That no credible secular rationalization has grown up to support an ancient morality, that the morality is not shared alike by other societies, by all religions, by religious and nonreligious, may be some evidence of abiding nonrational content identified with particular religious conceptions. Different laws may also retain, in different degrees, a present religious function in support of present religious practice or Church interest. In those instances, links between religion and morality, between religion and morality-legislation, are not wholly and clearly broken, In regard to morality laws, too, the separation of Church and State may require the drawing of constitutional lines and the measuring of constitutional degrees.

Perhaps the objection that some morals legislation imposes a religious morality is a facet of the earlier argument that morals legislation cannot be rationally supported. For in substantial part the effect, if not the purpose, of constitutional provisions forbidding religious establishment and guaranteeing the free exercise of religion is also to bar the interference of government in the realm of the nonrational, the sacred precincts of personal belief, the personal "Answer," even personal idiosyncrasy. The domain of government, it is suggested, is that in which social problems are resolved by rational social processes, in which men can reason together, can examine problems and propose solutions capable of objective proof or persuasion, subject to objective scrutiny by courts and electors. I ask whether legislation that is based on a particular religion, even on what is common to many religions, on what is supported by history only, on what is not capable of reasoned consideration and solution, is rendered unto government by the Constitution.

IV. Conclusion

Laws against obscenity reflect values of morality, decency, and modesty inherited from an earlier age and from religious ancestors. These laws reflect, too, assumptions about the nature of character and morals; they assume a concept of "corruption of morals" and assume that obscene material has such a corrupting effect. The roots, the purposes, and the assumptions must be taken into account in any considerations of the constitutionality of obscenity laws. These are relevant in regard to the freedom of communication affected by obscenity laws. They must be considered, too, in relation to the freedom of the individual to obtain and indulge -- at least privately -- even in what others may consider obscene. I have asked whether the morality that is the concern of obscenity laws, and of other morals legislation, is still the law's business and so a valid purpose for legislation under the due process clause. I have asked whether the perpetuation by government of a morality religious in origin and having no present social purpose is a form of establishment of religion, and interference with the free exercise of "nonreligion," forbidden to both state and federal governments. I have suggested that perhaps the Constitution denies to government and to majorities the domain of the nonrational, leaving private morality to Church, and Home, and Conscience. I suggest that perhaps, at least, legislatures might be required to re-examine old laws based on moral and religious views of an earlier day, to identify motives and purposes for regulation presently acceptable, and to determine anew whether and which regulation is now called for.

That the "morals" character of obscenity laws should have been considered in determining their validity as exceptions to the freedom of communication seems obvious; the further hypothesis that at least when applied to private indulgence obscenity laws may raise serious questions of liberty and privacy is perhaps novel. What is suggested implies that in the generalities of "due process of law" may lie unexplored limitations on government to regulate individual action in the name of "morals," and that when the morals protected are rooted in particular religious dogma and reflect no utilitarian social purpose there is substantial question whether the separation of Church and State has been breached. Of course, any such limitations would further increase the claim of liberty against the claims of representative democracy. But that appears to be the direction of the Constitution. While substantive due process long ago ceased to imply limits on government regulation for general economic and social welfare, it has increasingly provided doctrine to support individual freedom of action or expression, frequently even against regulations claiming some utilitarian, social purpose. Substantive due process has, in particular, provided protection for liberties and privacies claimed by one who would be let alone, who does not seek freedom to impinge on others. Clearly the Constitution, both in the first and fourteenth amendments, has been read liberally to limit government when it interferes with freedom of religion, including freedom from religion. But if the doctrine is novel, its consequences need not be revolutionary. It aims particularly at the intrusion of law into private indulgence by adults in acts that are not apparently antisocial. Public activity, commercial exploitation, the "morals" of children, involve additional questions that may suggest differences of degree and the drawing of lines.

Of course, it should be clear, I have asserted hypotheses for further consideration. That the government may act only for social purpose, for the protection of persons and property, is doctrine easy to state, and perhaps no more difficult to apply than some other constitutional doctrine. But the right of the state to legislate in the field of morals, to deprive the citizen of liberty or property for the sake of accepted notions of morality, is deeply part of our law; some will argue that it is beyond question or need for justification. It asks much of the Supreme Court to tell legislators, and communal groups behind them, that what has long been deemed the law's business is no longer, that even large majorities or a "general consensus" cannot have their morality written into official law. And a reluctant Court can find support in history, and some among the philosophers.

The philosophers are not irrelevant. I have attempted, it will have been observed, to set forth the constitutional arguments against laws that govern private morals without injecting the differences which regularly agitate the universe of political philosophy. One must yet note the current controversy, across the seas from our Constitution, where Lord Devlin and Professor Hart have provided a contemporary version of nineteenth century debate: whether it is proper, justified, desirable, even necessary, for government to enforce by law the common nonutilitarian morality. By my hypotheses, the United States would be a polity nearer the heart of Professor Hart, and of John Stuart Mill. To their philosophical arguments, we have added the special concerns of the American Constitution: that government shall be limited; that the limitations should be subject and susceptible to judicial scrutiny and enforcement; that legislatures shall therefore be limited to the rational and the reasonable; that, in addition -- for reasons particular to our society -- legislatures are debarred from enacting those nonrationalities of the majority which reflect its religions. Lord Devlin, of course, might dismiss us as, for these reasons, a special case. But Lord Devlin may find himself, instead, adopted by Supreme Court Justices reluctant to accept the hypotheses proposed. They may respond to his view that the enforcement by law of a people's morality is essential to the existence of a society, and accept his deduction that therefore "the suppression of vice is as much the law's business as the suppression of subversive activities"; if so, they are not likely to find that the Constitution stands in the way. With Professor Hart, I might accept Lord Devlin's proposition that the preservation of a nation's "morality" is essential to its ultimate cohesiveness, but I could hardly agree that "morality" as there used includes every element of popular attitude which is called "morals," particularly those few and special attitudes to the private indulgences which are our subject. In any event, whether on grounds rooted in history or in philosophy, the Supreme Court might yet proclaim that even under our Constitution the morals of the people, whatever they are and in all respects, may be enforced by law. The Court will still have to justify this pronouncement under today's Constitution; it will have to struggle, in particular, to distinguish and divide between the people's morals and its religions, its superstitions, its prejudices.

What is important is that the underlying questions be recognized and considered, in the context of concrete cases, in the light of new facts, new insights, new views of morality, new readings of the Constitution. Obscenity laws, at least those directed at private adult acts done privately, provide the Supreme Court an occasion to recognize and wrestle with the problem of morals legislation under the Constitution. If the Court will not look afresh at obscenity laws, particularly in its private aspects, other morals legislation may soon afford the court another occasion. It is time to begin to examine -- if only in order to justify -- the right of constitutional government to legislate morality which has no secular, utilitarian, or social purpose. It is time to attempt to define and articulate the extent to which the religious antecedents of our values may continue to motivate our governments in the enactment and enforcement of law. The Court, one may hope, will begin to attempt to disentangle and separate crime from sin in a secular country having warm feelings toward its religions and its religious ancestry, and having the strong conviction that the wall between Church and State is a good fence making good neighbors.

Notes

1. For the prohibitions on incest, sodomy, and adultery see particularly *Leviticus*, chs. 18 & 20. See also Leviticus 19:29, Deuteronomy 23:17 (prostitution). The prohibition on polygamy is also of old standing and has religious sanction although it is postbiblical. *But see* 1 *Timothy* 3:2. Since polygamy was not forbidden, the original biblical prohibition of adultery applied only to extramarital cohabitation by a married woman, not be a married man. In the King James translation, the word "adultery" appears sometimes to be used for any forbidden sexual act. *Cf.*, *e.g.*, *Exodus* 20:14. For the prohibitions on usury see *Exodus* 22:25, *Leviticus* 25:35-37, *Deuteronomy* 23:19-20. (Compare, for example, an old usury statute, 13 Eliz. c. 8, which included: "all usury, being forbidden by the law of God, is sin and detestable....") The use of intoxicating liquors was forbidden to one who took the Nazirite vows, see *Numbers* 6:3-4, and to the priests in service. *Leviticus* 10:9.

Also relevant, as sources of religious authority for other prohibitions an "immorality," are general exhortations and commandments, *e.g.*, "Ye shall be holy." *Leviticus* 19:2.

2. When the Supreme Court upheld the application of antipolygamy laws to the Mormons, it saw no question about the power of Congress to enact such laws and to apply them generally. The only issue the Court dealt with was the claim that these laws invaded the religious freedom of the Mormons. In that context it justified these laws as clearly proper because polygamy has always been "odious" to the nations of Western Europe, and because of its social consequences. See Reynolds v. United States, 98 U.S. 145, 164-66 (1879). Blending social and moral objections, the Court also found polygamy "to shock the moral judgment of the Community," and referred to "acts, recognized by the general consent of the Christian world in modern times as proper matters for prohibitory legislation." Davis v. Beason, 133 U.S. 333, 341, 343 (1889); *cf.* Cleveland v. United States, 329 U.S. 14, 18-19 (1946). *But cf.* Musser v. Utah, 333 U.S. 95 (1948)....

The American Law Institute has devoted considerable effort to developing a model code of criminal laws. Here, Professor Schwartz discusses the rationale which guided the morals offenses section of the 1962 draft of the Model Penal Code. This article was written as a companion piece to the previous article by Professor Louis Henkin.

Professor Schwartz's article is reprinted from 63 Columbia Law Review (1963) with the kind permission of the editors of Columbia Law Review and the author, grateful acknowledgment is made for permission to reprint here.

Louis B. Schwartz is Professor of Law, University of Pennsylvania and Co-Reporter, Model Penal Code.

Morals Offenses and the Model Penal Code

by Louis B. Schwartz

What are the "offenses against morals"? One thinks first of the sexual offenses, adultery, fornication, sodomy, incest, and prostitution, and then, by easy extension, of such sex-related offenses as bigamy, abortion, open lewdness, and obscenity. But if one pauses to reflect on what sets these apart from offenses "against the person," or "against property," or "against public administration," it becomes evident that sexual offenses do not involve violation of moral principles in any peculiar sense. Virtually the entire penal code expresses the community's ideas of morality, or at least of the most egregious immoralities. To steal, to kill, to swear falsely in legal proceedings -- these are certainly condemned as much by moral and religious as by secular standards. It also becomes evident that not all sexual behavior commonly condemned by prevailing American penal laws can be subsumed under universal moral precepts. This is certainly the case as to laws regulating contraception and abortion. But it is also true of such relatively uncontroversial (in the Western World) "morals" offenses as bigamy and polygamy; plural marriage arrangements approved by great religions of the majority of mankind can hardly be condemned out-of-hand as "immoralities."

What truly distinguishes the offenses commonly thought of as "against morals" is not their relation to morality but the absence of ordinary justification for punishment by a non-theocratic state. The ordinary justification for secular penal controls is preservation of public order. The king's peace must not be disturbed, or, to put the matter in the language of our time, public security must be preserved. Individuals must be able to go about their lawful pursuits without fear of attack, plunder, or other harms. This is an interest that only organized law enforcement can effectively safeguard. If individuals had to protect themselves by restricting their movements to avoid dangerous persons or neighborhoods, or by restricting their investments for fear of violent dispossession, or by employing personal bodyguards and armed private police, the economy would suffer, the body politic would be rent be conflict of private armies, and men would still walk in fear.

No such results impend from the commission of "morals offenses." One has only to stroll along certain streets in Amsterdam to see that prostitution may be permitted to flourish openly without impairing personal security, economic prosperity, or indeed the general moral tone of a most respected nation of the Western World. Tangible interests are not threatened by a neighbor's rash decision to marry two wives or (to vary the case for readers who may see this as economic suicide) by a lady's decision to be supported by two husbands, assuming that the arrangement is by agreement of all parties directly involved. An obscene show, the predilection of two deviate males for each other, or the marriage of first cousins -- all these leave nonparticipants perfectly free to pursue their own goals without fear or obstacle....What the dominant lawmaking groups appear to be seeking by means of morals legislation is not security and freedom in their own affairs but restraint of conduct by others that is regarded as offensive.

Accordingly, Professor Louis Henkin has suggested that morals legislation may contravene constitutional provisions designed to protect liberty, especially the liberty to do as one pleases without legal constraints based solely on religious beliefs. There is wisdom in his warning, and it is the purpose of this article to review in the light of that warning some of the Model Penal Code sections that venture into the difficult area of morals legislation. Preliminarily, I offer some general observations on the point of view that necessarily governed the American Law Institute as a group of would-be lawmakers. We were sensitive, I hope, to the supreme value of individual liberty, but aware also that neither legislatures nor court will soon accept a radical change in the boundary between permissible social controls and constitutionally protected nonconformity.

I. Considerations in Appraising Morals Legislation

The first proposition I would emphasize is that a

statute appearing to express nothing but religious or moral ideas is often defensible on secular grounds. Perhaps an unrestricted flow of obscenity will encourage illicit sexuality or violent assaults on women, as some proponents of the ban believe. Perhaps polygamy and polyandry as well as adultery are condemnable on Benthamite grounds. Perhaps tolerance of homosexuality will undermine the courage and discipline of our citizen militia, notwithstanding contrary indications drawn from the history of ancient Greece. The evidence is hopelessly inconclusive. Professor Henkin and I may believe that those who legislate morals are minding other peoples' business, not their own, but the great majority of people believe that the morals of "bad" people do, at least in the long run, threaten the security of the "good" people. Thus, they believe that it is their own business they are minding. And that belief is not demonstrably false, any more than it is demonstrably true. It is hard to deny people the right to legislate on the basis of their beliefs not demonstrably erroneous, especially if these beliefs are strongly held by a very large majority. The majority cannot be expected to abandon a credo and its associated sensitivities, however irrational, in deference to a minority's skepticism.

The argument of the preceding paragraph does not mean that all laws designed to enforce morality are acceptable or constitutionally valid if enough people entertain a baseless belief in their social utility. The point is rather that recognizing irrational elements in the controversy over morals legislation, we ought to focus on other elements, about which rational debate and agreement are possible. For example, one can examine side effects of the effort to enforce morality by penal law. One can inquire whether enforcement will be so difficult that the offense will seldom be prosecuted and, therefore, risk of punishment will not in fact operate as a deterrent. One can ask whether the rare prosecutions for sexual derelictions are arbitrarily selected, or facilitate private blackmail or police discriminations more often than general compliance with legal norms. Are police forces, prosecution resources, and court time being wastefully diverted from the central insecurities of our metropolitan life -- robbery, burglary, rape, assault, and governmental corruption?

A second proposition that must be considered in appraising morals legislation is that citizens may legitimately demand of the state protection of their psychological as well as their physical integrity. No one challenges this when the protection takes the form of penal laws guarding against fear caused by threat or menace. This is probably because these are regarded as incipient physical attacks. Criminal libel laws are clearly designed to protect against psychic pain; so also are disorderly conduct laws insofar as they ban loud noises, offensive odors, and tumultuous behavior disturbing the peace. In fact, laws against murder, rape, arson, robbery, burglary, and other violent felonies afford not so much protection against direct attack -- that can be done only by self-defense or by having a policeman on hand at the scene of the crime -- as psychological security and comfort stemming from the knowledge that the probabilities of attack are lessened by the prospect of punishment and, perhaps, from the knowledge that an attacker will be condignly treated by society.

If, then, penal law frequently or typically protects us from psychic aggression, there is basis for the popular expectation that it will protect us also from blasphemy against a cherished religion, outrage to patriotic sentiments, blatant pornography, open lewdness affronting our sensibilities in the area of sexual mores, or stinging aspersions against race or nationality. Psychiatrists might tell us that the insecurities stirred by these psychic aggressions are deeper and more acute than those involved in crimes of physical violence. Physical violence is, after all, a phenomenon that occurs largely in the domain of the ego; we can rationally measure the danger and its likelihood, and our countermeasures can be proportioned to the threat. But who can measure the dark turbulences of the unconscious when sex, race, religion or patriotism (that extension of father-reverence) is the concern?

If unanimity of strongly held moral views is approached in a community, the rebel puts himself, as it were, outside the society when he arraigns himself against those views. Society owes a debt to martyrs, madmen, criminals, and professors who occasionally call into question its fundamental assumptions, but the community cannot be expected to make their first protests respectable or even tolerated by law. It is entirely understandable and in a sense proper that blasphemy should have been criminal in Puritan Massachusetts, and that cow slaughter in a Hindu state, hog-raising in a theocratic Jewish or Moslem state, or abortion in a ninety-nine per cent Catholic state should be criminal. I do not mean to suggest a particular percentage test of substantial unanimity. It is rather a matter of when an ancient and unquestioned tenet has become seriously debatable in a given community. This may happen when it is discovered that a substantial, although inarticulate, segment of the population has drifted away from the old belief. It may happen when smaller numbers of articulate opinion-makers launch an open attack on the old ethic. When this kind of a beach-head has been established in the hostile country of traditional faith, then, and only then, can we expect constitutional principles to restrain the fifty-one per cent majority from suppressing the public flouting of deeply held moral views.

Some may find in all this an encouragement of approval of excessive conservatism. Societies, it seems, are by this argument morally entitled to use force to hold back the development of new ways of thought. I do not mean it so. Rather, I see this tendency to enforce old moralities as an inherent characteristic of organized societies, and I refraim from making moral judgments on group behavior that I regard as inevitable. If I must make a moral judgment, it is in favor of the individual visionaries who are willing to pay the personal cost to challenge the old moral order. There is a morality in some lawbreaking, even when we cannot condemn the law itself as immoral, for it enables conservative societies to begin the re-examination of even the most cherished principles.

Needless to say, recognizing the legitimacy of the demand for protection against psychic discomfort does not imply indiscriminate approval of laws intended to give such protection. Giving full recognition to that demand, we may still find that other considerations are the controlling ones. Can we satisfy the demand without impairing other vital interests? How can we protect religious feelings without "establishing" religion or impairing the free exercise of proselytizing faiths? How can we protect racial sensibilities without exacerbating race hatreds and erecting a government censorship of discussion? How shall we prevent pain and disgust to many who are deeply offended by portrayal of sensuality without stultifying our artists and writers?

A third aspect of morals legislation that will enter into the calculations of the rational legislator is that some protection against offensive immorality may be achieved as a by-product of legislation that aims directly at something other than immorality. We may be uneasy about attempting to regulate private sexual behavior, but we will not be so hesitant in prohibiting the commercialization of vice. This is a lesser intrusion on freedom of choice in personal relations. It presents a more realistic target for police activity. And conceptually such regulation presents itself as a ban on a form of economic activity rather than a regulation of morals. It is not the least of the advantages of this approach that it preserves to some extent the communal disapproval of illicit sexuality, thus partially satisfying those who would really prefer outright regulation of morality. So also, we may be reluctant to penalize blasphemy or sacrilege, but feel compelled to penalize the mischievous or zealous blasphemer who purposely disrupts a religious meeting or procession with utterances designed to outrage the sensibilities of the group and thus provoke a riot. Reasonable rules for the maintenance of public peace incidentally afford a measure of protection against offensive irreligion. Qualms about public "establishment" of religion must yield to the fact that the alternative would be to permit a kind of violent private interference with freedom to conduct religious ceremonies.

It remains to apply the foregoing analysis to selected provisions of the Model Penal Code.

. . . .

The obscenity provisions of the Model Penal Code best illustrate the Code's preference for an oblique approach to morals offenses, i.e., the effort to express the moral impulses of the community in a penal prohibition that is nevertheless pointed at and limited to something else than sin. In this case the target is not the "sin of obscenity," but primarily a disapproved form of economic activity -- commercial exploitation of the widespread weakness for titillation by pornography. This is apparent not only from the narrow definition of "obscene" in section 251.4 of the Code, but even more from the narrow definition of the forbidden behavior; only sale, advertising, or public exhibition are forbidden, and noncommercial dissemination within a restricted circle of personal associates is expressly exempt.

Section 251.4 defines obscenity as material whose "predominant appeal is to prurient interest...." The emphasis is on the "appeal" of the material, rather than on its "effect," an emphasis designed explicitly to reject prevailing definitions of obscenity that stress the "effect."[1] This effect is traditionally identified as a tendency to cause "sexually impure and lustful thoughts" or to "corrupt or deprave."[2] The Comments on section 251.4 take the position that repression of sexual thoughts and desires is not a practicable or legitimate legislative goad. Too many instigations to sexual desire exist in a society like ours, which approves much eroticism in literature, movies, and advertising, to suppose that any conceivable repression of pornography would substantially diminish the volume of such impulses. Moreover, "thoughts and desires not manifested in overt antisocial behavior are generally regarded as the exclusive concern of the individual and his spiritual advisors."[3] The Comments, rejecting also the test of tendency to corrupt or deprave, point out that corruption or depravity are attributes of character inappropriate for secular punishment when they do not lead to misconduct, and there is a paucity of evidence linking obscenity to misbehavior.[4]

The meretricious "appeal" of a book or picture is essentially a question of the attractiveness of the merchandise from a certain point of view: what makes it sell. Thus, the prohibition of obscenity takes on an aspect of regulation of unfair business or competitive practices. Just as merchants may be prohibited from selling their wares by appeal to the public's weakness for gambling, so they may be restrained from purveying books, movies, or other commercial exhibition by exploiting the well-nigh universal weakness for a look behind the curtain of modesty. This same philosophy of obscenity control is evidenced by the Code provision outlawing advertising appeals that attempt to sell material "whether or not obscene, by representing or suggesting that it is obscene."[5] Moreover, the requirement under section 251.4 that the material go "substantially beyond customary limits of candor" serves to exclude from criminality the sorts of appeal to eroticism that, being prevalent, can hardly give a particular purveyor a commercial advantage.

It is important to recognize that material may predominantly "appeal" to prurient interest notwithstanding that ordinary adults may actually respond to the material with feelings of aversion or disgust. Section 251.4 explicitly encompasses material dealing with excretory functions as well as sex, which the customer is likely to find both repugnant and "shameful" and yet attractive in a morbid, compelling way. Not recognizing that material may be repellent and appealing at the same time, two distinguished commentators on the Code's obscenity provisions have criticized the "appeal" formula, asserting that "hard core pornography," concededly the main category we are trying to repress, has no appeal for "ordinary adults," who instead would be merely repelled by the material.[6] Common experience suggests the contrary. It is well known that policemen, lawyers, and judges involved in obscenity cases not infrequently regale their fellows with viewings of the criminal material. Moreover, a poll conducted by this author among his fellow law professors -- "mature" and, for the present purposes, "ordinary" adults -- evoked uniformly affirmative answers to the following question: "would you look inside a book that you had been certainly informed has grossly obscene hard-core pornography if you were absolutely sure that no one else would ever learn that you had looked?" It is not an answer to this bit of amateur sociological research to say that people would look "out of curiosity." It is precisely such shameful curiosity to which "appeal" is made by the obscene, as the word "appeal" is used in section 251.4.

Lockhart and McClure, the two commentators referred to above, prefer a "variable obscenity" concept over the Institute's "constant obscenity" concept. Under the "constant obscenity" concept, material is normally judged by reference to "ordinary adults."[7] The "variable obscenity" concept always takes account of the nature of the contemplated audience; material would be obscene if it is "primarily directed to an audience of the sexually immature for the purpose of satisfying their craving for erotic fantasy."[8] The preference for "variable obscenity" rests not only on the mistaken view that hard-core pornography does not appeal to ordinary adults, but also on the ground that this concept facilitates the accomplishment of several ancillary legislative goals, namely, exempting transactions in "obscene" materials by persons with scholarly, scientific, or other legitimate interests in the obscene and prohibiting the advertising of material "not intrinsically pornographic as if it were hard-core pornography."[9] The Code accomplishes these results by explicit exemption for justifiable transactions in the obscene and by specific prohibition of suggestive advertising. This still seems to me the better way to draft a criminal statute.

The Code's exemption for justifiable dealing in obscene material provides a workable criterion of public gain in permitting defined categories of transactions. It requires no analysis of the psyche of customers to see whether they are sexually immature or given to unusual craving for erotic fantasy. It makes no impractical demand on the sophistication of policemen, magistrates, customs officers, or jurymen. The semantics of the variable obscenity concept assumes without basis that the Kinsey researchers were immune to the prurient appeal of the materials with which they worked. Would it not be a safe psychiatric guess that some persons are drawn into research of this sort precisely to satisfy in a socially approved way the craving that Lockhart and McClure deplore? In any event, it seems a confusing distortion of language to say that a pornographic picture is not obscene as respects the blasé (sexually mature?) shopkeeper who stocks it, the policeman who confiscates it, or the Model Penal Code Reporter who appraises it.

As for the prohibition against suggestive advertising, this is certainly handled more effectively by explicitly declaring the advertisement criminal without regard to the "obscene" character of the material advertised than by the circumlocution that an advertisement is itself to be regarded as obscene if it appeals to the cravings of the sexually immature. That kind of test will prove more than a little troublesome for the advertising departments of some respectable literary journals.

If the gist of section 251.4 is, as suggested above, commercial exploitation of the weakness for obscenity, the question arises whether the definition of the offense should not be formulated in terms of "pandering to an interest in obscenity," i.e., "exploiting such an interest primarily for pecuniary gain...."[10] This proposal, made by Professor Henry Hart, a member of the Criminal Law Advisory Committee, was rejected because of the indefiniteness of "exploiting...primarily for pecuniary gain," and because it would clearly authorize a bookseller, for example, to procure any sort of hard-core pornography upon the unsolicited order of a customer. "Exploiting...primarily for pecuniary gain" is not a formula apt for guiding either judicial interpretation or merchants' behavior. It is not clear what the prosecution would have to prove beyond sale of the objectionable item. Would advertising or an excessive profit convert sale into "exploitation"? Would the formula leave a bookseller free to enjoy a gradually expanding trade in obscenity so long as he kept his merchandise discreetly under the counter and let word-of-mouth publicize the availability of his tidbits? Despite these difficulties, it may well be that the Code section on obscenity has a constitutional infirmity of the sort that concerned Professor Henkin insofar as the section restricts the freedom of an adult to buy, and thus to read, whatever he pleases. This problem might be met by framing an appropriate exemption for such transactions to be added to those now set forth in subsection (3).

The rejection of the Hart "pandering" formulation highlights another aspect of section 251.4, namely, its applicability to a class of completely noncommercial transactions that could not conceivably be regarded as "pandering." This ban on certain noncommercial disseminations results from the fact that subsection (2) forbids every dissemination except those exempted by subsection (3), and subsection (3) exempts noncommercial dissemination only if it is limited to "personal associates of the actor." Thus, a general distribution or exhibition of obscenity is prohibited even though no one is making money from it: a zealot for sex education may not give away pamphlets at the schoolyard gates containing illustrations of people engaged in erotic practices; a rich homosexual may not use a billboard on Times Square to promulgate to the general populace the techniques and pleasures of sodomy. Plainly, this is not the economic regulation to which I have previously tried to assimilate the Code's anti-obscenity regulations. But equally, it is not merely sin-control of the sort that evoked Professor Henkin's constitutional doubts. Instead, the community is merely saying: "Sin, if you must, in private. Do not flaunt your immoralities where they will grieve and shock others. If we do not impose our morals upon you, neither must you impose yours upon us, undermining the restraints we seek to cultivate through family, church, and school." The interest being protected is not, directly or exclusively, the souls of those who might be depraved or corrupted by the obscenity, but the right of parents to shape the moral notions of their children, and the right of the general public not to be subjected to violent psychological affront. [Professor Schwartz also discussed private immorality, prostitution, and abortion.]

Notes

1. See MPC [sec.] 207.10, comment 6 at 19, 29 (Tent. Draft No. 6, 1957) ([sec.] 207.10 was subsequently renumbered [sec.] 251.4).

2. See MPC [sec] 207.10, comment 6 at 19 n.21, 21 (Tent. Draft No. 6, 1957).

3. MPC [sec.] 207.10, comment 6 at 20 (Tent. Draft No. 6, 1957).

4. MPC [sec.] 207.10, comment 6 at 22-28 (Tent. Draft No. 6, 1957).

5. MPC [sec.] 251.4(2) (e). Equivalent provisions appear in some state laws. _E.g._, N. Y. Pen. Law [sec.] 1141. There is some doubt whether federal obscenity laws reach such advertising. See Manual Enterprises, Inc. v. Day, 370 U.S. 478, 491 (1962). _But see_ United States v. Hornick, 229 F.2d 120, 121 (3rd Cir. 1956). [Also, _Ginzburg v. United States_, 383 U.S. 463 (1966).]

6. See Lockhart & McClure, _Censorship of Obscenity: The Developing Constitutional Standards_, 45 Minn. L. Rev. 72-73 (1960).

7. The Model Penal Code employs the "variable obscenity" concept in part, since [sec.] 251.4(1) provides that "appeal" shall be judged with reference to the susceptibilities of children or other specially susceptible audience when it appears that the material is designed for or directed to such an audience.

8. Lockhart & McClure, _supra_ note 27, at 79.

9. _Ibid._

10. MPC [sec.] 207.10(1) (Tent. Draft No. 6, 1957) (alternative).

The case of Ginzburg v. U. S., 383 U. S. 463 (1966) created a virtual storm among legal scholars. Some damned it, others accepted it but noted its questionable elements and implications, and a few found it good. The following series of articles, and excerpts thereof, illustrate the reaction of the legal estate to Ginzburg, and suggest many unsolved problems.

The attention given to Ginzburg may seem excessive; however, the case is worth study for it illustrates how a trend may be reversed, and how complex are the implications of any given case.

For examination of the Ginzburg case in non-legal journals, see Jason Epstein, "The Obscenity Business," 218 Atlantic Monthly (August, 1966), pp. 65-70; Leon Friedman, "The Ginzburg Decision and the Law," 36 American Scholar (Winter, 1966-67), pp. 71-91; and "Playboy Interview: Ralph Ginzburg," 13 Playboy (July, 1966), p. 13ff.

In the following article Professor Henry P. Monaghan points out how inadequacies of the Roth test came to roost in the 1966 cases. The article is reprinted by permission of The Yale Law Journal Company and Fred B. Rothman and Company from The Yale Law Journal, Vol. 76, pp. 127-157; grateful acknowledgement is made to The Yale Law Journal, to Fred B. Rothman and Company, and to the author for permission to reprint here.

Henry P. Monaghan is Assoc. Professor of Law, Boston University.

Obscenity, 1966: The Marriage of Obscenity Per Se and Obscenity Per Quod

Henry P. Monaghan

In a widely admired article, Harry Kalven argued that the New York Times case[1] embodies the "central meaning" of the First Amendment. On his view, in a free, open society, maximum protection must be accorded to "political" speech. He concluded that the right freely to criticize the government must lie at the center of any adequate theory of the First Amendment.

It is not so easy to make a comparable claim about the relationship between obscenity and the First Amendment. The Supreme Court's conception of obscenity is partially responsible. While the Court in Roth v. United States (1957) explicitly barred "obscenity" from the protection of the First Amendment, it defined the term so that only a marginal class of writings warranted the label. Obscenity was given enough precision so that obscenity prosecutions were unlikely to result in the loss of much of value, a result which was reinforced by the Court's parallel concern with local enforcement methods -- a First Amendment due process, if you will. In this respect, the 1966 obscenity decisions, Memoirs v. Massachusetts, Ginzburg v. United States and Mishkin v. New York, do not appear to portend fundamental changes. Attempts to suppress Eros, The Housewife's Handbook on Selective Promiscuity, and Mr. Mishkin's collection of So Firm So Fully Packed and The Strap Returns, etc., are not to be equated with the attempted suppression of Lady Chatterley's Lover, Memoirs of Hecate County or Strange Fruit, all of which felt the censors' crushing heel but a few short years ago. Nor is the literary importance of Edmund Wilson and Lillian Smith likely to be confused with that of Ralph Ginzburg and Edward Mishkin. Obscenity litigation in 1966 remains concerned with writings of little or no importance, as it has for nearly a decade.

The foregoing analysis is, however, unsatisfying.

Many people have no desire whatever to read Ulysses or Memoirs of Hecate County; their tastes run to Eros or The Strap Returns. And the 1966 decisions, even more than Roth, permit the state severely to restrict their reading fare. The existence of this governmental power of suppression demands explanation in any coherent "general theory" of the First Amendment.

Before 1966 the crucial question in obscenity prosecutions centered on the book itself; was it obscene per se? The new rulings have added another category -- a form of variable obscenity or obscenity per quod -- books assumed not to be obscene per se but which because of extrinsic facts ("the circumstances of production, sale and publicity") may be treated as such. The question is whether obscenity doctrine, vintage 1966, can be reconciled with the First Amendment.

I. Obscenity and a "General Theory" of the First Amendment

Though others disagree, I think that in terms of result Roth stands as one of the liberal hallmarks in Supreme Court history. The important question there was not whether obscenity would be sheltered by the First Amendment, but rather how broadly that term would be defined. . . . the Court explicitly rejected the view of The Queen v. Hicklin, which allowed the obscene character of a book to be judged by the effect of isolated excerpts upon particularly susceptible persons -- a standard which would threaten much serious literature. The First Amendment barred such a definition, said Mr. Justice Brennan, because it protects works unless they are "utterly without redeeming social importance." Thus, at a minimum, any book possessing literary, artistic or scientific value could not be classified as obscene, whatever its erotic characteristics. Moreover, Justice Brennan refused to measure obscenity by the impact of isolated passages on the particularly susceptible. Rather, the inquiry must be:

> whether to the average person, applying contemporary community standards, the dominant theme of the material taken as a whole appeals to the prurient interest.[2]

Soon thereafter Justices Harlan and Stewart added a third

ingredient to the constitutional definition of obscenity: books could not be pronounced obscene unless they were patently offensive -- "so offensive on their face as to affront community standards of decency."[3]

The crucial result of Roth seems to me beyond contradiction. No serious, complex work may be suppressed as obscene. But result is one thing, and adequacy of opinion quite another. The Court scarcely made an attempt to reconcile governmental power to repress obscenity with a comprehensive theory of the First Amendment. Nor, as a substitute, did it even construct a "special" theory for obscenity adequate to resolve future obscenity problems.

The inadequacy of Mr. Justice Brennan's opinion in Roth becomes evident from its context. When the case was in the court of appeals,[4] Judge Frank, in an elaborate and learned concurring opinion, questioned whether obscenity prosecutions could on principle be reconciled with the First Amendment. He particularly attacked the assumption that obscenity triggered anti-social conduct, and argued that the supporting evidence was far too insubstantial to justify suppression. Framed in these terms, the constitutional question presented to the Supreme Court was most difficult; why could speech be repressed where there was no solid basis for believing that it caused immediate harm? This question raises the sharpest problems of the relationship between the legislature and the Court on civil liberties questions. A legislative finding that obscenity is harmful might fairly be inferred from the pervasiveness of obscenity legislation. But, as Dennis v. United States held, a legislative finding of harm cannot be conclusive on the courts in First Amendment cases, for then the First Amendment would exist only at legislative sufferance. Rather, speech may be suppressed only after a judicial determination that it presents a clear and probable danger of serious harm. And Judge Frank demonstrated that on the available evidence, obscenity legislation failed this test.

The Supreme Court responded that Judge Frank had been asking the wrong questions. Obscenity, wrote Mr. Justice Brennan, is unprotected by the First Amendment not because it is harmful, but because it is worthless:

> All ideas having even the slightest redeeming social importance -- unorthodox ideas, contro-

> versial ideas, even ideas hateful to the prevailing climate of opinion -- have the full protection of the guaranties, unless excludable because they encroach upon the limited area of more important interests. But implicit in the history of the First Amendment is the rejection of obscenity as utterly without redeeming social importance.[5]

Judge Frank's impressive analysis was thus neatly laid to one side. But Justice Brennan's reply is perhaps a little too tidy.

In excluding obscenity from the shelter of the First Amendment, Justice Brennan resorted to what Professor Kalven has aptly termed a "two-level" theory of speech -- certain classes of speech are within the protection of the First Amendment and certain classes are not. Justice Brennan sought to identify obscenity with other excluded classes of speech. He quoted from Mr. Justice Murphy's opinion in Chaplinsky v. New Hampshire:

> There are certain well-defined and narrowly limited classes of speech, the prevention and punishment of which have never been thought to raise any Constitutional problem. These include the lewd and obscene, [the profane, the libelous, and the insulting or "fighting words" -- those which by their very utterance inflict injury or tend to incite an immediate breach of the peace]. It has been well observed that such utterances are no essential part of any exposition of ideas, and are of such slight social value as a step to truth that any benefit that may be derived from this is clearly outweighted by the social interest in order and morality.

Interestingly, Mr. Justice Brennan's opinion omits the bracketed material from his quotation. But the omitted material is instructive, because it demonstrates that, even assuming the validity of the two-level theory, obscenity is not in fact comparable to the other classes of excluded speech. The comparison of obscenity with "fighting words" is unpersuasive, since fighting words in their nature provide a clear and present danger of social harm... the classes of speech other than obscenity referred to by Mr. Justice Murphy seem positively harmful. Accordingly, they provide weak scaffolding for any theory that obscenity is beyond the First Amendment simply because it is worthless.

Second, the term "without social importance" is imprecise, and seems insufficient to rationalize all the classes of speech which the Court has held fall outside the protection of the First Amendment. Commercial promotion of goods and services is denied First Amendment protection, but no one thinks that commercial speech lacks social value. The reply seems to be that commercial speech plays "no essential part in the exposition of ideas"; and ideas relating to the buying or selling of goods are not "ideas" in the constitutional sense. So the social value test relates not simply to the exchange of ideas, but to the exchange of certain types of ideas, principally those related to the art of self-government.

But the exclusion of speech not related to the exposition of ideas rests on too limited a conception of the purposes of the First Amendment. To be sure, the First Amendment is centrally concerned with protecting the untrammeled flow of political and social ideas. But Mr. Justice Brennan recognized in <u>Roth</u> and subsequent decisions that the First Amendment protects art and literature as well, although the "people do not need novels or dramas or paintings or poems because they will be called upon to vote." Freedom of expression is, as Professor Emerson notes, necessarily concerned not just with public matters, but with private life, with self-fulfillment as well as self-government.[6]

Third, if the First Amendment excludes what is worthless, the standard of review for determining obscenity should be articulated in those terms, and those terms alone. But the <u>Roth</u> test turns on something altogether different -- the prurient appeal of the challenged publication. Nowhere did the <u>Roth</u> Court explain how the prurient and social value tests related to one another. The result was that until 1966 it was impossible to say whether social value was a separate criterion, or merely some aspect or other of the prurient appeal standard. Most authorities came to believe that the two categories were independent. Such, at least, is the import of Mr. Justice Brennan's insistence in a later case that material having "any... form of social importance... may not be branded as obscenity,"[7] apparently without regard to how pruriently appealing it is. But at least two other Justices still interpret Roth to make pruriency decisive and value irrelevant; otherwise, says Mr. Justice Clark in the Fanny Hill case, Roth gives "the smut artist free rein to carry on his dirty business." Given such disagreements among the Justices over what Roth really held, it is probably best to say that Roth simply left the issue up in the air.

Finally, even if obscenity is itself unprotected speech, it is a term of considerable vagueness. In Roth vagueness was a principal constitutional argument: not only do obscenity statutes fail to give notice of what conduct is proscribed, but their vagueness infringes heavily on First Amendment interests by encouraging censors' attempts to suppress protected speech. The Court frankly conceded that obscenity was by no means a precise term. But it accepted a measure of vagueness here that it had refused to tolerate anywhere else in the First Amendment area. The Court recognized that it was not dealing with a simple, colorless problem of "worthless" speech, but with a problem about which there are deep-and-irrational feelings. Its sole response (albeit an important one) was that only materials "utterly without redeeming social importance" could be suppressed.

In sum, Roth insulates from prosecution any serious or complex work, and is therefore a contribution of considerable importance. But Roth does not fit obscenity prosecutions within any general theory of the First Amendment; the social value test does not provide an adequate explanation either historically or on principle. And in no event does the social value test explain why speech dealing with sex alone shoulders the burden of showing that it is not worthless. Moreover, the Roth approach to obscenity focuses exclusively on the nature of the publication itself. By not addressing itself to such questions as why a distinction should be drawn between public and private obscenity, or between commercial exploitation of sex and the sale of the same material for scientific study, the Court simply postponed to another day problems which cannot be adequately resolved within the simple per se framework of Roth.[6]

The 1966 obscenity cases mark a recognition of Roth's inadequacies and the beginnings of a recasting of doctrine. Does the revamped doctrinal structure fit more easily into a comprehensive theory of the First Amendment?

Any answer must begin by assessing the possible governmental interests in suppressing obscenity. Probably no single purpose underlies obscenity legislation. Like most legislation, obscenity laws rest on views and policies which are not only inarticulate but imperfectly understood. Nonetheless, three kinds of state policies may be distinguished for the sake of analysis.

1. The Nuisance Interest

Public sexual conduct may offend community sensibilities, and few, if any, doubt the state's power to prosecute public indecency or public exposure. It has been suggested that obscenity prosecutions vindicate similar interests, that offensive and aggressive marketing of sexually arousing materials is a "nuisance." This analysis has something to commend it, and is reflected in part in the 1966 decisions. But it hardly explains the pervasive character of obscenity legislation that generally makes no distinction between publicly and privately disseminated erotica, or between invited and uninvited commercial exploitation. It is, after all, one thing to prevent a man from being accosted on the public streets by a seller of erotica; it is quite another matter when that man is a customer who enters the seller's bookstore or answers his ad. In this context the nuisance argument is trivial. Moreover, a nuisance analysis does not jibe with the Roth per se approach, which focuses simply upon the book itself, not its manner of dissemination.

2. Anti-Social Conduct

The time-honored rationale for censorship asserts that obscenity triggers anti-social conduct, particularly violent crimes. As Judge Frank observed, this proposition has never found substantial evidentiary support. To be sure, Mr. Justice Clark believes that such evidence does exist, but he concedes that opinion is divided on the point, and an examination of his affirmative sources -- which include J. Edgar Hoover and Cardinal Spellman -- is unpersuasive.[8] The evidence in favor of a direct, immediate connection between obscenity and criminal behavior is no more compelling now than when Judge Frank wrote his concurrence. Indeed, in the 1966 cases, the United States made no attempt to argue the point, contenting itself to say that opinion is "sharply divided" on the question;[9] the excellent brief for the State of New York disavowed any reliance on the supposed connection. Any some argue that obscenity is not only harmless, but it has "redeeming social importance" by providing a harmless escape for sexual frustrations -- it dissipates rather than unleashes anti-social acts.[10]

3. Preservation of Character

Finally, the state may seek to prevent the long-range effect of obscenity on character. The argument is not that obscenity generates immediate anti-social conduct, but that, like group libel, it has an insidious effect on character, gradually predisposing individuals toward deviant conduct, sexual or otherwise.

The "character" analysis was first advanced by Mr. Justice Harlan in Roth, and it is the subject of a stimulating article by Professor Louis Henkin.[11] There are, however, significant differences between the two arguments. Justice Harlan seems impressed with the state's interest in the prevention of character change because of its possible long-range effect on conduct. But even if obscenity can alter character, so can innumerable other stimuli, and Justice Harlan does not explain why the state has a peculiar interest in shielding character from change through obscene expression alone. Nor is his analysis consistent with Kingsley Pictures v. New York, where the Court vetoed New York's attempt to bar a showing of Lady Chatterley's Lover because it depicted adultery as desirable conduct under the circumstances. Mr. Justice Stewart wrote that New York had "struck at the very heart of constitutionally protected liberty" in attempting to shield the character of its citizens from change through exposure to attacks on present standards. Presumably, therefore, the First Amendment protects a direct appeal for character change which falls short of incitement to specific conduct, and there is very little evidence that the obscenity directly incites to action.

Professor Henkin pushes the analysis considerably further. He argues that obscenity legislation is designed to shield character from corrupting influences, not because such change would ultimately result in proscribable conduct, but because communities seek to preserve the traditional morality. What is more, Professor Henkin is satisfied that the traditional morality is quasi-religious in origin, and he is concerned that the legislation violates our concepts of separation of church and state as well as freedom of speech.

From these premises Professor Henkin concludes that discussion of obscenity has focused on the wrong issues. For him, the issue is substantive due process, not free speech: can the state enforce the morality of the community without showing that this enforcement serves some independent, "utilitarian" aim? He suggests that it cannot.

I do not find Professor Henkin's analysis persuasive. It may be conceded that much morals legislation, including obscenity legislation, was not and is not passed for "utilitarian ends," but as Professor Henkin recognizes, "If the challenge had been seriously pressed, some utilitarian reason for these laws might have been found." Most, if not all, morals legislation, including that relating to obscenity, can be assigned reasons falling within an accepted "utilitarian" framework. Mr. Henkin's only response is that these reasons "would have been rationalizations and might have been recognized as such." This is no answer, unless we are willing to abandon the "minimum rationality" standard of due process cases, and to permit the Court, in the fashion of *Lochner v. New York*, to pass on the "real" purposes of the legislation.

Moreover, even if we were to structure the question baldly in terms of the state's power to enforce the secular morality, is it not rational for a community to decide to enforce that morality so as to preserve the community's moral cohesiveness? Following Mill, some liberals suggest that it is improper for government to interfere with individual liberty except to restrain conduct threatening others. But the Constitution no more enacts Mill's *Essay on Liberty* than it did Herbert Spencer's *Social Statics*. Professor Henkin recognizes that the state may "promote general economic or social welfare." To what end? To promote the dignity and full development of its citizens. Does the constitution, then, forbid the state to promote -- even define -- virtue among its citizens? I think not. With Mr. Justice Douglas, "I assume there is nothing in the constitution which forbids [a state] from using its power... to proscribe *conduct* on the grounds of good morals."[14]

Unlike most other "morals" legislation, however, obscenity involves not conduct, but speech. And whatever the state's interest, the state cannot shield that interest from ideological assault. If the state cannot suppress advocacy of change, I fail to see why it may shield itself from images which in turn arouse one to question or reject his present view.[12]

II. The 1966 Decisions

1. Memoirs v. Massachusetts

The Fanny Hill case presented for review an attempt by the Commonwealth to suppress John Cleland's Memoirs of a Woman of Pleasure. History seemed to be repeating itself, for the Massachusetts court's determination that Fanny Hill was obscene mirrored the position it adopted in 1821 when first confronted with the book[13]... On appeal, the Supreme Court reversed.

The Fanny Hill case was a classic model of the old obscenity proceeding; the sole question was the nature of the book itself, without regard to the conduct of those who published or sold it. As Mr. Justice Brennan noted... neither party had presented evidence on the "manner and form of ... publication, advertisement, and distribution." In the context, the Supreme Judicial Court's admission that Fanny Hill had a modicum of social value necessitated reversal; the book could not be suppressed, wrote the Justice, unless it were found to be utterly without redeeming social value. Given the importance Mr. Justice Brennan seemed to attach to this pronouncement, it is surprising that he did not go on to consider how much social value Fanny Hill did have, or even to explain what "social value" is.

Perhaps the abstractness of the judicial discussion stemmed from the narrow confines of the proffered evidence. The case presented no questions on a crucial part of the obscenity problem -- the commercial exploitation of erotica. At this juncture Mr. Justice Brennan first considered, by way of dictum, the possibility that such additional evidence might have been determinative.

> It does not necessarily follow from this reversal that a determination that Memoirs is obscene in the constitutional sense would be improper under all circumstances. On the premise, which we have no occasion to assess, that Memoirs has the requisite prurient appeal and is patently offensive, but has only a minimum of social value, the circumstances of production, sale, and publicity are relevant in determining whether or not the publication or distribution of the book is constitutionally protected. Evidence that the book was commercially exploited for the sake of prurient appeal, to the exclusion of all other values, might justify the conclusion that the book was utterly without redeeming social importance. It is not that in such a setting the social value test is relaxed so as to dispense with the requirement that a book be utterly devoid of social value, but rather that, as we elaborate in Ginzburg v. United States... where the purveyor's sole emphasis is on the sexually provocative aspects of his publications, a court could accept his evaluation at its face value.[14]

2. Ginzburg v. United States

The idea that the manner in which the book is marketed -- its manner of production, distribution and advertising -- could be dispositive in a case moved from the level of dictum in Fanny Hill to holding in Ginzburg. Here the defendant was convicted on twenty-eight counts of violating the federal obscenity statute by mailing Eros (a hardcover magazine dealing in "literary pornography"), Liaison (a bi-weekly newsletter digesting articles on sex), and The Housewife's Handbook on Selective Promiscuity (an autobiography recounting the author's sexual history and philosophy in great detail).

The Supreme Court upheld Ginzburg's conviction: speaking for the majority, Mr. Justice Brennan said that in addition to the testimony centering on the books themselves, there was

> abundant evidence to show that each of the accused publications was originated or sold as stock in

> trade of the sordid business of pandering -- 'the business of purveying textual or graphic matter openly advertised to appeal to the erotic interest of their customers.'[15]

Here was the crucial shift in theory. The language quoted by Justice Brennan is taken from the brief concurring opinion of Chief Justice Warren in Roth. In that opinion the Chief Justice made plain that in his view the "conduct of the defendant is the central issue, not the obscenity of a book or picture." To put it differently, such prosecutions are concerned with the suppression of dirty businesses, not dirty books. The Chief Justice had no doubt that destruction of the business of exploiting erotica lay within the state's power. But, except for a passing bow at the nuisance theory, Mr. Justice Brennan makes no effort whatever to identify the state's interest in curtailing this business. Simply to denounce it as a "sorid business" is not enough. One suspects that the Court's consistent refusal to face the question of the nature of the state's interest rests on its feeling that any such attempt would open a Pandora's box.

From the foregoing premise, the result in Ginzburg was inevitable. The "leer of the sensualist" permeated Ginzburg's entire operation, particularly his advertising. And his evidence, Mr. Justice Brennan concluded, was relevant not only to the issue of redeeming social importance as it had been in the Fanny Hill dictum, but to the issues of prurient interest and patent offensiveness as well.

At several places in the opinion, the Court indicates that the "variable" or "per quod" factors of production, sale and advertising are to be considered only in "close" cases. This illustrates one of the difficulties of Roth: if a book must be "utterly without redeeming social importance" and if one emphasizes "utterly," as Mr. Justice Brennan does in Fanny Hill, it is difficult to imagine how the question of social value vel non can be analyzed in terms of close cases. "Utterly" seems to presuppose that the question is not one for dispute -- that a book is not "utterly" beyond the pale unless no reasonable man could fairly conclude that it had social value, and thus "close cases" should be accorded constitutional protection.

Moreover, it is interesting to note what the Court

found by way of a close case. Judging by Roth, Eros was not a close case; its "literate," artistic style might have saved it. Indeed, on appeal the government conceded as much. But under the revamped standards that was not enough. Moreover, the trial judge expressly found that only four of the fifteen articles appearing in the volume were obscene, and even these findings were by no means incontrovertible. What Ginzburg tried to do is, of course, evident. Roth required that the question of obscenity be determined on the basis of the "dominant theme of the book as a whole." Ginzburg sought to invoke that standard on the magazine level and to insulate Eros from condemnation by including within its covers some admittedly protected material, thereby preventing a judgment that, taken as a whole, any volume of Eros was without redeeming social value. On appeal, the United States did not go so far as to argue that on the magazine level the Roth standards should be applied on an article-by-article basis -- a position which has much to commend it. Rather, the government argued that

> in a publication, like Eros, which is a composite of independent works tied together only by the fact that they all treat sex in some manner, a judgment of obscenity as to the whole may thus be based upon some of its parts -- so long as they are significant in light of the whole.... The opposite rule would, on the other hand, privilege obscene material because of its physical connection with non-obscene material.[16]

The Court's response to the question of Roth's applicability on the magazine level is, to put it mildly, vague. Mr. Justice Brennan accepted the trial judge's finding that the inclusion of non-obscene material was a "deliberate and studied arrangement...for the purpose of appealing predominantly to prurient interest," and that the record demonstrated that "Eros was created, represented and sold solely as a claimed instrument of... sexual stimulation." But at this point his opinion suddenly trails off into obscurity:

> Petitioners' own expert agreed, correctly we think, that '(I)f the object (of a work) is material gain for the creator through an appeal to the sexual

> curiosity and appetite,' the work is pornographic. In other words, by animating sensual detail to give the publication a salacious cast, petitioners reinforced what is conceded by the Government to be an otherwise debatable conclusion.

This, of course, is no answer. The case is not "close" simply because the government "concedes" that it is. More importantly, Mr. Justice Brennan does not respond to the argument that the magazine must be judged as a whole, and that four of fifteen articles (themselves "close cases") do not render the book obscene.

The Court's sudden attempt to recast its obscenity doctrine in terms of a limited per quod theory raises problems of the sharpest order. As the dissents point out, it seems to fly in the face of the federal obscenity statute which apparently assumes an in rem approach -- i. e., that the only question is the nature of the book itself. Certainly Congress had not explicitly directed its attention to the possible impact of production and advertising on the question of obscenity. The Court's construction of the federal statute not only redraws it so substantially as to suggest a denial of due process for lack of fair warning, but is also inconsistent with First Amendment traditions.

The Court has always insisted that restrictions on speech be embodied in precisely drawn legislation directed at specifically defined evils, and has invalidated statutes containing broad, sweeping language. Closer to the point here, the Court has reversed a conviction where a state court has attempted the narrowest "enlargement" of a statute beyond its plain terms. Plainly, the Court's construction of the federal obscenity statute has little in common with these decisions.

Ginzburg is an attempt to preserve the essence of Roth -- that no serious work may be proscribed as obscene -- and at the same time to permit the states to prosecute the commercial exploiters of erotica. It purports to rationalize this result by treating the commercial exploitation of erotica as relevant in a close case, which case, in turn, is resolved by the defendant's own "evaluation" or "admission" that his work is obscene. These admissions are generally found in the circumstances of production and marketing. Over and over the Court emphasizes that defendant's "evaluation" of his work discloses that it lacks social value. But this refrain alone cannot harmonize obscenity per se and obscenity per quod. Under Roth, it is hardly self-evident that a book's social value is affected by the circumstances of its production or publicity, and to convict a publisher on the strength of his binding "admission" of obscenity is to indulge in the most naked of fictions. It is impossible to see why "admissions" should be binding only in "close" cases, nor why the "admissions" of a manufacturer should be binding on the First Amendment rights of his potential customers.

While the Court has abandoned a straight Roth approach, it has still confined pandering evidence to "close cases" -- that is, to cases involving books the social value of which is marginal. Thus we end up with the strange marriage of obscenity per se and obscenity per quod. The offspring of this marriage is the following: no serious or complex work may be suppressed as obscene, but a state has the power to suppress the business of manufacturing or distributing offensive erotica.

Despite Mr. Justice Brennan's protestations to the contrary, Ginzburg does result in some loosening of the soical value test. In candor, Roth has proved inadequate and its rationale has been recast.

3. Mishkin v. New York

Like Ginzburg, Edward Mishkin was in the business of manufacturing and distributing erotica. But his business was of a somewhat different character. His books dealt not simply with sex, but with "sick" or aberrational sex. Sex was the focus around which sadistic and masochistic themes were elaborated. These so called "bondage" books can be found in any drugstore and most bookstores. They include such titles as Strange Passions, Hours of Torture, So Firm So Fully Packed, The Violated Wrestler, and Pleasure Parade No. 2. Mr. Mishkin was convicted on the rather staggering total of 141 counts of hiring others to prepare obscene books, possessing them and publishing them, all in violation of the New York criminal obscenity statute. He received a three-year prison term and $12,000 in fines. The Supreme Court affirmed his conviction, three justices dissenting.

What was only hinted at in Ginzburg comes clearly to light in Mishkin. Despite the Court's disclaimer, Mishkin's intent was controlling. He sought to engage in the business of pandering, and that can be proscribed, at least where the books involved posses only minimal social value. Once again Justice Brennan wrote for the Court, and his opinion shows the great leeway now permitted the state. He made little reference to questions of advertising or of "admissions." Rather, he treated the various parts of the New York statute as a unitary effort to eliminate the manufacture and distribution of sado-masochistic materials, and on that basis sustained the convictions. Justice Brennan said:

> Appellant instructed his authors and artists to prepare the books expressly to induce their purchase by persons who would probably be sexually stimulated by them.... Not only was there proof of the books' prurient appeal, compare United States v. Klaw,... but the proof was compelling; in addition appelant's own evaluation of his material confirms such a finding. See Ginzburg v. United States....

A few rationalizations may be offered. Unlike Ginzburg, the books involved in Mishkin did not present a "close" case. They were obscene per se.... But Justice Brennan does not analyze the problem in those terms; he is centrally concerned with Mishkin's conduct, not the status of the books.

Mishkin's argument on appeal was principally restricted to the meaning of "prurient appeal." He made no effort to argue that his collection had social value. Thus, the Court was able to avoid dealing with a question of the most crucial importance: what is the "central meaning" of the social value test? But that question did not escape all notice. Dissenting in Fanny Hill, Mr. Justice White had pickishly inquired in passing why the fact that the books had a market did not demonstrate their social value. But it was left to Mr. Justice Douglas, dissenting in Mishkin, to lay bare the unexamined premises of the majority:

> Some of the tracts for which these publishers go to prison concern normal sex, some homosexuality, some masochistic yearning that is probably present

> in everyone and dominant in some....Why is it unlawful to cater to the needs of the group? They are, to be sure, somewhat offbeat, nonconformist, and odd. But we are not in the realm of criminal conduct, only ideas and tastes....(W)hy is freedom of the press and expression denied them? Are they to be barred from communicating in symbolisms important to them? When the Court today speaks of 'social value,' does it mean a 'value' to the majority? Why is not a minority 'value' cognizable?...If we were wise enough, we might know that communication may have greater therapeutical value than any sermon that those of the 'normal' community can ever offer. But if the communication is of value to the masochistic community or to others of the deviant community, how can it be said to be 'utterly without any redeeming social importance'? 'Redeeming' to whom?

Mr. Justice Douglas' questions cannot be brushed aside with the flourish that he misunderstands the social value test -- that this test protects only the interest in the exchange of ideas, not other interests however significant. But does purely literary or artistic value qualify for protection? And even if the interests catalogued by Justice Douglas are not entitled to protection under the First Amendment, are they not sufficiently important to warrant some protection under the Due Process Clause? If so, what are the interests which the legislature found -- or might have found, to use the traditional formulation -- which require suppression of these books? The Court's opinion offers answers to none of these questions.

III. Obscenity and The Law: Unfinished Business

Plainly, the 1966 obscenity decisions are not the last word on the relationship between obscenity and the First Amendment. Like Roth, the 1966 cases could not reconcile the existence of obscenity prosecutions with a principled general theory of the First Amendment. Indeed, the 1966 decisions merely "adjust" Roth to permit the states considerable latitude in suppressing the commercial exploitation of erotica having minimal social value. Against this general backdrop one must assess some of the important legal problems which still demand resolution.

1. Evidentiary and Related Problems

The role of the judge in an obscenity prosecution is a critical evidentiary question bearing on the scope of First Amendment protection. The typical obscenity prosecution has been a trial of the book itself, even though in form a proceeding against the distributor or retailer. The earliest trials apparently amounted to no more than a submission of the book to the judge, but recent trials have featured elaborate evidentiary hearings. Fanny Hill illustrates the pattern. The Commonwealth introduced the book and the testimony of one marginally qualified expert. The defense introduced notices by literary critics, and the testimony of professors at Harvard, Brandeis, Williams, and Boston University, each of whom affirmed Fanny Hill's social value. Ginzburg involved an even more extensive hearing along the same lines. The critical question never faced under Roth was the scope of judicial review given records of this character. In the typical case, the trial judge heard the testimony as though he were being given a short course in English literature, but then made up his mind about the book quite independently of the record evidence. In Fanny Hill the amici urged the Massachusetts court to reject this approach and direct the trial judge to dismiss the prosecution so long as the record contained substantial evidence of the book's redeeming social value, unless the judge could conclude that the record testimony was irrational. Any other standard, they insisted, would give too narrow a protection to freedom of speech. Their argument is persuasive, and deserves better treatment than it received in last term's decisions.

The substantial evidence approach won support from two of the three dissenting judges in Massachusetts, and a subsequent opinion of that court involving Naked Lunch was more favorable. Unfortunately, however, the argument that the judge was bound by the record evidence was not pressed in the Supreme Court. In Ginzburg, the United States did argue, almost in passing, that the judge must make an independent determination on the question of obscenity. The decisions, in turn, contain little explicit discussions of this problem. Mr. Justice Harlan indicated that he was aware of and rejected the argument that the judge is bound by the "substantial" record testimony. Mr. Justice Douglas reached the opposite conclusion.

While Mr. Justice Brennan's opinion in Ginzburg does not treat the problem directly, it did sustain convictions over considerable record evidence that Eros as a whole, and each of the four questioned articles, had social value. Thus Ginzburg raises the question whether the book's social value must be "self-demonstrating" if pandering evidence is to be irrelevant. But if this is so, then record evidence will be of virtually no significance on the question of social value. In a clear case (where a book has obvious value), supporting evidence is superfluous, while in a "close" case (where social value is not obvious), the book will not be saved by the record testimony if it is being sold by a panderer. In other words, the only cases where record evidence would really be helpful are those where it will probably do no good. But this need not be the practical result of Ginzburg, for the Court did not squarely address itself to the standard by which the trial judge should evaluate the record testimony and, despite its implications, it should not be taken to have settled the point.

The Court has paid even less heed to evidentiary and appellate review problems stemming from the prurient appeal and patent offensiveness criteria. In Ginzburg the United States argued that the Court should independently review social value, but should accept the lower court's determination on pruriency and patent offensiveness unless clearly wrong. If adopted, this rule would still leave open difficult evidentiary questions. Must evidence be introduced on prurient appeal or is it a proper subject for judicial notice? Must patent offensiveness be "so gross as to be self-demonstrating," as Justice Harlan has suggested? To the extent that an obscenity prosecution involves other than "hard-core" pornography, expert testimony on patent offensiveness seems necessary. Certainly the patent offensiveness of Eros cannot be fairly characterized as "self-demonstrating." But if evidence is relevant on the question of national community standards, what kind of evidence is it? Can the publisher introduce other books bought and sold in the market place as evidence of what national standards are? What of book reviews, or sociology studies? The Court has not addressed itself to any of these evidentiary questions, or, for that matter, to the proper relation between judge and jury in federal prosecutions.

2. Ginzburg at Retail

The potential impact of the 1966 cases is also complicated by the fact that Ginzburg and Mishkin presented only one facet of the commercial exploitation of sex; they dealt with the suppression at the manufacturing, not the retail, stage of the business. Mr. Justice Brennan noted that manufacturers and distributors of erotica were not in any position to complain about the "residual vagueness" of obscenity. Whether they were or not, the same cannot be said of the retail seller, as Smith v. California recognized. There the Court invalidated the conviction of a book seller under an ordinance prohibiting the sale of obscene books on the ground that scienter was not required. The Court left open what mental element would suffice, but it recognized that imposition of strict liability would have disastrous consequences. Smith suggests that the states either confine their prosecutions to manufacturers and distributors, or adopt a procedure comparable to the Massachusetts in rem proceedings against the book itself, which allows criminal proceedings against retailers only after the book is adjudged obscene. The great advantage of the Massachusetts procedure is that it eliminates the vagueness otherwise inherent in a prosecutory scheme. Indeed, I was of the opinion that in rem proceedings were a constitutional requirement -- part of the emerging First Amendment due process. Otherwise, fear of criminal prosecution would induce publishers and retailers to avoid the wide danger zone created by the definitional vagueness of obscenity. This self-censorship could deprive the community of protected materials. But the 1966 cases indicate that the Court no longer entertains this view.

The retailer, however, is not in the same position as the manufacturer of erotica. As a practical matter he is unable to cope with the residual vagueness of obscenity, except by means of the most drastic self-censorship. Accordingly, if no prior in rem approach is constitutionally required, Smith should be strongly reaffirmed. The Court will have this opportunity in a number of cases involving prosecution of retailers which it has agreed to review.[17] These new cases must, of course, take into account the sharp impact of Ginzburg and Mishkin on the mens rea question. Thus, if "appeal to prurient interest" means no more than sexual "stimulation," is the local seller on sufficent notice because he is selling Mishkin-type ("bondage") books, whose covers alone spell out their probable content? And is the cover -- or general class of the book -- sufficient to warn the retailer that it lacks social value?[18] And, of course, if patent offensiveness is not properly a matter for judicial notice, what kind of evidence must the state introduce on the question of national community standards? In any event, can the retailer defend on his lack of knowledge of community standards?

The difficulty of the foregoing questions will be aggravated because of the Court's enlargement of the obscenity statute to embrace the manner in which a book is advertised. Lacking legislative guidance, the Court must define the kind of advertising indicating an "admission" by the publisher that the book is not entitled to First Amendment protection. Is it sufficient that the cover alone have the "leer of the sensualist"?[19] What of advertising with the _quiet_ "leer of the sensualist"?[20] More to the point, what is the relationship between the advertising of the publisher or the distributor on the one hand and that of the retailer on the other? Can the advertising of the distributor be "imputed" to the retailer? Suppose one panders and the other does not? Whose advertising will be decisive? Or suppose that, as is sometimes the case, a book appears in both hard cover and paperback editions from different publishers, or appears in more than one paperback edition? Must the prosecution show that the publisher's advertising affected customers -- or potential customers -- of the retailer being prosecuted?

IV. Conclusion

Like _Roth_, the 1966 cases do not succeed in fitting obscenity prosecutions within any comprehensive theory of the First Amendment. But, in principle, they do permit the states wide leeway to move against the commercial exploiters of erotica. Their actual impact is, of course, difficult to assess at this juncture. But, as Professor Emerson reminds us, repression takes place in a live context, and "those who are assigned the task already have or soon develop a tendency to pursue it with zeal." Any ground yielded to the censor unquestionably means that he will demand more. It is, therefore, safe to assume that the censors will take the 1966 decisions as further encouragement to go about their good works. But, as yet, obscenity prosecutions are still of marginal concern; it still remains unlikely that any "significant" book will be suppressed. That may not be enough, but it is a good deal.

Notes

1. Harry Kalven, Jr. "The New York Times Case: A Note on the 'Central Meaning of the First Amendment'," 1964 Supreme Court Review, pp. 191-221.

2. [354 U. S.] at 489.

3. Manual Enterprises v. Day, 370 U. S. 478, 482 (1962) (opinion of Harlan, J.). . . .

4. 237 F. 2d 796 (2d Cir. 1956).

5. 354 U. S. at 484. Mr. Justice Brennan sought to buttress this position with an historical argument, id. at 482-83, but his effort has been roundly criticized. . . .

6. Emerson, "Toward a General Theory of the First Amendment," 76 Yale Law Journal 877 (1963).

7. Jacobellis v. Ohio, supra note 30, at 191.

8. Memoirs v. Massachusetts, 383 U. S. at 451-54 (dissenting opinion).

9. Brief for Respondent, p. 15, Ginzburg v. United States, supra note 7.

10. See E. Kronhausen & P. Kronhausen, Pornography and the Law 273-74 (1959).

11. Louis Henkin, "Morals and the Constitution: The Sin of Obscenity," 63 Columbia Law Review (1963).

12. Two recent decisions have raised the problem of private immorality in an obscenity context. In Redmond v. United States, 384 U. S. 264 (1966), a husband and wife were convicted under the federal obscenity statute for mailing negatives and receiving through the mails developed films of

each other posing in the nude. Their convictions were vacated by the Supreme Court on the suggestion of the Solicitor General that, as a matter of policy, the statute was enforced only against "repeated offenders." Mr. Justice Stewart, with whom Mr. Justice Black and Mr. Justice Douglas concurred, filed a brief memorandum stating that they "would reverse this conviction not because it violates the policy of the Justice Department but because it violates the Constitution." Id. at 265. Less than a month later the California Supreme Court reversed on statutory grounds a trial court instruction that a jury could find the defendant guilty of possessing obscene materials even if he had prepared the materials without any intent to distribute. In re Klor, 51 Cal. Rptr. 903, 415 P. 2d 791 (1966). In dicta, the court suggested that a statute making mere possession a crime would be unconstitutional. Id. at 906, 415 P. 2d at 794. See also Mapp v. Ohio, 367 U. S. 643, 673 (1961) (dissenting opinion).

13. Commonwealth v. Holmes, 17 Mass. 271 (1821).

14. 383 U. S. at 420. It should be noted that Mr. Justice Brennan here cited the per quod aspects as relevant only to the question of social value, not to those of pruriency and patent offensiveness. That limitation is abandoned in Ginzburg. . . .

15. 383 U. S. at 467.

16. Brief for Respondent, p. 31, Ginzburg v. United States. . . .

17. See Redrup v. New York. . . cert. granted, 384 U. S. 916 (1966); Austin v. Kentucky, Civ. Ct. McCracken Co., Ky. (unreported), cert. granted, 384 U. S. 916-17 (1966).

18. In this respect, it should be recalled that the advertising itself need not be obscene. In Ginzburg the government conceded that the advertising was not obscene, so that a book not itself obscene marketed by advertising also not obscene may result in a conviction for violating an obscenity statute.

19. See Books, Inc. v. United States, 358 F. 2d 935, 938 (1st Cir. 1966).

20. Consider The Story of O, said to be one of the most pornographic books ever written. This book is marketed in a plain white cover with the title alone appearing on the front page. An advertisement showing only the cover of the book appeared in the New York Times accompanied by a book review describing its erotic qualities. See, e. g., New York Times, August 28, 1966, Literary Supplement, p. 21.

Professor Richard B. Dyson submits a series of hypothetical cases, and discusses the possible effect Ginzburg would have upon them.

This article is reprinted from 28 University of Pittsburgh Law Review (October 1966), p. 1-8; reprinted here by permission of the editors of the University of Pittsburgh Law Review and the author, to whom grateful acknowledgment is made.

Richard B. Dyson is Associate Professor of Law, Boston University School of Law.

Looking-Glass Law: An Analysis of the Ginzburg Case

by Richard B. Dyson

In the nine years since the decision in Roth v. United States, the Supreme Court's guidelines for deciding whether printed or pictorial matter is protected by the first amendment has become considerably clearer. At least the requirement that to be censored as obscene a work must be "utterly without redeeming social importance" was one that probably could be applied by a court as easily as most constitutional tests, although some important questions remain concerning the proper relation between judge, jury and expert witness on this point. It seemed that the remaining problems were largely those of application of the rules to concrete situations, piecing out workable limits of permissible censorship on a case-by-case basis.

Ginzburg v. United States, decided last term, had a shock effect, however, that has blurred the freedom-of-press picture considerably. All that was immediately clear was that the Supreme Court, on the basis of the defendant's advertising methods, had affirmed his conviction under the federal mailing-obscene-materials statute for selling a book and two magazines that the majority assumed without deciding were not obscene under the Roth tests. The majority holding left lawyers and laymen confused, and gave rise to four sharply dissenting opinions. I will first explore what the decision is taken to mean, and then evaluate its soundness.

The ambiguity that surrounds the Ginzburg decision centers, as is usual in these cases, on the meaning and significance of the legal concepts embodied in the word "obscene." In the Roth case, and those cases applying Roth to attempts to suppress literary or artistic works, obscenity has two legal meanings, constitutional and statutory. The statutory meaning varies from case to case depending on the judicial interpretation of the statute involved. The constitutional concept is a complex one, which can in one sense be thought of in purely conclusory terms: that which is obscene does not receive first amendment protection, and that which is not, does. The process of arriving at this category of "constitutionally obscene" involves, according to recent opinions, three tests: (1) "prurient appeal," an archaic term for what seems to be approximately equivalent to sexuality; (2) candidness -- whether the material exceeds the limits beyond which people generally find it offensive; and (3) whether the material is "utterly without redeeming social value." The Ginzburg opinion, while purporting to be merely an embellishment of these concepts,[1] raises important new questions concerning the consequences of a finding of obscenity.

Before Ginzburg, the consequences of such a finding seemed to be fairly simple and clear. If a work was ultimately found not obscene, a question of law in the determination of which the Supreme Court participated directly, any contrary determination by other courts, state or federal, was reversed, and the work could not be suppressed anywhere in the country. If the Supreme Court upheld a determination that a work was obscene,[2] then it was open season for censorship of that work under whatever state or federal statutes might be applicable. But considerations of policy and reason, I will suggest, along with language in the opinion, deny such effects to the Ginzburg case. What, then, does a case such as this decide? It did affirm that Ralph Ginzburg would serve a five-year term in a federal penitentiary, but the Supreme Court presumably exists to give precedent and guidance, and to settle questions of law, functions more important than the disposition of individual cases. If, as the opinion stated, the case was deciding that the material was obscene, what was the significance of that decision, if not to "suppress" the material? In other words, obscene for what purposes, and to what extent?

The most difficult aspects of these questions did not have to be faced in the Ginzburg decision. Ralph Ginzburg was the producer, promoter, and original seller of Eros and Liaison, the two periodicals in question, and performed the last two of these functions in regard to the Housewife's Handbook on Selective Promiscuity. Where one man is responsible for both the promotion and the distribution of the publications in question, any theory of the case would apply to him. The difficulties arise in trying to assess the immediate precedential effect of the case. To test the scope of the Ginzburg doctrine, one might consider what relevance it would have to the following cases arising after the decision:

> Case 1. The prosecution for selling obscene materials of the owner of a bookstore who sells Eros and the Housewife's Handbook, with or without knowledge of the publisher's advertising, and with or without secondary use of it.
>
> Case 2. Prosecution of an advertising firm that produces advertising for the Housewife's Handbook substantially similar to that used by Ginzburg.
>
> Case 3. Prosecution of a competing publisher for selling the Housewife's Handbook in paperback edition without objectionable promotion.
>
> Case 4. A statutory civil action, in rem, to have the Housewife's Handbook and Eros declared obscene, with other statutes ready to be used to prosecute one found selling material thus declared obscene. This was, in fact, the Massachusetts setting of the Memoirs v. Massachusetts (Fanny Hill) case, decided the same day as Ginzburg.
>
> Case 5. Prosecution of the new head of Ginzburg's firm for selling the same publications through the same channels, one month, one year, or five years later, but without further use of the objectionable advertising methods.

To begin, the possibility that the case does have the effect of permanently suppressing the material in question should be considered. To be more precise, the question is whether the book and the two periodicals in question, in any form or context, have been deemed, on the basis of their promotion, unworthy of first amendment protection, so that their public sale[3] can be prohibited and punished by whatever state or federal action conforms with "first amendment due process." The argument for this proposition would be based on the language of the opinion. In several passages Mr. Justice Brennan used language that strongly implied that the Court had decided that the materials in question were obscene; e.g., "We perceive no threat to First Amendment guarantees in thus holding that in close cases evidence of pandering may be probative with respect to the nature of the material in question and thus satisfy the Roth test." Such a use of evidence of promotional methods would not, perhaps, be wholly irrational. From an evidentiary perspective, if the fact question is whether the book is obscene, and the proffered evidence is that its publisher, distributor, or almost anyone else for that matter, has expressed or implied the idea that it is, such evidence probably would not be held irrelevant, although it might be inadmissible for other reasons.

Such an interpretation of the Ginzburg opinion nevertheless seems untenable. First, whether a book is "obscene" is not a unitary factual question, such as whether it is "sexy." It is, as already mentioned, a complex legal conclusion, whose main components arise from the issues whether it is "utterly without redeeming social importance" and whether it transgresses the "customary limits of candor and offensiveness." Granted that social importance is not without ambiguity (though, perhaps, far less than is often injected by courts and others), it must be a term that comprises an objective literary, artistic, and historic judgment for which witnesses are avialable who are far more expert than those in the chain of distribution. In short, though the actions of the publisher or distributor may not be totally irrelevant to such questions as the social importance of material purveyed, it is evidence so weak as to be insignificant.

Second, there would be an unbearable capriciousness about deciding whether a given work were constitutionally prohibitable for all times, persons and places (always excepting the hypothetical scholar), on the basis of a particular local promotional scheme. Would the result of such a decision be res judicata on all subsequent litigation concerning the material? If it were not, zealous prosecutors could keep attacking a book on the basis of each new advertisement, and harass it out of existence. If it were, an early suit where promotion had been restrained by the advertiser would insulate all subsequent advertising, while on the other hand, one pandering bookseller could seal the book's fate for the entire country. Either answer would be intolerable. The Court's prior decisions seem to have established, moreover, that a decision on the ultimate constitutional status of a literary or artistic work must rise above the petty prejudices of a locality or a particular time.

Finally, one passage in Mr. Justice Brennan's opinion seems to contradict the implication that the Court was deciding the fate of the material in question:

> A conviction for mailing obscene publications, but explained in part by the presence of this element, [*i. e.*, pandering] does not necessarily suppress the materials in question, nor chill their proper distribution for a proper use.... All that will have been determined is that questionable publications are obscene in a context which brands them as obscene as that term is defined in *Roth* -- a use inconsistent with any claim to the shelter of the First Amendment.

The statement that such a conviction does not necessarily suppress the materials seems definitive, though it leaves open the question why Mr. Justice Brennan persisted in saying that the Court was deciding that "publications are obscene."

This brings us to the difficult question: If the *Ginzburg* case did not decide whether the publications in question were not protected by the first amendment and subject to suppression by summary statutory action, what did it decide? The opinion is redolent with inscrutable epigrams that purport to explain but only confuse. What does it mean to say "questionable publications are obscene in a context which brands them as obscene"? It is clear that evidence of obscene promotional methods was used to convict Ralph Ginzburg, but where censorship is in question, society's more lasting concern is what happens to the book, not what happens to the defendant.

One possibility is suggested by the passage quoted above. The words could be taken to mean that the book might be considered together with its promotional "context," such that the obscenity *vel non* of the compositional picture is put at issue. As an example, a picture of a girl in a bathing suit might be entirely inoffensive, but by adding captions, or retouching the picture, or superimposing other pictures, the compositional result could be made legally obscene. Such a decision would actually be that the "material is obscene," but its precedential effect -- its in rem effect -- would be limited to reproductions of the composition that were found to be substantially similar. This interpretation finds support in the opinion. At one point it quotes from Mr. Chief Justice Warren's concurrence in Roth: "The nature of the materials is, of course, relevant as an attribute of the defendant's conduct, but the materials are thus placed in context from which they draw color and character. A wholly different result might be reached in a different setting." The last substantive paragraph of Mr. Justice Brennan's opinion also suggests this position:

> It is important to stress that this analysis simply elaborates the test by which the obscenity vel non of the material must be judged. Where an exploitation of interests in titillation by pornography is shown with respect to material lending itself to such exploitation through pervasive treatment or description of sexual matter, such evidence may support the determination that the material is obscene even though in other contexts the material would escape such condemnation.

This interpretation raises some difficult problems, however. One is its application to the real world. If we assume that book-plus-advertising can be obscene where the book alone is not, how far in time and space does the taint of the promotion extend. Suppose that Tropic of Cancer is advertised in the New York Times in such a way that the book taken in context with its advertising becomes, by this interpretation of Ginzburg, obscene in the Roth sense. Does that mean that a bookseller who sells the book in a brown wrapper and with no reference to the advertisement (case one above), or the competing publisher (case two), can be prosecuted? It seems unlikely since the book, out of the context of its advertising, has been adjudged not obscene by the Supreme Court.[4] Is it not absurd to say that because someone can mark up our picture of the bathing beauty so as to make it obscene, all the unmarked copies of it at that moment also become obscene? What about later sales without further advertising (case five)? How long does the mental image take to fade? In reality, most advertising is not like a marked-up picture. While a publisher is physically delivering copies of a book to sales outlets across the country, he is also advertising through mass media that are quite separate from these outlets. The buyer-reader does not encounter the advertising at the same time that he does the book, except for that which appears on the cover. I also suggest that once a person has bought the book and opened the cover to read it, the effect of the advertising largely fades from his mind, and is not a significant factor in his impressions. In short, publisher matter does not live "in context" with its promotional materials in the sense that they form a compositional whole that can be judged obscene or not obscene.

Another objection to this "context" interpretation of the Ginzburg case is that it does not seem to fit the facts. We must assume, as did the Court, that the material in question was not obscene when viewed alone. This must mean (1) that it did not appeal to prurient interest, (2) that it did not exceed customary limits of candor, or (3) that it was not utterly without redeeming social value. It seems extremely unlikely that the material could pass test (1) while failing tests (2) and (3); i. e., that its only reason for protection would be its lack of prurient appeal. In fact, where, as here, the material deals almost exclusively with sex, it would seem logically impossible for it not to "appeal to prurient interest," while at the same time it does "exceed customary limits of candor." The most likely characterization of it would probably be that while it definitely appealed to prurient interest, it had a modicum of social (perhaps artistic) value, and was on the borderline of candor and offensiveness.

At one point Mr. Justice Brennan suggested how advertising might affect the obscenity of the material itself. He stated:

> The deliberate representation of petitioners' publications as erotically arousing, for example, stimulated the reader to accept them as prurient; he looks for titillation, not for saving intellectual content. Similarly, such representation would tend to force public confrontation with the potentially offensive aspects of the work; the brazenness of such an appeal heightens the offensiveness of the publications to those who are offended by such material. And the circumstances of pre-

> sentation and dissemination of material are equally relevant to determining whether social importance claimed for material in the courtroom was, in the circumstances, pretense or reality -- whether it was the basis upon which it was traded in the marketplace or a spurious claim for litigation purposes.

If, as I have suggested, the material is openly and concededly intended to be erotically stimulating, it would probably "appeal to prurient interest," with or without advertising. The battle would center on the other two tests, and it is there that the reasoning fails to deal with the evidence presented. The advertising in question was simply to the effect that the publications were frankly and candidly erotic, that the courts had ruled that they could be sold, and that if you were enlightened enough you would find them sexually stimulating and should buy them. To say that this "heightens the offensiveness" of them twists the concept completely out of shape. If the bathing beauty picture were sold with advertising that said, "You will find this picture sexually stimulating," is there any meaningful sense in which it would make the _picture_ more offensive? Offensiveness as developed in _Manual Enterprises, Inc. v. Day_, refers to the explicitness and crudeness of the material. As Mr. Justice Brennan uses offensiveness, it seems to refer to the reaction of the public to the _existence_ of the publications, regardless of their content. But this has nothing to do with the question whether they "exceed the customary limits of candor." The ultimate question to be decided is the extent to which public hostility to the existence of material may give rise to censorship of it. To determine this on the basis of the degree of hostility would be to make freedom of the press a hollow and evanescent concept indeed.

The last quoted sentence of Mr. Justice Brennan, concerning the social value test, is a fascinating one that on close reading seems to mix two unrelated questions. The first clause looks to whether the claimed social importance is "pretense or reality." That is, restated simply, does the material actually have social importance? As I have already suggested, the "circumstances of presentation and dissemination" may be "relevant" to that point, but it is evidence so weak as to be virtually immaterial. The other question, "whether it was the basis upon which it was traded in the marketplace," is quite another matter, unrelated to the underlying reality of social importance, or any other objective characteristic of the material. It is not related to any question whether the material, in or out of "context," is obscene. Thus, the hypothesis that the *Ginzburg* case was a decision concerning the obscenity of printed material in context with its advertising does not, on close examination, seem viable from the standpoint either or practical workability or application to the facts of this case.

In order to achieve a logically tenable interpretation of the *Ginzburg* case, we must shift our focus from the material in question to its purveyor, the defendant. That Mr. Justice Brennan was actually doing this is suggested by an interesting passage from his opinion in the *Fanny Hill* case:

> Evidence that the book was commercially exploited for the sake of prurient appeal, to the exclusion of all other values, might justify the conclusion that the book was utterly without redeeming social importance. It is not that in such a setting the social value test is relaxed so as to dispense with the requirement that a book be *utterly* devoid of social value, but rather that, as we elaborate in *Ginzburg v. United States, post,* pp. 470-473, where the purveyor's sole emphasis is on the sexually provocative aspects of his publications, a court could accept his evaluation at its face value.

At first glance, this description of the *Ginzburg* case, like much of the majority opinion in it, is difficult to grasp. It scarcely needs repeating that in a censorship case the chief issue is not whether a particular individual goes to prison, but whether 150 million adult Americans shall be denied access to a publication, be it *Ulysses, Fanny Hill,* or *Eros* magazine. Having reached the sensible position that a work can only be suppressed if it is devoid of social value, how can the Supreme Court turn around and say that they can justify the conclusion that a book is utterly without social value on the basis of the way it is commercially exploited? The answer might lie in the second sentence quoted, if by adding a crucial phrase (in italics) to Mr. Justice Brennan opinion, it were to read: "Where the purveyor's sole emphasis is on the sexually provocative aspects of his publications, a court could accept his evaluation at its face value, as against a later assertion by him to the contrary." So worded the doctrine is put into a category relaxingly familiar to any lawyer -- estoppel. It would be absurd to find that a particular work was without social value because any one person said so, but it is a common device for courts to say that a party's words will be held against him, that he will not be "heard" to assert the contrary, that his prior representations will be taken at their "face value." I suggest that this is the only rationally defensible interpretation of Ginzburg.

On this theory, a decision such as this would say little or nothing about the material involved, either in or out of context. This might be qualified by Mr. Justice Brennan's suggestion that the Ginzburg approach only applied to "questionable" materials. In light of the favorable attention given by the opinion to a 1940 opinion by Learned Hand,[5] in which a conviction under the predecessor statute was upheld where the material being sold was recognized scholarly work, this qualification would not seem to be very meaningful. Perhaps anything dealing with sex would do. At any rate, the offense that would strip away first amendment protection would be implying, in advertising materials, that the material is sexually exciting. So viewed, Ginzburg is not a censorship case at all. It allows an act -- "pandering" -- to be punished, rather than a book to be suppressed. In terms of my hypotheticals testing the precedential effect, Ginzburg would be relevant to none of them except case three, the similar advertising case. This use of pandering as a constitutional offense, without regard to what is sold, is strongly suggested by the Model Penal Code provisions and comments cited by Mr. Justice Brennan's opinion, and by frequent references in the opinion to defendant's acts.

Having thus put forth the only theory of the Ginzburg case that appears to make sense, I must admit that there is much language in the majority opinion that is inconsistent with it, language that eventually must be disregarded if the case is to stand for any coherent rule. No matter how Mr. Justice Brennan says it, it makes no sense whatever to judge the social value of a publication, and the public's consequent right to read it, on the basis of the "face value" of the publisher's representations. And in the end, the admission in the opinion that the publications are not themselves being suppressed defeats any suggestions that books, rather than people, are being judged.

At first impression, the paragraph in the Fanny Hill opinion in which Mr. Justice Brennan considers the application of the Ginzburg case seems to contradict this in personam theory. After the passage quoted above, where it is stated that a court might take the purveyor's evaluation at its face value, the opinion goes on to say:

> In this proceeding, however, the courts were asked to judge the obscenity of Memoirs in the abstract, and the declaration of obscenity was neither aided nor limited by a specific set of circumstances of production, sale, and publicity. All possible uses of the book must therefore be considered, and the mere risk that that book might be exploited by panderers because it so pervasively treats sexual matters cannot alter the fact -- given the view of the Massachusetts court attributing to Memoirs a modicum of literary and historical value -- that the book will have redeeming social importance in the hands of those who publish or distribute it on the basis of that value.

It is important to note that the Massachusetts proceeding was purely in rem; the attorney general brought a statutory civil action to have the book declared obscene. If my suggested in personam version of Ginzburg is correct, it would obviously have no application to a proceeding with no defendants at all. The passage seems to imply that further evidence of distribution practices under the Massachusetts in rem procedure might have changed the result. Such an inference, however, though certainly possible, is by no means mandatory. By "in this proceeding," the Court might have meant any proceeding under such a statute. Massachusetts contemplates in its statute a permanent statewide banning of the publication in question, and a "specific set of circumstances of production, sale, and publicity" would not appear relevant to that from the standpoint of either the statute or the Supreme Court.

To summarize this interpretive effort, Mr. Justice Brennan's majority opinion in Ginzburg cannot be taken to mean what it seems to mean on first reading: that a book's obscenity, that is, whether or not it is worthy of first amendment protection, can be judged on the basis of the way it is advertised. The express declaration that the words in question were not to be considered "suppressed" by the case, coupled with language about taking the defendant's promotional statements at their face value, leads inevitably to the conclusion that Ralph Ginzburg's conviction was upheld not because of what he was selling, but rather how he was selling it.

In evaluating the Ginzburg case, the question immediately arises why Mr. Justice Brennan wrote a confusing, self-contradictory opinion to announce a doctrine which, though novel, is not especially complex. Why did he need to insist that he was only "elaborating" an existing test when he was obviously treading new ground? Why try to establish by repeated assertions, contrary to common sense, that advertising crucially reduces a publication's social value, or increases its offensiveness? A more basic question is why the doctrine was found necessary at all; although the obscenity issue has caused some furor in recent years, no great pressures have appeared in the area of advertising.

The answers, it is submitted, lie in the friction between some deep moral convictions and the legal materials out of which the case was built. In previous opinions Mr. Justice Brennan made it clear that the presence of sexual themes or imagery was not enough to deprive material of first amendment protection, but the use of this sexual content to sell the material was, to him, beyond the pale.[6] He manifested in his opinion a deep sense of outrage, a great emotional need to condemn Ralph Ginzburg's activities. The opinion rings with pejorative phrases such as "leer of the sensualist," "the sordid business of pandering," and "titillation by pornography." He was disturbed not by the fact that Ginzburg had committed a crime, which was not at all clear as the case came up, but rather that he had committed a sin -- and a mortal one at that.

On the other hand, Mr. Justice Brennan was faced with facts and a statute that gave him little room to maneuver. The statute describes, by the familiar string of adjectives, obscene things, and declares them, and notices telling how to obtain them, to be non-mailable matter. The "things" in question, the two periodicals and the book, were, it seems fair to say, not really close to the outer limits of constitutional protection,[7] and therefore not "non-mailable matter" within the prohibition of the statute as it previously had been construed. Given that Mr. Justice Brennan was aroused at the thought of selling something on the basis of its sexual content, how was he to justify its incrimination under such a statute? As Mr. Justice Stewart was to point out cogently in his dissent, no federal statute made pandering or titillating a criminal offense.

The answer was a device worthy of a seventeenth-century chancellor. Reduced to its simplest terms, which Mr. Justice Brennan sedulously avoided doing, it was, "If you say that the matter you are mailing is obscene, we will punish you under the statute barring the mailing of obscene matter, regardless of the actual nature of the matter." A statute incriminating the distribution of obscene matter was extrapolated to cover the obscene distribution of matter. He thus managed to uphold a conviction without even reaching the main argument raised by the defense, that the material in question was not obscene and therefore constitutionally protected. In justification of this line of reasoning, he mounted the collage of rather inconsistent ideas that have been discussed above, drawing from Chief Justice Warren's *Roth* concurrence, the Model Penal Code, and a 1940 Learned Hand opinion, to suggest that advertising is somehow relevant to the obscenity of the thing advertised.

As an attempt to rationalize an anomalous result, the device and its accompanying reasoning are a failure; whether they will endure is another question. In the first place, the violence done to the statute, and therefore to the defendant's right to due process of law, is notable -- in Mr. Justice Harlan's words, "an astonishing piece of judicial improvisation." Ginzburg was perfectly justified in believing that the only issue raised by his activities was the obscenity of the materials he was selling, and that the chances that the issue would be decided against him were remote. To pack him off to prison for a long term on the basis of a tortured construction of a familiar statute raises grave questions of *ex post facto* justice. Our legal system is not improved by Mr. Justice Brennan's justification of the result by his opinion that Ginzburg was a nasty man in a "sordid business," an opinion that many do not share. Ginzburg was not a wretch on the fringes of society, but a well-known and successful publisher.[8]

Furthermore, the opinion is defective even in terms of its internal logic. Its key idea is that if a seller characterizes his produce as obscene, that characterization will be taken at its face value. But to say that Ginzburg's advertising implied obscenity is to ignore the definition of obscenity on which the whole doctrinal structure rests -- a definition whose chief author is Mr. Justice Brennan himself. For the key test of obscenity here was not whether the material was sexually stimulating in nature ("prurient", in Brennanite terms); there was no question about that. It was, rather, whether the publications possessed redeeming social value, and here the advertisements in question loudly proclaimed the affirmative. While speaking of taking them at their face value, the opinion ignored what was plainly on their face.

Finally, the advertisements described did not fit the lurid descriptions attached to them by Mr. Justice Brennan. They invited the reader to buy publications frankly and candidly concerned with sex, which recent court decisions had rendered marketable. In his references to the courts' decisions, Ginzburg was quite correct. His felony, then, was declaring that he was doing something that the courts had said, and for the purposes of this decision we must assume, he could do. The additional matter about attempts to use towns such as Intercourse, Pa. for a mailing address is, I submit, a weak joke too trivial to merit serious discussion, not to mention five years in prison. Any suggestion that Ginzburg's advertisements were more leering than the standard Madison Avenue product in the mass media would betray a certain insulation from that product.

Beyond its obvious failures of logic and justice, the most disturbing thing about Ginzburg is its simplistic importation of personal values into the Constitution. The opinion has a syllogistic foundation strongly reminiscent of Lochner v. New York: The Constitution does not exist to protect evil activities; what he was doing was evil; therefore the Constitution cannot protect him. Value judgments are inescapable in constitutional decisions, however much we might long for purely "neutral" principles. But there is a crucial difference between making necessary choices between competing goods, such as fairness to an accused versus prosecutory effectiveness, and gratuitously taking sides, in the name of the Constitution, in a value dispute where reasonable men differ. There is a point at which a wise judge must say: Although I feel strongly about this particular value-choice (e. g., whether this activity is unequivocally bad), there is a significant body of respectable opinion on the other side and I must, therefore, refrain from making my feelings on this point the basis of a constitutional rule. To fail to do so is to place the Constitution on one side or the other of contemporary disputes about economics, religion, or, heaven forbid, sex. And if the choice happens to be a bad one, the court appears not only wrong but foolish. Here there was no broadly recognized norm that Ralph Ginzburg violated; in fact, the place of sex in our current literature, art, and theater, coupled with the preponderant opposition to censorship of the academic and literary world, seems to indicate that a majority of the literate public disagrees with Mr. Justice Brennan's values. Mr. Justice Peckham in Lochner at least had the conventional wisdom of the day on his side.

In the long view, the Ginzburg case may be viewed as an expression of revulsion by the Court at the "exploitation" of its own broad interpretation of the first amendment. The majority appears to tolerate freedom of expression, but not the attempt to popularize sex and profit by it with broad appeals through the mass media. The underlying validity of the Court's position, aside from the problems of lawmaking discussed herein, is likely to be judged by the view one takes of what Ginzburg was doing. I suggest that the majority, distracted by Ginzburg's immediate commercial goals, failed to recognize that he is in the mainstream of a broad and significant social movement. Freedom of expression is an integral part of the current drive to change freedom from a familiar slogan to an activist credo, and of the rejection of the traditional primacy, in Western society, of self-control and obedience for that of self-expression and creativity. Thus, it is inseparable from the movements for political and social freedom that are causing a notable upheaval in America today. The function of law, especially constitutional law, in the face of social upheaval should not be to enforce the personal codes, the traditional mores, that are under attack, but to limit the degree of direct impingement on person and property that such movements cause. Books, pamphlets, and magazines are among the least obnoxious channels of radicalism; once the limits of tolerance of their contents are set, there is no wisdom in further examining the methods and motives of their distributors.

Notes

1. "All that will have been determined is that questionable publications are obscene in a context which brands them as obscene as that term is defined in Roth -- a use inconsistent with any claim to the shelter of the First Amendment." 383 U. S. at 475. "It is important to stress that this analysis simply elaborates the test by which the obscenity vel non of the material must be judged." Ibid.

2. Mishkin v. New York, 383 U. S. 502 (1966), was the first case in which the Supreme Court held flatly that a work was constitutionally obscene.

3. It is speculated, although it apparently has never been expressly decided, that serious scholarly study of even hard-core pornograph would find some constitutional haven. The more marginal area of pornographic material created privately and quietly distributed to acquaintances, probably will receive separate treatment also....

4. Grove Press, Inc. v. Gerstein, 378 U. S. 577 (1964) (per curiam).

5. United States v. Rebhuhn, 109 F. 2d 512 (2nd Cir. 1940), discussed in 383 U. S. at 472-74.

6. A curious feature of Mr. Justice Brennan's thinking is illustrated by the passage from the Fanny Hill opinion quoted above.... He distinguishes the "exploitation by panderers" of a book from its "social importance in the hands of those who publish or distribute it on the basis of that value." The focal point of his thinking thus appears to be how a book is "used" by its sellers. There is an apparent analogy to the contrast between the use of a gun by a policeman and that by a criminal. But the anomaly is obvious. The analogy to the policeman or criminal is not the seller, but the reader of a book. His are the relevant "hands." And the underlying premise of press freedom is that society's interests are best served by having the fewest possible obstacles to the distribution of books (as sharply contrasted

with guns) to the adult public. To face the matter squarely, once given that a book is not objectively obscene, i.e., valueless, is it rational to say that it will be valueless if obtained from one seller, but valuable if obtained from another? Is this not nonsense in the garb of reason?

7. One might compare the homosexual-oriented stories and pictures described in One, Inc. v. Olesen, 241 F.2d 772,777 (9th Cir. 1957), rev'd, 355 U.S. 371 (1958), and Manual Enterprises, Inc. v. Day, 370 U.S. 478, 480-81 (1962), with the nudist pictures vividly described in Sunshine Book Co. v. Summerfield, 128 F. Supp. 564, 571-72 (D.C. Cir. 1955), rev'd, 355 U.S. 372 (1958), all of which were held not obscene by the Supreme Court.

8. Another of his publications, Fact magazine, has a current reported circulation of 140,000. N.W. Ayer & Sons, Directory 736 (1966).

In the following excerpt from his article, "Obscenity and the Supreme Court: Nine Years of Confusion," Raymond F. Sebastian examines some of the questions raised, but not resolved, by the Ginzburg decision. The original article is commended to the interested reader, since it contains an excellent survey of some peculiar post-Roth decisions.

From 19 Stanford Law Review (November, 1966), pp. 182-189.

"Obscenity and the Supreme Court: Nine Years of Confusion."

By Raymond F. Sebastian

2. The relevant-audience problem

Clearly the Court will now [after Ginzburg] look to the specific segment of the general public at which the material is directed to determine whether the material has prurient appeal. This approach reflects an increasing acceptance of the concept of variable obscenity.[1] According to the variable obscenity theory nothing is inherently obscene, but only becomes so according to its distribution and audience.

...assuming that variable obscenity is a valid concept, there are real problems of application. Identifying the factors which are to be considered as variables in analyzing commercial exploitation or delineating the relevant audience would seem to be an almost hopeless task....

Mr. Justice Douglas' objections to the variable obscenity theory are more basic, challenging the very concept of the specific audience. Because "[m]an was not made in a fixed mold,"[2] Douglas argued that he should be able to reject any social mores as long as he does not interfere with the rights of others. Douglas also questioned whether rejection of the values of the socially deviant subgroup by censorship of material that appeals to that subgroup does not result in majority control of the meaning of social value. Material that represents deviant values to the majority may or may not be pruriently appealing to the deviant group. One could surmise that deviancy is rejected by the "normal" person. If so, how is he to judge whether material is pruriently appealing to a deviant? And if the material in fact is pruriently appealing to the "normal" person, how can it be so deviant that it supports a finding of patent offensiveness because of its portrayal of deviant practices?

3. "Close cases" which make evidence of distribution relevant

A further confusing factor is the Court's statement in Ginzburg that evidence of pandering is relevant in "close cases." Immediately the question is raised of just what a close case is. One, at least, is where the work in question is found to possess the requisite prurient appeal and is patently offensive, yet has some "minimal" social importance.[3] This minimal importance cannot save the work when its distributor has emphasized its prurient appeal.

The real target of the Court in including this pandering element is undoubtedly the person who, falsely or otherwise, makes a blatant "appeal to the erotic interest of [his]... customers."[4] Why, then, is the degree of social importance relevant at all? If conduct and not the work itself is to be condemned, why can the panderer of minimally important works be punished, while the panderer of a great work who is guilty of the same conduct presumably cannot? If the answer is that in the latter case some net social good results from the distribution of great works, a claim of denial of equal protection might be valid.

4. Commercial exploitation: a fourth element.

The probative value of commercial exploitation in determining obscenity is a validation of the position taken in Mr. Chief Justice Warren in his Roth dissent and echoed by numerous commentators through the years. Weighty objections to adding the factor of commercial exploitation to the obscenity standard, however, came from within the Court itself. Dissenting Justices argued that consideration of commercial exploitation rewrites the obscenity statutes, is unconstitutionally vague, and is in any case irrelevant.

In "Memoirs" Mr. Justice Brennan intimated that Fanny Hill, a book of minimal social importance according to the Massachusetts court, might constitutionally be termed obscene if it had been commercially exploited. Thus, while the commercial-exploitation test is formulated in evidentiary terms as being only of probative value, in fact evidence of commercial exploitation would completely negate the minimal social importance of a book such as Fanny Hill. Because the commercial-exploitation element is applicable only to close cases, when no clear decision can be made on the basis of the three original elements -- prurient appeal, patent offensiveness, and social importance -- the operation of this fourth element of necessity assumes some prior affirmative finding of social importance; otherwise the case would not be a close one. Yet, if obscenity can be constitutionally prohibited only because it is in fact "utterly without redeeming social importance," how can a work of even "minimal" importance be prohibited merely because of its method of distribution?

The commercial-exploitation element is so grossly inconsistent with the original rationale for finding some regulation of obscenity constitutional -- namely, that obscenity was not worth protecting -- that one must conclude that the phrase "utterly without redeeming social importance" now should be read "utterly without above-minimal social importance." The addition of the element of commercial exploitation and its application to close cases have made the standards for identifying obscenity, already vague, now hopelessly abstruse.

The inherent vagueness of the commercial-exploitation concept as applied in close cases will undoubtedly discourage some expression which might otherwise have occurred. A finding of obscenity and affirmance of a conviction in a commercial-exploitation context would greatly discourage anyone else from distributing the same material. With such vague standards at work, who is to know what weight was given to the exploitation element as opposed to the other elements? Was the work judged obscene only because it was exploited, or was it inherently obscene? If the answer is not clear, will the material ever be distributed again?

It might also be argued that advertisements which indicate the prurient appeal of a publication are actually valuable because they give advance warning of the contents. Such an argument is predicated on the assumption that the only value of antiobscenity laws is the removal of material which would be offensive to some members of society. If this is so, condemnation of advertising which in fact does warn the reader may be a disservice.

Moreover, if advertising is emphasized, promoters

of filth will simply change the labels and not the contents of their packages. Consumers who are "salaciously disposed" will probably soon learn to identify the familiar old product in the new wrapping. Advertising that attempts to dispel an otherwise clear appeal to normal prurient interest or deviant sexuality is not likely to turn the consumer's attention away from "titillation" to "saving intellectual content."

Finally, Mr. Justice Douglas was most likely correct when he stated that the method of distribution is irrelevant to a determination of the obscenity of particular material. Regardless of the desirability of prosecuting the commercial purveyors of smut who are the real target of the obscenity laws, the statutes in the Ginzburg and "Memoirs" cases related only to publications which were inherently obscene. No statutory mention was made of the manner of distribution. A statute reaching commercial exploitation may or may not be constitutional, but some legislation directed at specific conduct would be preferable to the current practice of labeling material obscene which is not on its face obscene in order to reach those who exploit the material. For instance, if the exploitation concept were by statute limited to circumstances analogous to common-law nuisance, commercial exploitation as a limitation of distribution might be acceptable. The state can regulate nuisances and can even constitutionally regulate the time, place, and manner of distribution of religious or political literature. Thus, distribution of material to unwilling recipients advertising sexual works in an erotic manner could probably be proscribed. Such a statute is merely suggested here as a more acceptable alternative to the exploitation concept. Even this alternative involves some of the objections already discussed, such as whether legitimate distribution would be inhibited.

5. The scope of Supreme Court review of obscenity cases

The Supreme Court may find itself overburdened by review of obscenity cases, since it appears to adhere to the theory of independent review in this area. To alleviate some of the burden, the Government suggested in "Memoirs" that the Court limit its independent review to the question of social importance.[5] In view of this concern, do the standards set forth in the new cases help to ease the work load?

Conceivably the limitation of the commercial-exploitation element to close cases may indicate a step in the direction of Supreme Court review of only those cases which are not close and in which the standards clearly were erroneously applied. In the gray area where material of questionable value was commercially exploited, the lower courts would have free rein. This hypothesis, however, runs counter to the Court's own admonition in Roth that "[t]he door barring federal and state intrusion into this area... must be kept tightly closed and opened only the slightest crack necessary to prevent encroachment upon more important interests." Allowing the lower courts to have free rein would seem on the contrary to open the door almost all the way.

It seems more likely the Court will continue to adhere to independent review, in which case it has certainly not eased its own burden. Now a fourth factor must be considered, a factor wholly apart from the obscenity of the publication itself. Not only must the publication be examined, but extrinsic evidence of advertising and distribution must also be considered.

Moreover, and contrary to the suggestion that review could be limited because of the exploitation element, the same publication could theoretically reach the Court an infinite number of times. Although one adverse decision based on exploitation might keep the material from being distributed at all, in an extreme case the Court would have to consider the same publication anew each time it was distributed in a different way. If the pandering concept is to be retained, the Supreme Court must either accept the lower court findings on the question or drastically restrict the meaning of the close case. Otherwise, the burden of review might be staggering.

6. The "community" in community standards.

Although in "Memoirs" the Government contended that the scope of community standards was national,[6] the Court did not discuss the question, perhaps because of the probable division within the majority had it been considered. Of the Justices presently on the Court, only Justices Brennan and Harlan had previously supported the national standard. Mr. Chief Justice Warren and Mr. Justice Clark had favored a local community standard on the theory that there is no national standard.

Whatever the scope of the community, an expert on contemporary community standards is hard to identify. He might be a sociologist, a psychologist, a minister, or anyone else who could rationally be thought to provide information over and above that derived from his position as an individual member of the community. A new finding in each case of the current state of community standards involves a great deal of time and effort; if some kind of expert testimony is not taken and a finding made, however, the community-standards element in operation contemplates nothing more than the subjective attitudes of the trier.

Moreover, application of the community-standards element will be paradoxical. Presumably the Government, limited in time the resources, will move only against publications it feels pose the greatest threat to society. Publications posing the greatest threat are most likely those with the widest circulation and thus the most general impact. Yet, if a publication <u>does</u> circulate widely, does this not mean that it <u>is</u> within limits which the community will tolerate?

IV. Where Do We Go From Here?

One solution is to do away with obscenity censorship in most instances. Obscenity could be retained as a classification, but no obscene work, absent a showing of clear and present danger of criminal conduct, could be prohibited, and no distributor could be prosecuted unless he caused the material to be distributed to an involuntary receiver who was offended by it. The problem of nonobscene material being advertised as obscene could be solved by a separate statute dealing with fraudulent and misleading advertising. Emphasis on the involuntary receiver would preserve the distribution of obscenity to willing receivers in order not to inhibit the distribution of nonobscene material.

It is unlikely, however, that society would in the near future accept such a near absence of obscenity censorship. Thus, assuming censorship, some standard should be promulgated which will protect literature of any importance from censorship by lower courts and yet still relieve the Supreme Court of case-by-case disposition of obscenity litigation. With these goals in mind, the following is presented as a workable standard.

First, the commercial-exploitation element should be discarded as irrelevant to a determination of whether any given work is obscene. If a finding of obscenity is made by reference to a factor unrelated to a publication's contents, the first amendment has been violated and the public done a disservice. A statute limited to condemnation of conduct, based on theories of nuisance or the concept of the unwilling receiver, could be enacted in order to reach commercial exploitation of sex.

Second, the means of determining social importance and the weight given to social importance must be clarified. The appelant in "Memoirs" suggested that expert testimony be weighed by the courts and further that the quantity of critical reviews of a work be considered highly indicative of its importance.[7] However, if serious works are to be saved from censorship, some other standard than the usual weighing of the evidence must be adopted. After all, "[t]here are among us individuals who, by training and experience, are better qualified than most to appraise the literary or artistic or other merit of a book."[8] This much is agreed -- some people are better equipped to judge than courts and juries. The real question is how much weight is to be given to their testimony. There are two alternatives other than weighing the evidence of a work's social importance: (1) such evidence is conclusive if substantial, although not predominating, or (2) if there is a scintilla of such evidence it is conclusive.

The scintilla test is impractical because someone of at least some repute could probably be found to testify in favor of the social importance of almost anything. Therefore, expert testimony in favor of the social importance of a work should be conclusive if it is credible and substantial, although on balance definitely not predominating. "Credible" means the witness' status as a reputable expert is acknowledged. Such an evidentiary test should ensure that works of at least arguable merit would be protected, thus protecting minority access to these works. If it is true that public, and perhaps also critical, acclaim in the area of sex runs behind important expression,[9] such a test is especially important.

Third, the patent-offensiveness test should be retained, with objective evidence of widespread national circulation being conclusive of its acceptance by the community and of its inclusion within the limits of candor.

Fourth, the appeal to prurient interests test should be retained despite the criticism that obscenity repels rather than attracts, with the exception that evidence of shock and repulsion in a particular case may be introduced in place of the prurient-appeal element if exposure to the material was involuntary. Agreeing that in almost every case the prurient-appeal element invites the highly personal reaction of the trier, such a personal reaction will be of some utility at least in weeding out works which never should have been subjects of prosecution.

Fifth, each of the above elements should be independent of the others so that, for example, a finding of patent offensiveness and prurient appeal could be negated by a finding of even minimal social importance.

Sixth, social importance, in turn, should be negated only by a finding that the publication presents a clear and present danger of illegal action (sexual or otherwise) or of destruction of the moral fiber of society.

Seventh, the Supreme Court should treat lower court findings on patent offensiveness and prurient appeal as matters of discretion, but should make an independent judgment on social importance and clear and present danger. Alternatively, the Supreme Court could further restrict itself and limit review to two classes of cases: (1) where the social-importance element had been misapplied to prohibit a serious work and (2) where a serious and potentially provable allegation of clear and present danger had been made.

Operation of these standards should achieve the goal advocated in this Note: making censorship of any publication of even minimal social importance extremely difficult.

Notes

1. For the original and probably most comprehensive statement of this theory, see Lockhart & McClure, Censorship of Obscenity: The Developing Constitutional Standards, 45 Minn. L. Rev. 5, 77-88 (1960).

2. Ginzburg v. United States, 383 U. S. 463, 491 (1966) (dissenting opinion).

3. See A Book Named "John Cleland's Memoirs of a Woman of Pleasure" v. Attorney Gen., 383 U. S. 413, 419 (1966).

4. Ginzburg v. United States, 383 U. S. 463, 467 (1966), quoting from Roth v. United States, 354 U. S. 476, 495-96 (1957) (Warren, C. J., concurring).

5. Brief for the United States 27-28, A Book Named "John Cleland's Memoirs of a Woman of Pleasure" v. Attorney Gen., 383 U. S. 413 (1966).

6. Brief for the United States 20, A Book Named "John Cleland's Memoirs of a Woman of Pleasure" v. Attorney Gen., 393 U. S. 413 (9166).

7. Brief for Appellant 22-23, A Book Named "John Cleland's Memoirs of a Woman of Pleasure" v. Attorney Gen., 383 U. S. 413 (1966).

8. Id. at 22.

9. See Comment, Free Speech and Obscenity: A Search for Constitutional Procedures and Standards, 12 U. C. L. A. L. Rev. 532, 552 (1965).

Professor Henry P. Monaghan's view of the _per se_ and _per quod_ elements of _Ginzburg_ is complemented by Charles P. Schiller's "Case Note," in which Schiller notes a merging of a "variable" and a "constant" view of obscenity, and suggests that the merging of the two in _Ginzburg_ could make obscenity law more realistic.

From 16 _American University Law Review_ (1966), pp. 126-128, to which grateful acknowledgement is made for permission to reprint here.

"Case Notes: Constitutional Law - First Amendment...."

By Charles P. Schiller

It is accordingly evident that Ginzburg can be considered as an adoption of a line of cases expounding the "variable" approach to obscenity, and represents for the first time the recognition and acceptance of that approach by a majority of the Supreme Court....With the decision in Ginzburg the Supreme Court has in effect moved away from the solely subjective standards enunciated in Roth and, while not abandoning the Roth test, has supplemented it "by another test that goes to the question of whether the mailer's aim is to 'pander' or to 'titillate' those to whom he mails questionable matter." In addition, as noted by Mr. Justice Harlan in dissent, as a result of the Court's holding, "material must now also be examined in light of the defendant's conduct, attitude, motives."

Ginzburg is significant, therefore, in that it represents a merging of the two legal approaches to obscenity, the "variable" and "constant" concepts. Borderline material can now be examined in light of its creator's or disseminator's motives and intent when it fails to be found obscene under the criteria set forth in Roth. The "variable" approach cannot intrinsically be considered as more stringent or rigid than the "constant" approach; for, under the "variable" approach, even admittedly hard-core pornography might travel freely in the mails. Accordingly, it can no longer be said that borderline material must be judged obscene or non-obscene in the abstract since Ginzburg, providing for a greater degree of flexibility in the area of obscenity, permits the evaluation of material based on the intent with which it was written or sold, and the purpose for which it is to be used by the recipient. Although it is questionable as to whether any form of censorship should exist, once that issue is answered in the affirmative, it can be said that Ginzburg must be regarded as breathing new life into a more realistic, certain and enforceable approach by which government may act as a censor in determining what remains accessible to the reading public.

Hugh McPheeters, Jr. also feels the Ginzburg opinion partakes of the "variable obscenity" concept advanced by Professor William B. Lockhart and Professor Robert C. McClure; see article from 7 Utah Law Review, pages 131-152 this anthology.

From 32 Missouri Law Review (1967), pp. 129-130, to which grateful acknowledgement is made for permission to reprint here.

"Recent Cases -- Obscenity"

By Hugh McPheeters, Jr.

Justice Brennan insisted that Ginzburg was merely an elaboration of the Roth standards; however, the effect and impact of the decision reaches beyond this. Its importance is found in the realization that Ginzburg indicates a major shift in the legal doctrine of obscenity. This is a shift from a concept of constant obscenity to a concept of variable obscenity.[1] The concept of constant obscenity views obscenity as an inherent quality of the material, remaining the same regardless of time or circumstances. The variable obscenity concept views the question of obscenity as dependent upon the setting and the conduct of the defendant; a publication might be obscene in one setting and not in another.

The extent to which this concept of variable obscenity will dominate future obscenity determinations depends upon whether the courts apply the standards of Roth first and bring Ginzburg to bear only in a "close case." If this is the intention of the Court, there arises the question of what is a "close case." In view of the inability of a majority of the Court to concur in the meaning of Roth, this question might produce much litigation and appeal.

It is probable, however, that Ginzburg will dominate future obscenity determination. Justice Brennan indicated in Fanny Hill that evidence of exploitation of, or appeal to, prurient interest might justify a different result in that case, but the Court had been asked only to judge the book in the abstract. An indication of the future use of Ginzburg is seen in Books, Inc. v. United States, in which the court of appeals found there was sufficient evidence in the text of a book, Lust Job, that the three separate tests set forth above were met, and the book was obscene. The court in dicta said that under Ginzburg, the text of Lust Job could be declared obscene because a consideration of the front and back covers of the paperback justified a conclusion "that there were [sic] pandering and an exploitation of interest in titillation."

An approach to obscenity based upon a variable concept is more realistic than one based upon a constant concept. In the area of obscenity, the courts are called upon to reconcile the rights of persons to freely express themselves under the First Amendment with the right of the people to maintain a decent society. Freedom of expression demands the widest possible latitude within this context. Conviction under a variable concept, as set forth in Ginzburg, would not suppress a publication for use in a different setting, a setting where there was a "serious endeavor to advance human knowledge or understanding...." The approach in Ginzburg should help dispel the "inherent vagueness of Roth," which appears to be a major concern of the Court. A variable obscenity approach would be helpful in determining the true dominant theme of the material and its true social value despite attempts to disguise them. The dominant theme of the material under a variable approach would vary according to the material's primary audience, but the material would still be considered as a whole.

Extended to its logical conclusion, the Court's opinion in Ginzburg, with its emphasis upon the setting and the defendant's conduct, raises the question whether a publication might be declared obscene without any consideration of the text. In Ginzburg, the Court mentioned the content of the publications, as it did briefly in Mishkin v New York. The ultimate limiting factor would be whether or not a "close case" must be established under Roth before Ginzburg is brought into play.

The legal problem of obscenity is difficult to resolve due to definitional difficulties surrounding the word itself and to the need to protect freedom of expression. Ginzburg, by adopting a variable concept of obscenity, has placed the pressure upon the panderer and the purveyor. This approach gives the widest possible latitude to persons honestly attempting to express themselves.

Notes

1. See generally Lockhart & McClure, "Censorship of Obscenity, The Developing Constitutional Standards," 45 Minn. L. Rev. 5, 68 (1960).

The following excerpt from an article in 80 _Harvard Law Review_ discusses the implications of the "pandering" element in _Ginzburg_, and examines the suggestion that _Ginzburg_ was convicted of an offense for which he had not been charged. The commentator suggests that civil proceedings may partially resolve some of the difficulties of criminal proceedings against allegedly obscene material.

"The Supreme Court, 1965 Term:
Freedom of Speech and Association -- Obscenity"

The landmark decision in Roth settled the constitutionality of obscenity legislation, but the guidelines announced have proved difficult to apply.... In part...due to the nature of the standards developed by the Court: that a book must be "patently offensive" and "appeal to a prurient interest" adds little to the test that it must be "obscene"; and "national community standards" and "social importance" are difficult criteria to apply in a heterogeneous society....also due to practical difficulties peculiar to the obscenity area. The only evidence available is difficult to work with: "dominant theme" must be judged on the basis of the work "taken as a whole" -- not an easy task for materials of any complexity and not a task for which judges and juries have any special competence. Moreover, the relatively recent phenomenon of the introduction of expert testimony has raised many problems. On some of the issues relevant under the Court's test -- for example, whether material is patently offensive -- the "experts" allowed to testify are frequently unqualified....On the other hand, the issue of social importance...seems particularly well suited for resolution in light of expert testimony, but the factfinders in obscenity cases have apparently been hesitant to follow even qualified expert opinions.

The "pandering" modification of the Roth test is another attempt to elucidate a constitutional standard that the Court has itself recognized is "not perfect." The relationship of "pandering" to the Roth test, however, is not made completely clear by the Court's opinions. Conceptually, the relevance of pandering to prurient appeal can be based upon the proposition that a book is more likely to arouse a reader erotically if it is presented as a book that ought to arouse him erotically. This is a plausible psychological hypothesis for which there is some empirical support, and there is no apparent reason why the standards of obscenity cannot be made to incorporate it.

The Court also indicated that evidence of pandering was relevant on the issue of social importance. Pandering might indicate that the alleged social value was a spurious claim for litigation purposes. If there are to be obscenity laws there must be some way to deal "as a whole" with a magazine that contains, for example, both a political commentary on the Constitution and pornographic selections from the Marquis de Sade. The lower court in Ginzburg used evidence of pandering to determine whether the inclusion of nonobscene materials in Eros was merely an attempt to evade the obscenity laws. But it is difficult to construe the Court's emphasis on the relevance of pandering to social importance in so narrow a fashion, since it found pandering relevant in discussing the Handbook even though it accepted that the book had social importance in some contexts: its claim to social importance could not, therefore, have been a "spurious claim for litigation purposes." Instead, the Court in effect "elaborated" the constitutional test of social importance to read: Does the material have social importance in the context presented to the Court by this litigation? If this is the test, it only confuses to say, as Mr. Justice Brennan did in Fanny Hill, that a book that has a minimal social importance could be found to be utterly devoid of social value on the basis of its having been pandered. A book does not lose its social importance to literary scholars because it is exploited to the sexually immature. More accurately, the book has a minimal social value in the context of sale to literary scholars but has none in the context of its exploitation as a sexual stimulant.

The Court's "pandering" analysis may on a practical level be seen as a first attempt to change the existing disharmony between the constitutional standard of obscenity and the evidence actually available to satisfy that standard, by extending the scope of evidentiary inquiry as well as further elucidating the standards themselves. Evidence that a defendant commercially exploited the sexually provocative aspects of a book will frequently be "objective": Ginzburg, for example sought mailing privileges in the town of Intercourse, and Mishkin instructed his writers to emphasize scenes involving sexual perversions. Such evidence may, of course, necessitate careful evaluation, but it is closer to the types of evidence used to prove other common questions of fact than is evidence which reflects only a value judgment concerning a book's literary merits. Accepting the relevance of pandering to determining obscenity may therefore ameliorate the Court's burden of decision in a difficult area of the law, without foreclosing all regulation of obscenity as would the still more easily applied standard advocated by Justices Black and Douglas.

Elaborating the Roth standard in terms of particular "contexts" does, however, raise difficult problems. Where evidence of pandering is used, it is no longer the book's importance that is being evaluated. Realistically, the question is not, "Does the book have value to society?" Rather it is, "Does the defendant's activity contribute to the value that the book may have for society or does it detract from that value?" Focusing on the defendant's activity in this fashion may serve to protect those, such as the medical practitioner or literary scholar, whose use of erotic literature is worthy of protection. It may, however, tend to disregard the interests of the reading public. Many of the people who buy a book that has been pandered may appreciate its nonprurient appeal -- its value to them may be the same as if it had not been exploited, and the right of free speech guaranteed by the first amendment includes the listener's right to hear. Also, the Court's statement that a conviction based upon evidence of pandering should not inhibit others from disseminating the materials for proper use is perhaps too optimistic. A conviction based in part upon such evidence is not equivalent to a determination that the materials would be constitutionally protected if disseminated differently. If evidence of pandering is used, few publishers would be likely to issue the book after another publisher has been sent to prison for disseminating it unless the courts specifically indicate -- rather than "assume" as the Court did in Ginzburg -- that the book is not in itself obscene. Reliance on evidence of pandering may therefore result in works of value to society never being published.

Allowing convictions in "close cases" to be based upon evidence of pandering may also adversely affect the publisher anxious to stay within the law, since it destroys the finality of the adjudication. A finding that a book is not obscene will not immunize a publisher from prosecution if he changes the manner in which the book is advertised .... This problem is especially serious in a society such as ours, where much commercially successful advertising makes an appeal based upon sexual interest. The line between mere "sexual appeal" and illegitimate "prurient appeal" is likely to be exceedingly fine if the book itself is "close" to being obscene. Nor will reliance on pandering have only a beneficial effect on the administration of obscenity laws since a finding based upon evidence of pandering will not prevent the courts from having to relitigate the status of the book in a different context....

Even if one accepts the logical and practical relevance of pandering to a determination of a book's obscenity, the Court's opinions raise the question whether convicting the defendants upon this evidence in the criminal cases before it was consistent with due process. The dissenting Justices contended that the Court's basis for affirming the convictions was not the basis upon which the defendants were tried. One difficulty in evaluating this contention is that Mr. Justice Brennan did not always make clear whether he was discussing the relevance of pandering to the cases before him or speaking of the possible logical relevance of pandering unrelated to any specific set of facts.... To some extent context was considered by the courts below. In Ginzburg, the lower court considered pandering relevant in determining whether non-obscene materials were included in the same magazine with obscene materials merely to evade the obscenity laws, and the lower court in Mishkin apparently considered the clandestine manner in which the materials were disseminated in reaching its conclusion that they were devoid of social value. At no point, however, did the lower courts consider pandering relevant to gauging the prurient appeal of the materials. Nor did they evaluate the materials only in the context before them: they apparently determined that the materials were in themselves obscene. For example, the lower court in Ginzburg explicitly rejected the expert testimony that the Handbook had any social value. And although the statute under which Mishkin was prosecuted contains a subsection, quoted by the Court, specifically directed at materials which "commercially exploit prurient interest," the indictment was not couched in terms of that subsection and the trial court found Mishkin guilty of violating two other subsections of the statute without mentioning that subsection in its opinion. Since the Supreme Court did not rest its holding on the nature of the books themselves, one cannot be certain that the lower courts, charged with the responsibility of weighing the evidence and determining guilt, would have found the evidence of pandering sufficient to support a finding that the materials were obscene if they had been instructed that the materials could not be deemed obscene in themselves. In addition, the defendants might have introduced other evidence had they been aware during their trial that guilt or innocence would turn on evidence of pandering.

Even assuming that the Court's basis for decision was the same as that relied on in the lower courts, it is still necessary to evaluate the dissenters' contentions that the Court's "pandering" analysis was not consistent with the federal statute and that the defendants were not afforded fair warning of the offense for which they were ultimately convicted. The Court itself noted that section 1461, which speaks of obscene matter, appears to deal with the materials in the abstract, and previous opinions of the Court generally appear to have disregarded context, focusing on the materials themselves. Nevertheless, if the emphasis of the Court has changed, it remains true that the courts have always considered context -- at least in the sense of the group to whom the materials were directed -- relevant to a determination of obscenity. The Court cited no prior cases invoking the theory that pandering itself may stimulate the reader to be erotically aroused. If the Court's causal proposition is accepted, however, it did not change the meaning of the statute but merely recognized as relevant a type of evidence that has probative value but had never before been presented. "Fair warning" does not require that a defendant be informed in advance of every type of evidence that may be found probative in relation to a defined crime, but the emphasis in the decisions since Roth upon the materials themselves may be regarded as so misleading in light of the Court's new emphasis upon context that in a realistic sense the defendants were not afforded "fair warning." Thus, the doctrine would appear to be weakened in practice if not in principle.

In the criminal cases before it, the Court gave little consideration to the possible "chilling effect" that convictions would have on freedom of expression. Because obscenity is not easily distinguished from constitutionally protected speech, statutes designed to control obscenity may inhibit protected speech. In light of the Court's recognition of this danger in previous obscenity cases, its failure adequately to consider the problem in the cases before it can only be considered surprising. The possibility of such a chilling effect suggests that methods of controlling obscenity other than criminal prosecution should be reexamined. One possibility is to amke greater use of civil proceedings. This could be accomplished either through legislation or by a court requirement that the method used to control obscenity be the alternative that is least restrictive of the rights guaranteed by the first amendment. To increase the deterrent effect, criminal penalties could be imposed on those who disseminate materials after they had been declared obscene in a civil proceeding. Such an approach presents certain difficulties, for the civil determination of obscenity would have to be broad enough to prevent an individual from continuing to disseminate a closely similar work or essentially the same work with minor changes. Perhaps this and other difficulties, such as the problem of deterring the first publications of obscene materials, would prove insurmountable, but a closer consideration of such an approach appears warranted. The effect of the Court's "pandering" analysis, however, is to weaken seriously the effectiveness of civil proceedings, and so it would seem that any new approach to controlling obscenity through civil proceedings would require a reconsideration of the principles underlying last Term's decisions.

Miss Leslie J. Crocker notes that Ginzburg apparently adds a fourth element to the Roth test; she also notes the Supreme Court's apparent dependence on Professors William B. Lockhart and Robert C. McClure.

From 17 [Case] Western Reserve Law Review (1966), pp. 1334-1341, with the permission of [Case] Western Reserve Law Review, to which grateful acknowledgement is made for permission to reprint here.

"Freedom of Expression"

By Leslie J. Crocker

An Evaluation

With Roth v. United States, in 1957, it appeared that the test established by the Supreme Court was intended to accomplish two goals. First, an attempt was made to set forth an objective standard which trial courts would be able to apply and which would obviate constant appeals to and review by the United States Supreme Court. Second, although obscenity was excluded from the purview of first amendment protection, there was a great interest in protecting freedom of expression by guarding anything not obscene from over-zealous censors. These two goals appeared to remain present in the Court's attitude toward obscenity in all decisions subsequent to Roth and prior to Ginzburg. It now seems entirely reasonable to assert that each of these goals has been seriously subverted by the Ginzburg group of cases.

With Ginzburg et. al., a highly subjective element has been engrafted onto the Roth test and standards for judging obscenity. This added element will further confuse trial courts -- already embroiled in an area which defies any real delineation -- and add to the Supreme Court's flood of censorship cases. And, as previously indicated, it will seriously deter freedom of expression and expose this area to the self-appointed "watch-guards" of the moral fiber of our society.

While Fanny Hill reaffirmed the three requisite elements of the test in Roth and subsequent cases, it held that all three elements must coalesce and must be independently satisfied before a determination of obscenity may be reached. But the Ginzburg decision added the new element: when objective examination of the three criteria is not conclusive, the courts may examine the publisher's intent and motives as established by his marketing and advertising practices. If he attempted to pander or to titillate the public's sexual interest, stressing this aspect of the material he is selling, then his own evaluation of the material may be taken "at its face value" and a finding of obscenity established. The Mishkin decision redefined the element of prurient appeal by asserting that it is really not the "average person" whose prurient interest must be aroused in order for a work to be obscene; a work may be obscene if it is designed for deviant sexual groups and appeals to the prurient interest of the "average member" of these groups.

In evaluating these three decisions, a preliminary question might well concern the source and reason for the engrafting of the new "pandering" element. It is submitted here that just as the Supreme Court has relied extensively on Lockhart and McClure the two leading experts in the constitutional area of obscenity, in all prior obscenity decisions, it again relied on them in the Ginzburg group of cases. Although the Court had avoided adoption of this facet of their ideas until this year, much of Roth and Jacobellis, for example, stemmed directly from their writings. In Jacobellis, the opinion of the Court did indicate a variable concept of obscenity, for the Court stated that had the film involved been directed toward minors, the standard employed and result attained might well have been different. But a concept of obscenity which is variable only on the basis of a distinction between adults and minors is far different from the one now adopted by the Court. For the concept now adopted by the Court is a totally variable one. In judging obscenity, the intrinsic nature of the material will depend on the audience to which it is directed via marketing and advertising. This is basically the position advanced by Lockhart and McClure: censorship should be limited to material "treated" as hard-core pornography, because it is the "manner in which it is marketed and the primary audience to which it is sold" which should be determinative of obscenity, not the intrinsic value of the material alone. It is by this means alone, they claim, that hard-core pornography may occasionally be distributed legitimately for scientific purposes, "while at the same time censorship of material that is not intrinsically hard-core pornography can be permitted when the manner of marketing and the primary audience to which it is marketed indicate that it is being treated as hard-core pornography -- that its function in that setting is to nourish erotic fantasies of the sexually immature."[1] It is submitted here that there are some basic problems inherent in a concept of obscenity this variable. Primarily, while the first goal of allowing occasional dissemination of even hard-core pornography may be achieved under this concept, there is every reason to believe that many "average" adults will effectively be prevented from all exposure to material which has intrinsic social value in order to "protect" the "sexually immature." The Lockhart and McClure theory assumes that it is necessary to protect the sexually immature in our society and that it is possible to determine who these people are.

It is urged here, first, that no reason has been shown for such protection of society. The only justification for censorship would arise from reasonably conclusive evidence of a correlation between obscene materials and antisocial behavior, for example, sex crimes. No such correlation has been proven and authoritative studies appear to negate the correlation, and occasionally even to support the value of obscenity.[2] It is urged that until this correlation is shown, only censorship of hard-core pornography directed at minors alone is justifiable. There is no other certain or objective way of discriminating among "types of audiences." Further, as pointed out elsewhere[3] and by Justice Stewart in his Ginzburg dissent, censorship inherently reflects a lack of self-confidence of a society in its people, a feeling that moral tutelage is necessary and that pluralistic standards of private conduct are impermissible. The more primitive or the more totalitarian a society, the more extensive its censorship. Let society expend its efforts in enforcing prohibitions on sales of certain materials to minors, rather than in limiting the individual's essential need for freedom of expression by proscribing materials for all. If no harm to others results from exposure to obscenity, let each individual guard his own "moral fiber." Government has no place here.

The addition of the "pandering" element to the obscenity test has even more serious faults. Despite pronouncements of the majority opinions in Ginzburg et. al. to the contrary, this element in practical effect negates the meaning of the Roth decision. For in "close cases" -- which must mean in almost every case -- there will inevitably be some doubt or question as to satisfaction of the three objective criteria set forth in and developed from Roth. And once this doubt or question appears, the courts may examine the advertising involved. If it is not clear whether a work appeals to the prurient interest, sexually stimulating advertising will be held to determine the point. And if the advertising dwells on the sexual aspects of a work, this will be considered to support its "patent offensiveness." Finally, it is submitted that the third Roth criterion -- "redeeming social value" -- is now totally nullified. A work is no longer examined for its intrinsic value alone. Thus, a determination that a work had some value, that it was not "utterly without redeeming social importance," may apparently be off-set by the circumstances of the marketing of the work. Publications with admitted social value may be suppressed, even though the advertising employed is not by itself obscene and even though the material by itself and by definition is not obscene. In 1966, this is a tragic defeat for those believing in the sanctity of freedom of expression....

One further aspect of the Ginzburg group of cases should be examined. This is the "redefinition" of the "average person" concept enunciated in Roth as related to the prurient appeal aspect of that test. In Mishkin v. New York, as previously discussed, material concerned with deviant sexual practices which allegedly appealed to the prurient interests of these groups -- and those groups alone -- was held to be obscene. The Court claimed that the terms "average" or "normal" person utilized in Roth were only intended to reject the "most susceptible person" standard enshrined by the Hicklin case. Prurient appeal must now be assessed in terms of "the sexual interests of its intended and probable recipient group," and since the group must be defined more specifically than merely as "sexually immature," the Court claims that it avoids the inadequacies of the Hicklin test.

It should first be admitted that the Court's view is entirely logical in its development. This is, the nature of the appeal to pruriency is no different under Roth than under Mishkin; it is the nature of the group that is different in its particular demands, tastes, and inclinations. In Mishkin, as previously in Roth, the Court did indeed reject the Hicklin standard. According to Hicklin, in order for material to be obscene, it would have to "deprave and corrupt" the susceptible;[4] according to Roth, it would have to stimulate the sexual interest of the average or normal person, not "deprave and corrupt"; and according to Mishkin, it could not deprave or corrupt, because the particular group established as the criterion would already be "depraved and corrupt." Under Hicklin, there could be no finding of obscenity given the Mishkin situation, because the materials could not deprave or corrupt a group which is already both. Under Roth, read literally and logically, there could be no finding of obscenity given the Mishkin situtation because the materials dealing with aberrant sexual practices could not (within the realms of knowledge in this area) appeal to the average or normal person -- they could only disgust. The result is different under Mishkin, because the nature of the group examined is different and the resulting definition of "average" is changed accordingly.

Is the Supreme Court's logic adequate? Is it based on a consideration of the whole meaning and import of the Roth test? The Roth test goes beyond pruriency to the question of redeeming social value. On this basis, although the Mishkin test appears logical as far as it goes, it is so narrowly focused as to ignore the concept of the total role of literature in society. This, it is submitted, is the real reason for the strong dissents and the general dissatisfaction with the decision. The real element of inadequacy in the Mishkin decision, as in Ginzburg, is that it results in the exclusion of certain groups, ipso facto, from the whole realm of social value. What is of value to these groups, namely, to homosexuals, sadists, and masochists, is declared to be of no value by the Court. Thus, the Court is making a sociological, rather than a legal, determination as to what has social value versus what does not -- and a sociological determination which has no sufficient basis and which cannot be supported. It is condemning entire groups of people by not allowing them free expression, essentially saying that they are "obscene," since anything which appeals to them becomes automatically obscene.

The repugnant nature of such a test is probably best expressed by Justice Douglas in his combined Mishkin-Ginzburg dissent. There he raises certain fundamental questions about the majority's outlook and analysis of this facet of the obscenity standards. Why is it unlawful to cater to the needs of deviant sexual groups? Even if their ideas are nonconforming or unappealing, should such groups be prevented from being able to communicate with each other "by the 'written word'"?

....

III. Conclusion

If the first amendment has any meaning, it is that ideas which are not utterly worthless or which do not incite to action must be allowed free expression -- whether they are "good," "bad," appealing, or non-appealing. The tragic aspect of the Ginzburg group of cases is that this basic protection of expression in our society has suffered a serious set-back.

It is not enough, however, merely to criticize the decisions; a substitute should be suggested. It is submitted here that obscenity should be considered within the ambit of the first amendment. If this were the case, the clear and present danger test could then be applied, so that any materials which might incite to "action" could be proscribed. All other material would be allowed free reign so that all members and groups in our society -- representing majority or minority views, normal or abnormal ideas -- could express themselves without fear of legal repercussions. Surely, our society is mature enough to tolerate in writing that same pluralism of private moral standards which obtains in fact in the realm of conduct. Why should a free society fear to write and read about the "darker" or deviant aspects of human emotions and conduct? Surely, the danger of such writings to our society is less than that of a capricious censorship which, with no sound basis in sociology, psychology, or law, would stifle the freedom of expression we consider to be our right. The day will come when Ginzburg will be considered a victim, not a criminal.

Notes

1. See Lockhart & McClure, supra note 13; Lockhart & McClure, "Obscenity Censorship: The Core Constitutional Issue -- What is Obscene?" 7 Utah L. Rev. 289, 298 (1961).

2. See studies by Margaret Mead and other leading sociologists and anthropologists, in Lockhard & McClure, "Censorship of Obscenity: The Developing Constitutional Standard," 45 Minn L. Rev. 5 (1960). See Murphy, "The

Value of Pornography," 10 Wayne L. Rev. (1964).

3. 16 W. Res. L. Rev. 780, 786 (1965).

4. Regina v. Hicklin, L. R. 3 Q. B. 360, 371 (1868).

Granting that Ginzburg partakes of the "variable" concept of obscenity, Tim K. Banner feels the concept is weakened by its application in Ginzburg, and that the net result of Ginzburg may be more confusion.

From 44 Texas Law Review (1966), pp. 1387-1389; reprinted with the permission of the Texas Law Review, and Fred B. Rothman and Company, to which grateful acknowlgement is made for permission to reprint here.

"Notes: Constitutional Law -- Criminal Law -- Obscenity...."

By Tim K. Banner

All of the publications which the Supreme Court has examined since the Roth decision have been evaluated under a standard of "constant obscenity." Obscenity under this standard is an inherent characteristic, and material so categorized is obscene at all times and places and in all circumstances. In comparison, the test adopted by the Court in Ginzburg would permit censorship whenever questionable material was disseminated in a manner which appealed solely to prurient interests. A standard of "variable obscenity" was first suggested by the concurring opinion of the Chief Justice in Roth. There it was contended that in a close case the conduct of the accused should be the deciding factor, and the nature of the material is only to be considered as an attribute of defendant's conduct. Under this approach, the method of sale determines the validity of a claim to first amendment protection, and obscenity becomes a chameleonic quality which changes with time, place, and circumstances. Theoretically, this doctrine should allow serious readers freedom to purchase. However, this freedom will last only until the material is censored because someone selling it seeks to profit by directing advertising and sales campaigns toward arousing prurient interests. One possible alternative would be regulation of the conduct of the disseminator instead of total suppression of material that has minimal social value; but whenever the disseminator is the only source of the literature, as Ginzburg was, the result will be the same.

The theory of variable obscenity appears to have been weakened by its application in a difficult case. The most beneficial effect of this theory could be to free the members of the Court from their disliked and oft-criticized roles as "super-censors" because, under this theory, the aesthetic tastes of the individual judge are no longer the controlling factor in a determination of obscenity. However, the Ginzburg decision will encourage litigation to determine if "questionable" material is close enough to the line to permit an evaluation of the accused's conduct in order to push the material into the area of illicit merchandise. Moreover, there must now be a decision on the type of scienter necessary to sustain an obscenity conviction. The scienter requirement must be clearly defined for protection of vendors who neither pander nor commercially exploit, but who quietly offer for sale literature of minimal social value.

In Ginzburg the Court apparently assumed that the prurient-appeal requirement had been satisfied, because it made no attempt to delineate the primary audience to which the materials were directed. Had there been a delineation, the Court would have had great difficulty in affirming the conviction, because although Ginzburg had engaged in a nation-wide campaign of advertising and selling his publications, the contents of the letters were directed toward "intelligent, educated adults." Therefore, the prurient interests of the hypothetical average person of this primary audience must be found to have been aroused before petitioner could have been convicted of selling obscene materials under the Mishkin definition of the prurient-appeal requirement. The Court reasoned that since petitioner had advertised and sold the publications in a manner to appeal to prurient interests, it was willing to accept petitioner's own proclamation of obscenity and hold that the prurient-appeal requirement had been satisfied. This conclusion was sharply criticized by the four dissenting justices who felt the conviction had been affirmed on a ground which was unrelated to the original indictment and conviction. Although the majority attempted to circumvent this argument by labeling the dissemination setting as "an aid to determining the question of obscenity," it appears that the minority is correct in concluding that the majority affirmed because it found the petitioner guilty of "pandering" and "commercial exploitation."

The Court's opinion in these cases may well return obscenity litigation to the confusion existing prior to the Roth test. Every questionable publication which has previously escaped censorship because it had some redeeming social value is now vulnerable to partial or total suppression if it is being sold in a titillating manner. Moreover, literature which previously had been adjudicated as not obscene is now subject to new censorship litigation whenever dissemination of the material is accompanied by salacious advertising. While the Court intimates that the conduct of the disseminator is controlling only where the material being sold is a "close case," it fails to offer any guidelines to assist lower courts in determining when this point is reached.

The decision in Mishkin permits censorship of literature under the Roth test when the material appeals to the prurient interests of its primary audience even though it has no effect on anyone else. The decision in Memoirs holds that censored material must be utterly without redeeming social value. However, the Memoirs holding is modified by the Ginzburg decision, which permits censorship of literature which is given a salacious cast by the conduct of the disseminator, even if the literature does have some social value. While the thrust of these decisions seems to be directed only toward those who seek to profit from "the shoddy business of pandering," the practical effect will be to limit the reading public's access to border-line literature. Until the Court decides to designate the limits of censorship permitted by these decisions, censors can exert more pressure in their attempt to control the sale of "questionable" literature by threatening vendors with prosecution under the Ginzburg test.

Quite possibly, the worst aspect of any criminal conviction for distributing obscene material is that such convictions encourage much extra-legal suppression that never gets to the courts. In the conclusion to his "Comment" on the Ginzburg opinion, Teddy M. Jones calls attention to that effect.

From 21 Southwestern Law Journal (1967) pp. 304-305, to which grateful acknowledgement is made for permission to reprint here.

"Comments: Obscenity Standards in Current Perspective"

By Teddy M. Jones, Jr.

IV. Conclusion

Questions concerning the necessity of censorship cannot be answered satisfactorily to those on both sides of the basic issues. A reading of the Supreme Court opinions certainly conveys the impression that each decision is permeated by a collective concern of the Justices for perserving freedom of expression. If the inquiry ended at this point, most observers could be relatively unconcerned except upon theoretical grounds of constitutional law. Yet it is a harsh reality that an inquiry into the validity of current obscenity statutes and decisions cannot stop with a reading of the United States Reports. The careful weighing of constitutional niceties and balancing of competing interests simply is not carried out at the administrative enforcement level. Obviously, much of the enforcement is entered into from a biased and prejudiced point of view. It is this feeling of indignation at the abuse to which the obscenity statutes have been subjected and at the attitude taken by the postal, state, and local enforcing agencies which causes many commentators to take a critical view of the current state of the law. Regardless of the careful judicial review given to state or federal obscenity decisions, most cases of literary suppression will never be reviewed al all. The coercive force of threatening a bookseller, drug store, magazine stand, etc., with a criminal prosecution acts almost as self-executing censorship in many areas. The cost of litigation and appeal leads one to believe that most censorship is sub-surface and is never reflected in reported cases. Too, where official censorship is condoned, the door is opened to informal and extra-legal suppression by private groups whose methods entail no notions of due process or of freedom of speech. Operating through the use of fear and coercion and playing on ignorance, the damage they have done to the intellectual climate in this nation is incalculable.

Against these objections must be weighed the possible valid control of some forms of expression. Certainly "hard-core pornography," as the term is generally understood, has no significant artistic, literary, or social value. Perhaps the most acceptable middle ground is that suggested by Mr. Justice Stewart in restricting the federal government and the states to censorship of hard-core pornography. Even in using such a test, the definition of "hard-core" pornography would have to be carefully formulated to avoid abuse of the censorship power on a local or administrative level. Viewing the abuses to which censorship power has given rise, the question of whether the game is worth the candle must be answered.

There is something disturbing and unsettling about the history of censorship, about the fact that private and public frenzy has been aroused over the issue of whether citizens should be free to choose what they will read and what they will see. Perhaps the strongest indictment of governmental censorship is carried in Mr. Justice Stewart's statement, "Censorship reflects a society's lack of confidence in itself."

As preceding articles have shown, *Ginzburg* created much uncertainty and confusion. In the following article, Thomas H. Baughman examines a decision which followed *Ginzburg* by about a year. Baughman finds the confusion of *Ginzburg* somewhat resolved by the later case.

The matter is still open, however; as Baughman notes, *Roth* still predominates as a measure of obscenity, and since the *Ginzburg* decision, the Supreme Court has had no occasion to elucidate that opinion. Contrarily, the Court seems to invoke *Ginzburg* rarely.

For a more recent case than the one cited by Baughman, see *Ginsberg v. New York*, 390 U. S. 629 (1968), which depends upon the variable obscenity concept.

Thomas Baughman's article is reprinted from 19 *Case Western Reserve Law Review* (1968) pp. 748-756, with the permission of *Case Western Reserve Law Review*, to which grateful acknowledgement is made for permission to reprint here.

"Obscenity -- Obscene Publications -- Pandering"

By Thomas H. Baughman

Books, Inc. v. United States, 388 U. S. 449 (1967).

On June 12, 1967, the last day of the October 1966 term, the United States Supreme Court rendered several two-line per curiam decisions in cases involving obscenity censorship. It appears that these short opinions may be useful in clearing up some of the confusion which exists in this area of constitutional law. The utility that these opinions may possess can be ascertained only after a perhaps unnecessarily rigorous examination and comparison of the facts, issues, and holdings of several cases. Although the Supreme Court's use of these very short per curiam opinions may be a rather vague method of clarifying its previous decisions, the procedure is not without precedent.

It is the purpose of this article to examine the contribution of one recent per curiam decision, Books, Inc. v. United States [388 U. S. 449 (1967).], toward reducing the confusion in the area of obscenity censorship. Briefly, it may be said that this case clarifies the rule announced in Ginzburg v. United States pertaining to evidential requirements in criminal prosecutions under obscenity statutes. It also appears that while the Ginzburg rule has survived, its scope may have been effectively limited to its facts. A further, but weaker, implication may be drawn that the Court is becoming more liberal in its outlook on censorship. Before preseting an analysis of Books, Inc. v. United States, it would be well to first examine the development of the common law regarding censorship of allegedly obscene material.

This area of constitutional law is concerned with the first amendment rights of freedom of speech and freedom of the press. In February 1957, the United States Supreme Court established in Butler v. Michigan the principle that first amendment protection (via the 14th amendment) would be afforded to persons prosecuted under State obscenity statutes. Although this first step was significant and carefully taken, many questions were yet to be answered.

After Butler, the question remained whether any statute would be proper. If this question were answered affirmatively, the Court would be faced with determining what standards a statute must meet so as not to violate the first amendment. The Court addressed itself to this issue in Roth v. United States. The most important part of the holding in Roth was that a federal statute making it a criminal offense to deposit obscene material in the United States mail was held constitutional. This established the principle not articulated in Butler that obscene material would not be afforded the protection of the first amendment. "[W]hether to the average person, applying contemporary community standards, the dominant theme of the material taken as a whole appeals to prurient interest."

Depending on how stringently the Supreme Court wished to apply this broad test, either a liberal or conservative standard of obscenity censorship could have resulted. It was generally felt that the Court meant to adopt a conservative standard; that is, one favoring broad powers of censorship.[1] But this interpretation was shortly proved wrong when, in 1957, the Supreme Court handed down four per curiam decisions[2] which reversed lower court decisions upholding obscenity censorship. In all of the cases the Court simply cited Roth v. United States, or Alberts v. California, a companion case to Roth, and gave no further opinion. After resorting to the lower court opinions for the facts and comparing them with the Roth standard for censorship, one might conclude that the Court intended to apply "the constitutional guarantees of freedom of expression [so as] to confine obscenity censorship, within very narrow limits...."[3] However, this conclusion would be based on more speculation than is usually necessary to ascertain a rule of law from a Supreme Court opinion.

Even though these short opinions indicated the Court's general approach to the censorship issue, neither did they indicate with certainty where the line lay between the obscene and the nonobscene, nor did they shed much light on some of the problems inherent in the Roth test. For example, was a book which had great literary value but whose dominant theme also appealed to prurient interest to be withheld from the reading public? Also, did the Court intend to make it impossible for research organizations to obtain admittedly obscene and pornographic material for study purposes?[4] To apply the Roth standard, even under the liberal interpretation given it by the 1957 term per curiam decisions, would have been to uphold censorship of both literarily valuable books and the pornographic material requested by the research organization. This was an unsatisfactory situation, and one that was probably not intended by the Court when it attempted to define obscenity in the Roth case.

The dilemma posed by the logical extention of the Roth test to cover these extreme cases, as well as some other problems concerning obscenity censorship, was solved by the Court in a set of three decisions in 1966. These three decisions were: A Book Named Memoirs v. Attorney General, Ginzburg v. United States, and Mishkin v. New York. In the first of these cases, Memoirs, the Court said that the Roth definition of obscenity, "as elaborated in subsequent cases," meant that there must be a coalescence of three elements:

> [I]t must be established that (a) the dominant theme of the material taken as a whole appeals to a prurient interest in sex; (b) the material is patently offensive because it affronts contemporary community standards relating to the description or representation of sexual matters; and (c) the material is utterly without redeeming social value.

Essentially this three-element test breaks the Roth definition of obscenity into two parts, (a) and (b), and adds a third element -- social value. It is important to note that this definition explicitly requires that the three elements must be established independently; a failure to establish any one of them will result in a judgment that the material involved is not obscene. The addition of the last element solves part of the dilemma posed by a strict interpretation of the Roth definition. If material must be "utterly without redeeming social value" to be held obscene, then the literarily valuable, but sex-oriented, book should not be condemned. This third element announced in Memoirs may even partially solve the hypothetical problem of the obscene material requested by the research organization.

Thus far in the discussion both criminal and civil actions have been considered without differentiation. The differences between these two kinds of actions becomes important in the next step in the evolution of the test for obscenity. In a civil action, such as a declaratory judgment where for example a book is sought to be condemned as obscene, it is the book that is on trial; it is examined in vacuo according to the current definition of obscenity. Other factors such as evidence of contemporary community standards may be considered, but these factors are relevant only as they aid the Court's understanding of the meaning and effect of the words of the book.

On the other hand, in criminal actions, such as a violation of an obscenity statute, it is a person, not a book, that is on trial; it is the defendant's conduct that is being examined. Until the Memoirs decision the Court, with few exceptions, looked at the nature of the material alleged to be obscene as a factor separated from the conduct of the defendant. The issue of obscenity in the criminal case was therefore treated the same as it was in civil cases.

This compartmentalized thinking strains the very fabric of the criminal case; it forces apart two elements that, united, form the basis of the crime. This process is unnatural, and causes the kind of dilemma posed by the research organization hypothetical mentioned previously. The only reason why this dilemma arose was the fact that the intended use of the pornographic material seemed quite proper; and yet under a strict interpretation of the Roth definition of obscenity, the material would have been condemned. The dilemma could have been avoided if the Roth standard had been flexible enough to give weight to the future conduct of the organization.

Likewise, a strict interpretation of the words of the Memoirs three-element test for obscenity would result in the same dilemma for the research organization. In all three elements of the Memoirs definition the word "material" is used; there is no mention of conduct. Thus the use that the hypothetical research organization planned for the pornographic material could not influence the result of the application of the new standard. The new "social value" element would not justify an exception to the rule; it is clear that "social value," under strict interpretation, applies to the material itself, not to the use of the material. This problem could, of course, be resolved if the Court did not insist upon separating conduct from the nature of the material.

Although the addition of the social value element solves the problem of the sex-oriented but literarily valuable book, it creates a new one. For material to be considered obscene, it must be "utterly without redeeming social value."[5] This means that if a book has any merit at all, either socially, literarily, or historically, then it cannot be judged obscene. The practical effect of this requirement could make it possible for any book to be saved from the censor's ban merely by the addition of a chapter on, for example, history. If such a chapter were totally unassociated with the rest of the book, the Court would probably ignore it as spurious. But it would not take much ingenuity to integrate this kind of material without destroying the dominant theme. It seems clear, therefore, that a strict interpretation of the Memoirs definition could have the practical effect of vitiating the whole concept of obscenity censorship. Unquestionably, the United States Supreme Court is not going to go this far; yet, strictly speaking, Memoirs does just that. It would appear reasonable that if the conduct of the person dealing with such a book were considered, then at least a partial solution to this newly created problem could be achieved.

In Ginzburg v. United States, Justice Brennan, writing for a majority of the Court, discussed the defendant's conduct in regard to the issue of obscenity. Specifically, the Court held that evidence of pandering would be relevant to the issue of obscenity "in close cases"[6] -- that is, in cases in which it is questionable whether or not the material is obscene. Justice Brennan even said, at the beginning of his opinion, that "standing alone, the publications themselves might not be obscene." Thus, under Ginzburg the Court can look at the material to see whether it is sex-oriented. If it is, then it can pass immediately to an examination of the defendant's conduct in relation to the material; a specific finding that the material is obscene, by itself, is not necessary.

Essentially, the elements of pandering which the Supreme Court felt relevant to the case can be grouped into two broad categories, as follow: (1) the presence of deliberate representations on the material itself indicating that it is erotically arousing and pruriently oriented without saving intellectual content, and (2) circumstances of presentation and dissemination which are obviously designed to attract the prurient minded. The Court did not say specifically whether proof of all or any one of the issues or categories of issues was necessary; all the Court said was that the evidence was "relevant in determining the ultimate question of obscenity." This ambiguity appears to have been resolved by a recent per curiam decision, Books, Inc. v. United States.

Books was a criminal case involving the prosecution of a paperback book distributor for violation of a federal statute prohibiting the transportation of obscene books in interstate commerce for the purpose of sale or distribution.[7] At a jury trial, the defendant had been found guilty of transporting the book Lust Job in interstate commerce. On appeal, the court of appeals affirmed the conviction.[8] District Judge Wyzanski, writing the opinion of the court, described the book in the following manner:

> [A] tale exclusively devoted to the sexual adventures of its principal characters. Adulteries, seductions, and orgies are the only events of importance. The contacts described include not only sexual intercourse, but sodomy and other perversions. There is not any serious effort to portray the reality of cultural or social conditions of even the most neurotic or sordid portion of the population.

Based on the results of this analysis of the contents of the book, the circuit court felt that a jury could find Lust Job obscene within the definition of obscenity announced in the Memoirs case. Judge Wyzanski went on to bolster the court's finding of obscenity by noting that according to Ginzburg, in borderline cases the circumstances under which the material is commercially exploited (pandering) can have a decisive effect upon the determination of the question of obscenity. Standing on this precedent, he then pointed to the district court's discussion of the front and back covers of the book and found therein evidence of pandering. He said that the title of the book itself, Lust Job, was suggestive, and that the illustration on the cover of the book enhanced this suggestion. Concerning the back cover, the court quoted the following description found thereon: "A time for shame and lust and everything that added up to wild bedroom orgies where nobody cared what anybody did as long as they did it and never stopped!"[9]

On appeal, the United States Supreme Court summarily reversed citing Redrup v. New York. The Redrup decision was a composition of three State obscenity cases.[10] In a per curiam opinion, the Court said that in none of these cases was there evidence of the sort of pandering which it had found significant in Ginzburg, nor did it feel that the material involved in the three cases was obscene.[11]

Since the Supreme Court in Books, Inc. cited the Redrup decision, and since Redrup dismissed the pandering doctrine announced in Ginzburg as not pertinent to its decision, one could arrive at only two conclusions: either the Court felt there was no evidence of any kind of pandering in Books, Inc., or the Court felt that there was no evidence of the sort of pandering which it had found significant in Ginzburg. Clearly, the first alternative is false because of the substantial evidence of pandering presented to the circuit court in Books, Inc. This leaves the second alternative, and there are two inferences that can be drawn from it, either one or both of which can be true. The first inference is that by the use of the word "significant," the Court may have indicated, in a subtle manner, the necessary elements to the proof of pandering. As mentioned above, in Ginzburg the Court discussed two elements which it considered evidence of pandering. But the Court did not say which of the elements or categories of elements were necessary to the proof of pandering. The circuit court in Books, Inc. presented evidence of pandering, consisting of a discussion of the front and back covers of the book Lust Job. Since the Supreme Court in Books, Inc. effectively disregarded, through reference to Redrup, the evidence of pandering discussed by the lower court, it might be fair to assume that the Court did not consider to be relevant to proof of pandering deliberate representations on the material that it is erotically arousing. If this is true, then the Court was saying retrospectively that it did not find the representations made on the material significant in the Ginzburg case. If this reasoning is correct, then only the evidence pertaining to the circumstances of dissemination of the material must be deemed significant to the proof of pandering. To carry this rationale one step further, it might be said that the Court was also distinguishing between the publisher-defendant and the distributor-defendant. Ginzburg involved the former; Books, Inc. the latter. If evidence pertaining to the circumstances of dissemination is all that is to be considered relevant to the proof of pandering, common sense dictates that a distributor such as found in Books will rarely fall within the purview of the Ginzburg doctrine. A distributor does not advertise to the public, he is a middleman; whereas the publisher prints the books, and the retailer sells them. Finally, distributors seldom engage in advertising.

A second inference that can be drawn from interrelating the three cases -- Books, Inc., Redrup, and Ginzburg -- is that the Supreme Court's use of the phrase sort of pandering in Redrup v. New York might indicate an intention to limit Ginzburg to its facts. First of all, it is clear that there was evidence of pandering in Books, Inc. Also, this evidence was of the same variety as some of the evidence of pandering found in Ginzburg. Therefore, if the Court was saying that the pandering in Books, Inc. was not the same sort of pandering in Ginzburg, it might have meant that all of the evidence of pandering in Ginzburg was to be treated as one unit, rather than several individual elements. The practical effect of treating all the little bits and pieces of evidence that support the verdict in a given case is to limit the case to its facts. However, the most important doctrine established by Ginzburg would still be left intact: a defendant's conduct in relation to obscene or almost obscene material can be relevant to the ultimate determination of obscenity.

It remains to be considered whether both inferences can be drawn at the same time, and , if so, what the implications would be. The first inference results in eliminating, as irrelevant to the proof of pandering, the consideration of deliberate representations on the material that it was erotically arousing. The second inference is that Ginzburg has been effectively limited to its facts. There seems to be no reason why these two inferences may not be drawn simultaneously. The result would be that representations on the material would not be considered in regard to the pandering issue. Pandering would only be found if the circumstances of distribution were essentially the same as those of Ginzburg.

Regardless of whether one draws the first, second or both inferences, the resulting Ginzburg rule on pandering would be more difficult to use to obtain a conviction for an obscenity statute violator. Therefore, so long as at least one inference is in force, one could say that Books, Inc. indicates that a subtle change has taken place in the Supreme Court's collective attitude toward obscenity censorship. This change is in the direction of a more liberal concept of what should be censored, or conversely, what should receive the protection of the first amendment rights of freedom of speech and freedom of the press.

Notes

1. For an excellent discussion of the other two cases and the other issues decided in Roth, see Lockhart & McClure, "Censorship of Obscenity: The Developing Constitutional Standards," 45 Minn. L. Rev. 18-32 (1960).

2. Sunshine Book Co. v. Summerfield, 355 U. S. 372 (1958); One, Inc. v. Olesen, 355 U. S. 371 (1958); Mounce v. United States, 355 U. S. 180 (1957); Times Film Corp. v. City of Chicago, 355 U. S. 35 (1957).

3. Lockhard & McClure, supra, Note 1, at 35. For a complete analysis of how this conclusion is supported, see id. at 32-39.

4. For a complete discussion of these and other problems raised by the Roth decision, see Lockhart & McClure, supra note 6, and Lockhart & McClure, "Obscenity Censorship: The Core Constitutional Issue -- What Is Obscene?" 7 Utah L. Rev. 289 (1961).

5. A Book Named Memoirs v. Attorney General, 383 U. S. 413, 418 (1966) (emphasis added).

6. 383 U. S. at 474 (emphasis added).

7. 18 U. S. C. [sec.] 1465 (1964).

8. Books, Inc. v. United States, 358 F. 2d 935, 936 (1st Cir. 1966), rev'd, 388 U.S. 449 (1967).

9. 358 F. 2d at 937.

10. The other two cases were Austin v. Kentucky, and Gent v. Arkansas.

11. 386 U. S. at 770. It is interesting to note the method the Court used to arrive at its conclusions that the material was not obscene. Although not mentioning them by name, the independent views of seven of the Justices on the definition of obscenity were succinctly set forth. (The views of Justices Clark and Harlan, who dissented in the case, were not included). The Court then said that no matter which of the views were applied to the cases under consideration, the finding would be that the materials were not censorable obscenities. Id. at 770-71.

The relationship of the trier of fact and the presumed "expert" in an obscenity trial, and the considerations involved when expert testimony is used, are discussed at length by Charles M. Stern in "Toward a Rationale for the Use of Expert Testimony in Obscenity Litigation." The conclusion to Stern's article is given here, as a summary of his discussion.

From 20 Case Western Reserve Law Review (1969), pp. 304-305, to which grateful acknowledgment is made for permission to reprint here.

"Toward a Rationale for the Use of Expert Testimony in Obscenity Litigation"

By Charles M. Stern

I have tried to point out that many uses of expert testimony in obscenity trials cause more confusion than enlightenment, and to suggest why this is so. It is now appropriate to draw some general conclusions concerning the proper function of expert testimony in the litigating process.

Virtually all of the difficulties explored -- conceptual, evidentiary, and practical -- result from the questionable notion that all the evidence at trial must be directed to the ultimate yes-or-no issue of obscene vel non. In a broad sense, of course, this is true; for the dispute over the obscenity of the work at issue is the underlying reason for the presentation of any evidence whatsoever. But the misconception, more precisely, is that the experts are expected to help the fact-finder decide the ultimate issue by participating in essentially the same kind of analysis of the fact-finder himself -- much as though the fact-finder where to say to the expert, "I must decide whether this work is 'obscene' within the meaning of our statute. What do you think?" Because the expert is welcomed to participate in the decisional process in the same way as the trier of fact, so that the latter's decision will somehow be bolstered by professional consultation with the former, the roles of fact-finder and expert witness have become fuzzy and overlapping.

Asking the expert whether or not he considers the challenged publication to be obscene is only the most superficial manifestation of the failure to differentiate between the roles of fact-finder and expert witness. Such failure is more graphically demonstrated by the phenomenon of "omniscient expertise," that is, the tendency of counsel and jury to overlook the particular competence of the witness and to regard him as a general expert whose wisdom will be summoned to join in the collective analysis of those less confident in judgment. This tendency was notable in the

Lady Chatterley trial in London, where the list of cognoscenti testifying was awesome. "[T]here had appeared," reports one observer, "a tendency to stop treating the witnesses as literary experts, or ethical experts, or 'other merits' experts, and just treat them as experts."[1] This merging of the fact-finder's and the expert's roles also underlies those warnings by commentators that import decisions concerning censorship may soon be turned over to a collection of randomly chosen Ph. D.'s. The warning was well expressed by Ernst and Seagle:

> At first glance, the critic as literary expert appears to have a great deal to recommend him. It seems absurd that a work of literary art should be judged not by liteary standards but by the rules of the criminal law which for the most part exclude him. Nevertheless the remedy is worse than the disease. The fact that vice societies at times have signified their entire willingness to have a board of literary men pass on manuscripts in advance should alone make us suspicious. A gift horse is to be looked very closely in the mouth even when he happens to be Pegasus.[2]

The response should be a clearer division of decisional responsibilities between experts and triers of fact. This division can best be dramatized by an analogy... of the legislative hearing. When the analogue is posited alongside the obscenity trial, it appears that what previously may have been thought to be a one-step process -- the summoning of experts to aid in the judgment of obscene vel non -- is more appropriately to be regarded as a two-step process: an initial gathering of information about the challenged publication, and a subsequent assessment of the witnesses' explanations and application of legal standards. The initial step requires the observations of specially trained experts. But the subsequent step requires that witnesses' opinions be excluded in order to give full scope to the responsibility of the triers of fact. This division of the litigation into two steps provides a means of summarizing, and synthesizing, the points raised in the course of this article:

(1) The expert has his own concept of obscenity and it is different from the legal concept, of which the essence is proscription. The expert must be allowed to discuss the

work at issue in his own terms, in order to utilize the educational value of his testimony and to avoid superfluous opinions which are ultimately not his to make.

(2) Unsubstantiated notions about the evils of obscene matter are not constitutionally permissible foundations for legal censorship; but where expert witnesses can provide specific information concerning the characteristics and effects of questionable publications, their professional observations may serve to provide an ad hoc determination of obscenity for the particular case at hand. Therefore, the goal of expert testimony is not to achieve a majority expert opinion on the question whether the work is objectionable, but to acquire an array of particularized perceptions which can be accepted or rejected by the trier of fact in his final task of applying the Roth test.

(3) Similarly, on issues such as the nature of the average person or the existence of social value, the expert should not be called upon to provide his own notions for acceptance by the trier of fact; for the expert is by definition not an average person and the meaning of social value extends far beyond literary merit, psychological benefit, or any other single-faceted element of social existence. The challenged work can be utterly lacking in literary merit, for example, and still possess social value. Rather, the expert should provide pieces of information with which the trier of fact is to construct his own idea of the average person or of social value.

(4) Statutory provisions for the admission of expert testimony, and common law rules of evidence, should work to allow a wide scope to the eliciting of specific information and no scope whatever to pronouncements which are either unconnected with the expert's particular competence or related to opinions concerning the ultimate legal issues.

(5) The undesirable side-effects of prestigious critics lining up on either side of the case are minimized by limiting their testimony to their respective areas of competence, by eliciting specific responses, and by purposefully avoiding dogmatic pronouncements which push rather than point the way.

The fact that judges and juries must bear the final

responsibility for the decisions of legal censorship may, as has been asserted, "shackle genius to the average prejudices of the times."[3] But if this is so, it is because juries and judges have been deemed by legislatures to be the proper bodies to determine, in Judge Learned Hand's words, "the present critical point in the compromise between candor and shame at which the community may have arrived here and now...."[4] I have tried to show that experts are not suitable participants in these decisions as to what is obscene, but are equipped to provide information upon which intelligent decisions can be made. Hopefully, this demarcation of roles shall keep all participants -- experts, judges, and juries -- within the confines of their repsetive abilities and appropriate functions. At the very least, the analysis should make clear that at the limits of expertise are the beginnings of the responsibilities of judge and jury.

Notes

1. The Trial of Lady Chatterley -- Regina v. Penguin Books Limited 117 (C. Rolph ed. 1961).

2. Ernst and Seagle, To the Pure ... A Study of Obscenity and the Censor (1928).

3. Ibid., 211.

4. United States v. Kennerley, 209 F. 119 (1913).

Index